Practical Ecocriticism

D1435764

Under the Sign of Nature: Explorations in Ecocriticism

Editors Michael P. Branch, SueEllen Campbell, John Tallmadge

Series Consultants Lawrence Buell, John Elder, Scott Slovic

Series Advisory Board Michael P. Cohen, Richard Kerridge, Gretchen Legler, Ian Marshall, Dan Peck, Jennifer Price, Kent Ryden, Rebecca Solnit, Anne Whiston Spirn, Hertha D. Sweet Wong

GLEN A. LOVE

Practical Ecocriticism

. . . .

Literature, Biology, and the Environment

University of Virginia Press • Charlottesville and London

University of Virginia Press
© 2003 by the Rector and Visitors of the University of Virginia
All rights reserved
Printed in the United States of America on acid-free paper
First published 2003

9 8 7 6 5 4 3 2 1

LIBRARY OF CONGRESS CATALOGING-IN-PUBLICATION DATA

Love, Glen A., 1932–
Practical ecocriticism : literature, biology, and the environment / Glen A. Love.
p. cm. — (Under the sign of nature)
ISBN 0-8139-2244-5 (cloth : alk. paper) — ISBN 0-8139-2245-3 (paper : alk. paper)
1. American literature—History and criticism. 2. Nature in literature. 3. Howells, William Dean, 1837–1920—Knowledge—Natural history. 4. Hemingway, Ernest, 1899–1961—Knowledge—Natural history. 5. Pastoral Literature, American—History and criticism. 6. Cather, Willa, 1873–1947. Professor's house. 7. Literature and science—United States. 8. Biology in literature. 9. Ecology in literature. I. Title. II Series.
PS163.L68 2003
810.9'36—dc21

2003007373

Contents

Acknowledgments

I wish to thank all those who have offered encouragement and advice for this book. I have profited from their suggestions, whether or not they have become part of the finished work. What remains, then, is my responsibility alone.

I owe a great debt to Lawrence Buell and Joseph Carroll, who read and commented upon the entire manuscript, offering invaluable advice. From that, and from their books and articles, I continue to learn.

Since my subject includes science, I am beholden to scientists for much of what I have to say. Their published work forms a considerable part of the argument, as will be apparent. I am also appreciative of the advice from my University of Oregon scientific colleagues, especially cognitive psychologist Ray Hyman and biologist John Postlethwait. Both are at the top of their professions, and fine teachers, as I can attest. Philosopher Maxine Sheets-Johnstone, with an extensive background in, and command of, evolutionary biology, has been a major personal and professional influence. Scientists in my own family, wife, Rhoda, biologist/ecologist; son, Stan, astrophysicist; and daughter-in-law, Jancy McPhee, neurobiologist, have contributed greatly to my education. Rhoda has been, as always, the best of colleagues and an exemplar of the scientific spirit, helpful, as well, with my computer ineptitudes and patiently willing to read draft after draft of my chapters. Without her . . .

I also want to acknowledge and thank a number of colleagues and friends who have read and commented upon parts of this book, including Bert Bender, Cheryll Glotfelty, William Howarth, Jonathan Levin, Jay McGarrigle, John Orbell, Susan Rosowski, Scott Slovic, and Kermit Vanderbilt. Support in many forms has come from many people, including Kerry Ahearn, Bruce Bennett, Jack Bennett, Peter Blakemore, Sam Boggs, Bob Bumstead, Bruce Carlson, Laird Christensen, Suzanne Clark, Jim Crosswhite, Ludwig Deringer, François Duban, Karen Ford,

John Gage, Hansjörg Gehring, Jim Harrang, Linda Kintz, Tom Lyon, Michael McDowell, David Copland Morris, Dan Philippon, Jarold Ramsey, Laurie Ricou, Forrest Robinson, Randall Roorda, Bill Rossi, Gordon Sayre, Gary Scharnhorst, Heinz Tschachler, George Wickes, and Henry Wonham. Louise Westling has been a constant source of encouragement and advice to me, as well as providing spirited leadership to our graduate program in literature and environment here at the University of Oregon. Boyd Zenner, Acquiring Editor at the University of Virginia Press, has been a very helpful and skilled guide through the acceptance process, as has Mark Mones in the book's final editing. I was also most fortunate to have Sarah Nestor as my copy editor. She has made this a better book.

Finally, I wish to thank the editors of the following journals for permission to reprint material, here revised, from my earlier articles. Portions of chapters 1, 3, and 5 were originally published in *Western American Literature* issues for Fall 1992, Fall 1990, Winter 1990, and Fall 1987. Parts of chapter 2 appeared in *ISLE*, Winter 1999, and in *New Literary History*, Summer 1999. Chapter 4 makes use of material reprinted from *Cather Studies*, volume 5, by permission of the University of Nebraska Press, © 2003 by the University of Nebraska Press. Chapter 6 is revised from an essay in the *Harvard Library Bulletin*, Spring 1994.

Practical Ecocriticism

Introduction

At the beginning of the third millennium and of a new century often heralded as "the century of the environment," a coherent and broadly based movement embracing literary-environmental interconnections, commonly termed "ecocriticism," is emerging. Environmental and population pressures inevitably and increasingly support the position that any literary criticism which purports to deal with social and physical reality will encompass ecological considerations.

Ecocriticism, as the editors of the journal *New Literary History* wrote in introducing their 1999 special issue on the subject, "challenges interpretation to its own grounding in the bedrock of natural fact, in the biospheric and indeed planetary conditions without which human life, much less humane letters, could not exist. Ecocriticism thus claims as its hermeneutic horizon nothing short of the literal horizon itself, the finite environment that a reader or writer occupies thanks not just to culturally coded determinants but also to natural determinants that antedate these, and will outlast them" (Tucker 505). Another way of saying this is that ecocriticism, unlike all other forms of literary inquiry, encompasses nonhuman as well as human contexts and considerations. On this claim, ecocriticism bases its challenge to much postmodern critical discourse as well as to the critical systems of the past.

The study of literature's relationship to the physical world has been with us, in the domain of the pastoral tradition, since ancient times. And academic attention to canonical works such as Thoreau's *Walden* and the fiction, poetry, and essays of the British and American Romantics has always had a place in the literary spectrum. But early beginnings of a distinctly contemporary, consciously environmentalist criticism, with its "spirit of commitment to environmental praxis," as Lawrence Buell characterizes it, seem to have first stirred in the 1960s, in widespread public concerns over nuclear annihilation, runaway population growth, loss of wild and natural areas, accelerated species extinctions, and increasing contamination of the earth's air, water, and land (*Environmental Imagination* 430). Rachel Carson's *Silent Spring*, published in 1962, which is now commonly regarded as the major work of the contemporary environmental movement, describes with a novelist's art and a scientist's knowledge the dangers posed by the indiscriminate use of chemical biocides.[1]

Like many other young academics during the 1960s, I came to literature influenced by pressing social considerations. By this time my wife, Rhoda, a biology teacher and plant ecologist, and I were both concerned about increased environmental degradation. Active in the conservation movement, we worked together to edit and publish the first anthology of readings on crucial ecological issues of the post–*Silent Spring* years.[2] Writing my doctoral dissertation in the sixties, I had been much influenced by Leo Marx's new book on the conflict in American life between technology and nature, *The Machine in the Garden*. Marx's powerful reading of American literature and culture, a crowning example of the same myth-symbol criticism to which I was attracted, was inspirational to me as a young scholar, working with environmental ideas in American literature. But Marx's last pages had seemed to me to sound a decidedly premature epitaph for the place of nature in American thought and culture.

In the dying fall with which Marx's book closes, the old pastoral idea is depicted as "stripped . . . of most, if not all, of its meaning," a victim of the inexorable "reality of history" (363). Marx was surely correct in delineating so memorably the increasing domination of machine civilization in America. What was to escape his conclusions was a sense of the ecological complexity of nature, the impossibility of its complete control by human beings, and the obstinacy with which Americans would resist any dismissal into history and literary irony what Marx had rightly called "the root conflict of our culture" (365). If, as Marx claimed, the old "simple" pastoral world of the nineteenth-century American mythos had been swept away, a complex of new and decidedly nonmythic forces was at work that would, along with civil rights and Vietnam war protests, keep the root conflict squarely before us. Ironically, *The Machine in the Garden* appeared in 1964, in the midst of the furor caused by Carson's best-selling *Silent Spring*, which had unsparingly documented widespread environmental threats deep enough, paraphrasing Robert Frost's "A Brook in the City," to keep this new-built America from both work and sleep.

By the end of the sixties the word *ecology* had surfaced from a subfield of biology to encompass the same root conflict whose history and cultural implications Marx had so effectively interpreted through the development of American literature from its beginnings to F. Scott Fitzgerald's *The Great Gatsby.* Culminating in the first Earth Day in 1970, "environmentalism," an awkward media term—which has nevertheless stuck—for the knot of issues surrounding the machine in the garden, signified not only a part of the pervasive political and social unrest of a decade, but a permanent national and global concern, a check to a blind faith in progress and to the juggernaut of technology.

In the decades following the sixties, much of literary criticism moved away from the New Criticism, archetypal studies, and the myth-symbol methodology of Marx, Henry Nash Smith, R. W. B. Lewis, and others. New waves followed, including structuralism and various manifestations of post-structuralism: deconstruction, reader-response theory, race-class-gender studies, new historicism. Curiously enough, while literary attention fastened upon the admittedly important social conflicts associated with race, class, and gender, there seemed little or no critical concern for literature that addressed the overarching and increasingly stressed natural systems within which these cultural conflicts were playing themselves out.

The notion that literature encompassed nonhuman as well as human contexts, nature as well as culture, found a few critical proponents during the 1970s and 1980s, including some senior scholars such as John Elder and others with longstanding interests in environmental literature, as well as younger scholars, often graduate students, who later became the impetus for forming the Association for the Study of Literature and Environment. But the crucial nexus between nature and culture was strangely off-limits to mainstream academic discourse at a time when the world's population was doubling, then tripling; when Cold War nuclear annihilation threatened; when water and air pollution, toxic wastes, deforestation, species extinction, global warming, urban sprawl were becoming worldwide issues; and when "The Year of the Environment" or "The Decade of the Environment" was being regularly proclaimed by the media. Practitioners of literary criticism, while concerning themselves with other contemporary issues, ignored the underlying single most important event of our times, one whose implications were latent in all literature. If anything, what kept environmental thinking alive in literary discussion, as Patrick D. Murphy reminds us, were the concerns of classroom teachers and students ("Forum" 1098).

There were, if one looks retrospectively, some important signs during these years of new critical attention to literature and the environment. Two significant early books were *The Comedy of Survival: Studies in Literary*

Ecology, published in 1974 by Joseph W. Meeker, a comparative literature scholar with a background in evolutionary biology, and Annette Kolodny's 1975 ecofeminist study, *The Lay of the Land: Metaphor as Experience in American Life and Letters*. A few early ecocritical journal articles appeared during the 1970s, including one by William Rueckert, who, in 1978, first coined the term "ecocriticism."[3] In 1986 Leo Marx, reflecting upon the twenty-two years that had passed since the publishing of *The Machine in the Garden*, recognized in contemporary American culture the resurgence of the old root conflict. Two years later, he published a collection of his essays from preceding years, *The Pilot and the Passenger;* several of these pieces threw more light upon ecological ideals and technological realities of the times. His recent work places him again at the forefront of significant activity in ecocriticism. The eighties also saw the publication of significant works such as Frederick O. Waage's collection, *Teaching Environmental Literature;* Leonard Lutwack's *The Role of Place in Literature;* John Elder's study of American nature poetry, *Imagining the Earth;* Daniel Halpern's anthology, *On Nature;* and Alicia Nitecki's *The American Nature Writing Newsletter*. Lawrence Buell's 1989 article, "American Pastoral Ideology Reappraised," examined the ideological position of pastoral criticism in recent times and carved out the direction for his 1995 book, *The Environmental Imagination: Thoreau, Nature Writing, and the Formation of American Culture*, the most important single ecocritical study thus far.

During the 1980s the Western Literature Association's annual meetings attracted an increasing number of scholars interested in literature and environment. Understandably so, since much of the serious western American literature confronts perhaps the greatest American environmental issue of the last 150 years: the fate of the vast resources of undeveloped public and private lands in the West.

Every part of the West, from its increasingly threatened natural wonders to its mushrooming urban centers, has been deeply involved in environmental conflict. The late nineteenth- and twentieth-century West witnessed the transfer of the old machine-garden conflicts into the immediate present, with battles over the fate of the West's native peoples; over the appropriation of its water; over wilderness, old-growth forests, mineral extraction, endangered species, pollution, toxic wastes, and spreading urban blight. The work of western writers like John Muir, Mary Austin, Aldo Leopold, Wallace Stegner, Gary Snyder, Edward Abbey, Leslie Marmon Silko, Barry Lopez, William Kittredge, and Terry Tempest Williams kept such issues at the forefront of the Association's meetings and publications during these years, when the early and influential frontier hypotheses of historian Frederick Jackson Turner were transmuted into new paths of awareness and interpretation.

At the 1989 meeting of the Western Literature Association, two papers called for literary scholars to bring environmental thinking into their work: Cheryll Burgess's [Glotfelty's] "Toward an Ecological Literary Criticism" and my Past President's Address, "Revaluing Nature: Toward an Ecological Criticism." Interest in ecocritical activity continued, and at the 1992 Western Literature meeting, the new Association for the Study of Literature and Environment (ASLE) was formed and within a year had more than 300 members. Three years later in 1995 its members numbered over 750 and ASLE held its first conference. During the decade of the nineties and at the turn of the century, the study of literature and the environment grew rapidly under vigorous leadership.[4] ASLE expanded in the 1990s to over a thousand members, with chapters in Japan, England, and Korea and one currently forming in Australia, and published its own journal, *Interdisciplinary Studies in Literature and Environment (ISLE)*. Ecocriticism was featured in articles in *The New York Times Magazine*, *The Chronicle of Higher Education*, *The Washington Post*, *PMLA*, and elsewhere.[5] An influential critical anthology and bibliography, *The Ecocriticism Reader*, edited by Cheryll Glotfelty and Harold Fromm, and a rapidly expanding number of scholarly books and articles on literature and the environment have marked these recent years.[6]

The present state of this movement, for which the blanket term *ecocriticism* has come to be accepted, is one of ferment and experimentation. What is emerging is a multiplicity of approaches and subjects, including—under the big tent of environmental literature—nature writing, deep ecology, the ecology of cities, ecofeminism, the literature of toxicity, environmental justice, bioregionalism, the lives of animals, the revaluation of place, interdisciplinarity, eco-theory, the expansion of the canon to include previously unheard voices, and the reinterpretation of canonical works from the past. As Buell notes, "the phenomenon of literature-and-environment studies is better understood as a congeries of semioverlapping projects than as a unitary approach or set of claims" ("Forum" 1091). Like many others, I find this rapid expansion of critical effort both necessary and exhilarating. Exploring all potentially rewarding perspectives is the appropriate course for an ascending new paradigm.

This book is a contribution to the mix. It stands against a recent past dominated by opposing critical tendencies, by which I mean those approaches that, for the most part, have little or nothing to do with the physical world. My own critical evolution as a literary scholar toward a better understanding of the natural sciences, particularly biology, is a case in point. The aggressive anti-anthropocentrism with which my earlier ecocriticism is associated, as Steven Rosedale argues in his new anthology, *The Greening of Literary Scholarship*, might well now make way for what he describes as "environmentally useful emphases on the human component of the human-nature relationship" (xvii).

I agree. What I have to say in the following pages is basically this: We have to keep finding out what it means to be human. And the key to this new awareness is the life sciences.

My attraction to a literal—that is, scientific—ecology and to the evolutionary biology upon which it is based has opposed a general coolness, even hostility, in the humanities toward the sciences in recent decades.[7] Much of this hostility is an anachronistic holdover from the wholly justified reactions to the social Darwinist distortions of a century ago. The lingering effects of such hostility tend to obscure the fact that it was the advance of science which, through its disciplinary methodology, repudiated the bigotry and racism of social Darwinism (see Barkan). In opposition to the motives of racists, science has made increasingly evident how biologically alike all human beings are. There are differences, but these are comparatively small. The world over, we are pretty much the same. Recent genetic research indicates that all the earth's people alive today are descended from a small group of modern humans originating in eastern Africa. This new science-based awareness of our overwhelming genetic commonality can be an important and progressive social force (Olson 3–7).

A lingering resistance to biological science is also reflected in an unfamiliarity with evolutionary biological research in the last several decades on the part of many humanists and social scientists. Many in these fields are still working under the assumptions of the so-called Standard Social Science Model (SSSM), which was dominant over the last century but has been increasingly challenged and replaced in recent years. The biological counter to the SSSM has arisen from the Darwinian awareness that humans are part of the animal world—that they, like all other creatures, evolved, body and brain. Correspondingly, human behavior is not an empty vessel whose only input will be that provided by culture, but is strongly influenced by genetic orientations that underlie and modify, or are modified by, cultural influences. This is no longer a dismissible minority view.

Pioneering scientific ecologist Eugene P. Odum, in a recent edition of his book, *Ecology: A Bridge between Science and Society*, calls attention to ecology as the underlying and integrating science of today's world. Odum points to the rapidly expanding number of ecological and environmental centers, institutes, schools, and departments in colleges and universities, bringing together the sciences, social sciences, and humanities in their programs. "Especially significant is the rise of 'interface' fields of study, with their new societies, journals, symposium volumes, books—and new jobs" (xiii). I believe that as one of these new interface territories, ecocriticism has the potential to contribute to the study of values in what we increasingly find to be a world where, to cite an ecological maxim, everything is connected to everything else.

My title, *Practical Ecocriticism*, deserves an explanation, especially to those who will recognize it as a play on the title of the 1929 book, *Practical Criticism*, by the eminent Cambridge University scholar I. A. Richards.[8] There, Richards had argued for the primacy of the words on the page, the literary work as an autonomous whole apart from contextual information, as the basis for literary criticism. His work was influential in establishing the close-reading style of the New Criticism in America, ascendant in the post–World War II years. Richards is also appropriately considered here, as Joseph Carroll has reminded us, for his support of the tradition of interdisciplinary study, which recognizes the influence of an external world on the mind of the writer (*Evolution and Literary Theory* 9, 55–56). While I, like nearly everyone else, have parted company with Richards on the issue of context and the autonomous whole, I still teach and practice the advantages of close reading and attention to rhetoric and style, as will be evident in the later chapters of this volume. But what attracts me to the term *practical* in today's literary climate is its evocation of a discourse that aims to test ideas against the workings of physical reality, to join humanistic thinking to the empirical spirit of the sciences, to apply our nominal concern for "the environment" to the sort of work we do in the real world as teachers, scholars, and citizens of a place and a planet.

Kate Soper, in her important book *What Is Nature?* has examined the contemporary critical conflict between what she terms the "nature-endorsing" view of nature and the "nature-skeptical" perspective. As Soper points out, there are various subcategories of contemporary theory that can fall on either side of this divide: "It is one thing to challenge various cultural representations of nature, another to represent nature as if it were a convention of culture" (4). My principal argument is with the latter view, and in opposing it I clearly belong with the nature-endorsers.[9]

But while I understand the relevance of other nature-endorsers exploring different cultural representations of nature, my position is once again "practical." It leads me toward ecological, naturalist, scientifically grounded arguments that recognize human connection with nature and the rest of organic life and acknowledge the biological sciences as not just another cultural construction. Rather, they are the necessary basis for a joining of literature with what has proven itself to be our best human means for discovering how the world works.

My benchmark is ecological relevance. In a real world of increasing ecological crisis and political decision making, to exclude nature except for its cultural determination or linguistic construction is also to accept the continuing degradation of a natural world that is most in need of active human recognition and engagement. Although I recognize that our perceptions of nature are necessarily human constructed, these constructions are also, necessarily, the product of a brain and a physiology that have evolved in close relationship to nature. Nature interacts with cultural influences in shaping human attitudes and behavior.

Kate Soper reflects that her title, *What Is Nature?* "should be construed more as a gesture towards a problem than as a promise to supply a solution to it. It is intended, that is, as an echo, or index, of the politically contested nature of 'nature' in our own times" (7). That is a reasonable philosophical position.[10] It has been sagely observed that all important problems are likely to be insoluble; that is why they are important. Yet I hope to contest the contesting. There may be a resolution in this case, wherein the discourse on one side, according to a steadily increasing body of evidence, has far greater explanatory capability than that on the other side. The nature-endorsers also gain crediblity in being drawn to real problems and in advocating and working toward analyses and solutions, while the nature-skeptics do not. Insoluble or not, problems often require consequential decisions and significant actions. With much at stake, it makes sense to act or in this case, as literary citizens, to write, read, teach—even in recognition of a mediated contextuality at work—with more attention to the biological and ecological context than has been previously evident in dominant nature-skeptical thinking.

Finally, the word *Practical* suggests accessibility to the general reader from the humanities as well as to the specialist. If the term also threatens an injudicious measure of prosaic pragmatism, I hope that it will be balanced by its connotations of ecological consequentiality. Although the title may conjure up the image of an authorial Gradgrind, busily assembling theory-squashing facts, the book manages a fair amount of theory.

I theorize following the lead of scientists like Edward O. Wilson, the world's foremost proponent of biodiversity and the conjoining of the two cultures, and following the example of groundbreaking literary scholars Joseph Meeker, author of *The Comedy of Survival*, and Joseph Carroll, whose monumental *Evolution and Literary Theory* calls for a new nature-endorsing scientific paradigm to replace that presently in ascendancy. I have also been significantly influenced by evolutionarily based scholars like philosopher Maxine Sheets-Johnstone and anthropologist Ellen Dissanayake.

Testing the nature-endorsers versus the nature-skeptics against the standard of explanatory power with regard both to the real world and to literary experience ought to be the best sort of critical work. Here, I side with the indispensable American philosopher William James in his advocacy of a pragmatism that "unstiffens all our theories, limbers them up, and sets each one at work" (28).

The chapters that follow divide into two sections. The first, comprising chapters 1–3, addresses broad questions, issues, and approaches encompassed by the emerging field of ecocriticism. Chapter 1 expands this introduction, pursuing ways in which an awareness of a rapidly changing world—witness the quantum jump in public environmental concerns about biological terrorism following the events of September 11, 2001—requires appropriate new ways of thinking about literature and its environmental context. This chapter also surveys some principal thematic concerns of literary/environmental studies and argues for an interdisciplinary ecocriticism as best representing the theory and approach of its namesake, the scientific field of ecology.

Ecology as a science may not generally concern itself with the issue of values. Values are often seen as the province of those in the humanities, including the teachers, scholars, and students to whom this book is addressed. But the work of environmentally concerned ecologists, biologists, anthropologists, psychologists, and others from the sciences and social sciences, along with the thinking of those of us from the humanities, should, I believe, help to replace the sense of sharp disciplinary distinctions with a new perception of commonality.

Chapter 2 follows Charles Darwin's basic assertion in *The Descent of Man, and Selection in Relation to Sex* that humans are descended from earlier forms of life, differing only in degree from other animals. The chapter urges an interdisciplinary pairing with the natural sciences, especially evolutionary biology and the new fields that it has spawned. Though I have a strong interdisciplinary interest in the sciences, I am a card-carrying literature teacher. As such, I am beholden to others who are expert in their scientific fields. The positions I take are, I believe, consonant with those that are now generally accepted in the biological sciences and are becoming increasingly so in the social sciences, though they have yet to make much headway—or even to be read—in the humanities. Much developing life science is intensely relevant to the work we do as scholars and teachers.

In chapter 3 the book's emphasis shifts toward more directly literary concerns. The chapter looks back at the long history of pastoral as a literary genre and at the much longer human history of our nature-oriented Pleistocene beginnings. Literary pastoral and the pastoral impulse in artistic creation may relate to what Edward O. Wilson hypothesizes in his book *Biophilia* is a human affinity for natural life-forms and what Ellen Dissanayake posits as the biogenetic origins of all art. Human nature, after a long period of excision from critical thinking in the social sciences and humanities by the nature-skeptics, makes its literary reappearance here and in the rest of the book.

The last three chapters center upon what many of us might do as teachers and critics of literature concerned not only with informed ecological thinking but with language and textual analysis. Here I work with the novels of three canonical American novelists of the modern period, Willa Cather, Ernest Hemingway, and William Dean Howells. None of them is considered a nature writer primarily, and that is why I have chosen them. Most of the pioneering work of ecocriticism thus far has centered upon nature writing. If there is a contribution to be made in this volume's final chapters, it is to join other ecocritics in extending the purview of environmental criticism, in this case by considering the work of some leading writers of the modern American novel. I recognize that the word *Literature* in my subtitle is more inclusive than my examples, but I hope that my critical approach will be seen to apply more widely as ecocriticism expands its borders of influence.

These ecologically oriented chapters on modern American novelists will, I hope, show the possibilities of a fresh rereading of established texts from perspectives that have been set forth in the preceding chapters. The later chapters explore, from a contemporary biocultural viewpoint, the intuitive understanding of human nature that literary artists have always shown in their works. Chapter 4 employs a scientifically informed approach to place and human nature in Willa Cather's *The Professor's House*, working from a phenomenological perspective that acknowledges all human thought as embodied. A consideration of Cather's experimental stylistic techniques in the novel's three distinctive "books" enhances our sense of the rhetorical interlacing of cultural/aesthetic and biological elements in the narrative.

In chapter 5 the young Ernest Hemingway, whose "iceberg principle"[11] closely resembled Cather's minimalist stylistic experiments, presents us with a far different encounter with nature. At its center is a unique tragic consciousness, which engages in a paradoxical and deadly ecological conflict with the author's avowed primitivism and with his love for animals and the natural world. This conflict emerges most memorably in Hemingway's late masterwork, *The Old Man and the Sea.*

The final chapter is a study of two late novels by the pioneering American realist W. D. Howells, one work realistic *(The Landlord at Lion's Head)* and the other Utopian *(The Traveler from Altruria).* This unlikely pairing takes us to the heart of what remains today, a century after Howells's novels were written, perhaps the most controversial and vexing issue of evolutionary theory and practice, as well as the center of political and moral discussion: the question of altruism versus selfishness in human nature and behavior.

As someone who has been an ecocritic of sorts for a long time, I have published articles on literature and environment in widely scattered journals over the years. Because my theoretical perspective has increasingly led me in the direction of the natural sciences, I have substantially revised earlier work used here for what is, along with much new material, serviceable and appropriate to my aim to ground today's ecocriticism in today's best science.

I do not attempt to construct a strictly scientific critical apparatus for testing the assumptions set forth in the book. Others are working in that direction.[12] I also want to avoid the "gotcha" manner of an eco-policeman, dragging past writers to the dock for violations of today's sense of environmental incorrectness. For the most part the thinking, or nonthinking, of past writers on nature-related matters was simply part of the cultural given of their times. This particular given, or the writer's unique diversion from it, however, may well be worth examining. My aim is to help initiate, on the ground level, a more biologically informed ecocritical dialogue about literature and its relationships to nature and to environmental concerns.

Memorable literature repays attention from succeeding generations in its capacity to speak to new readers in their own terms on issues which, nowadays, are unavoidably ecological. Human/nature interrelationships that are at the social forefront today may reveal something of their underlying importance, even universality, through their presence in earlier literary works that now open themselves to our reinterpretation.

1

Why Ecocriticism?

• • • • • • • • • • • • •

These stories have trees in them.—Single-sentence rejection letter received by Norman Maclean for *A River Runs through It*

In Melville's *Moby-Dick*, perhaps the greatest book on nature ever written, narrator Ishmael weaves various motives for a whaling voyage into his opening chapter, "Loomings": escape from personal neuroses; the appeal of water, that no land-based pastoral can satisfy; the satisfaction of being paid for one's troubles; tonic benefits from exercise and pure sea air; the itch of far away places; and above all, "the overwhelming idea of the great whale himself" (29). Ishmael conjectures that his whaling voyage may be set down by Providence as a "brief interlude and solo between more extensive performances." But as it happens this "shabby part" in a whaling scenario, where others are assigned magnificent or easy or comic roles in other productions, leads to a performance worth telling about, one that justifies the imminence suggested by "Loomings." Ishmael's story, once told, sweeps us out of our immaterial roles and presses us into a momentous drama in which we are confronted with the elements that link each of our lives to all life and to our place within a biotic community.

I believe that we are at such an "Ishmael moment" today, ready for a story that reconnects us to the human universals which, as Aristotle writes in his *Poetics*, are the province of literature. History tells us what *happened*, he says. Literature ("poetry") tells us what *happens*. "Poetry, therefore, is more philosphical and more significant than history, for poetry is more concerned with the universal, and history more with the individual" (IX, 17). The accelerating pace and now globalizing scale of history seems, to those of us who call ourselves ecocritics, to require a new look at literature, a fresh examination that presumably makes some sense of the human place within it all.

This is a book about literary interpretation, about what happened and is happening environmentally and what happens or does not happen in literature. Or in literary interpretation.

Gloomings

Start with a historian who is also concerned with universals. Renowned student of the past Arnold Toynbee, in his narrative history of the world entitled *Mankind and Mother Earth*, which was published in 1976 at the end of his long career and also at the time of the first worldwide recognition of the possibility of environmental disaster, reflected somberly upon the biological health of the planet. He concluded that humankind now has the power to "make the biosphere uninhabitable, and that it will, in fact, produce this suicidal result within a foreseeable period of time if the human population of the globe does not now take prompt and vigorous concerted action to check the pollution and the spoliation that are being inflicted upon the biosphere by shortsighted human greed" (9).

What was the late twentieth-century response to widespread appeals like Toynbee's for awareness and concerted action on pressing environmental issues? At the beginning of a new millennium and near the time I am writing this, Earth Day, 2001, one might look back and reflect that thirty-one Earth Days have passed since the first one in 1970. Despite a few progressive accomplishments, all of the signs announce that we are further behind than ever in efforts to protect Earth's ecosystems and thus our future on the planet. With the present United States president, an oil man who shows little or no interest in environmental concerns, our well-being is assessed from the top almost entirely in economic terms. But, as Alison Hawthorne Deming reminds us, "if we reported each year's progress not in terms of fiscal loss and gain but in terms of the earth's biological and cultural loss and gain, we would have a more accurate assessment of human success" (13).

The disquieting fact is that we have grown inured to the bad news of human and natural disasters. The catalog of actual and potential environmental crises is by now familiar to us all, so familiar as to have become dismissible. Ten, twenty, or thirty years ago we were regularly warned of spectres on the horizon: An unchecked growth of world population, tripling from 2 to 6 billion in the twentieth century and on its way to perhaps 10 billion in the next few decades, accelerating beyond the present rate of 247 new Earthlings every minute, nearly 250,000 every day, and 130 million per year. Indications of global climate warming of potentially enormous effects. The muted but still real threat of nuclear warfare. Actual instances of radiation poisoning, chemical or germ warfare, all rendered more threatening by the rise of terrorism. Industrial accidents like that in Bhopal, India, where the death toll lies between 20,000 and 30,000. Destruction of the planet's protective ozone layer. The overcutting of the world's remaining great forests. An accelerating rate of extinction of plants and animals, estimated at 74 species per day and 27,000 each year. The critical loss of arable land and groundwater through desertification, contamination, and the spread of human settlement. Overfishing and toxic poisoning of the world's oceans. Inundation in our own garbage and wastes. A tide of profit- and growth-driven globalization that overwhelms the principle of long-term sustainability, our best hope for the future. At each day's end, as David W. Orr summed it up, "the Earth will be a little hotter, its waters more acidic, and the fabric of life more threadbare".[1]

Where do we stand now? Population-growth estimates have fallen somewhat, to the range of 9 billion by mid-century, but that is still several times more than appears sustainable over a long period and takes no account of the inevitable associated threats of massive air and water pollution, food and resource shortages, runaway urbanization, and all of the other above-listed ills that increasing flesh is heir to.[2] Half the world's jobs are dependent on fisheries, forests, and small farms, but most of the world's fish, forest, and water resources are being used up at a rate much beyond sustainability. These trends leave increasing numbers of people in poverty and hopelessness, flash fuel for the spark of terrorism (Lash 1789). Gary Snyder assesses the current situation in an update to his 1969 essay, "Four Changes":

> Twenty-five years later. The apprehension we felt in 1969 has not abated. It would be a fine thing to be able to say, "We were wrong. The natural world is no longer threatened as we said then." One can take no pleasure, in this case, in having been right. Larger mammals face extinction and all manner of species are being brought near extinction. Natural habitat is fragmented and then destroyed. The world's forests are being cut at a merciless rate. Air, water and soil are all in worse shape. Population continues to climb. The few remaining traditional people with place-based sustainable economies are driven into urban slums or worse. The quality of life for everyone has gone down, what with resurgent nationalism, racism, violence both random and organized, and increasing social and economic inequality. There are whole nations for whom daily life is

> an ongoing disaster. I still stand by the basics of "Four Changes." (149–50)

What does all this have to do with those of us in the field of English, with the study and teaching of literature? As a cultural activity, like all other cultural practices, English teaching and research goes on within a biosphere, the part of the earth and its atmosphere in which life exists. In some of the literary texts that we study and discuss, this enveloping natural world is a part of the subject on the printed page before us. But even when it is not, it remains as a given, a part of the interpretive context, whether or not we choose to deal with it in our study and teaching. Worsening environmental conditions rub our noses in this contextual reality.

As the circumstances of the natural world intrude ever more pressingly into our teaching and writing, the need to consider the interconnections, the implicit dialogue between the text and the environmental surroundings, becomes more and more insistent. Ecocriticism is developing as an explicit critical response to this unheard dialogue, an attempt to raise it to a higher level of human consciousness. Teaching and studying literature without reference to the natural conditions of the world and the basic ecological principles that underlie all life seems increasingly shortsighted, incongruous.

As the introduction's arguments on behalf of practicality indicate, I believe that a generous share of pragmatism is necessary if we are to carry on the sort of meaningful teaching and research that our position within the biospheric envelope bespeaks. Unlike the buzz-saw irrationalism of global politics and nationalism, environmental issues *can* respond to rational means of solution (Huxley, "Politics" 330). Giles Gunn reminds us of William James's position that pragmatism proposes turning away from ultimate philosophical investigations, "translating questions of meaning and truth into questions of practice," thus directing them, as James said, " 'towards concreteness and adequacy, towards facts, towards action, and towards power' " (Gunn 38). Pragmatic awareness, as I see it, undergirds the discipline of ecocriticism, separating it from that devaluing of the real that characterizes much literary criticism of recent years.

"Contemporary critical theory fails to connect with the full human world," writes Mark Turner in *Reading Minds*, "to the extent that it treats objects in literature that can be seen only by means of the theory: in that case, if the theory vanishes, its objects vanish" (4). Turner notes a related story mentioned by Frank Kermode that caught my biologically attuned attention; the following was affixed to a laboratory door in the Life Sciences Building at UCLA: "'Les théories passent. Le grenouille reste.—Jean Rostand, *Carnets d'un biologiste.*' There is a risk that in the less severe discipline of criticism the result may turn out to be different; the theories will remain, but the frog may disappear" (Turner 264). Further irony intrudes from the real world, where the frogs actually *are* disappearing, for reasons which herpatologists are studying but which include human-caused environmental changes unrelated to critical theory (see Withgott).

Most of us, as current practitioners and students of literary criticism, have tended to insulate ourselves from environmental concerns so long as they remain on page nine of the newspapers rather than page one. In the face of increasing evidence of our imperilment, we continue, in the proud tradition of humanism, as David Ehrenfeld says, "to love ourselves best of all" and to celebrate the self-aggrandizing ego, placing private interest above public, even—irrationally enough—in matters of common survival (239). The main character in Don DeLillo's masterful postmodern spin, *White Noise*—a college professor and, wryly enough, a department head—refuses to believe that a lethally poisonous chemical cloud is invading his own tasteful suburban neighborhood rather than confining itself to someplace more appropriate. He reassures a worried family member as follows: "These things happen to poor people who live in exposed areas. Society is set up in such a way that it's the poor and uneducated who suffer the main impact of natural and man-made disasters. People in low-lying areas get the floods, people in shanties get the hurricanes and tornadoes. I'm a college professor. Did you ever see a college professor rowing a boat down his own street in one of those TV floods?" (114) Like him, we may refuse to believe that environmental reality has a claim upon our attention. And like him, we may be wrong.

A consideration of evolutionary biology and the long ages of human and prehuman history might suggest to us that we have neither the biological nor the cultural evolutionary experience to enable us to deal with long-term perils. "Our evolutionary history," as biologists Robert Ornstein and Paul Ehrlich write in *New World, New Mind*, "equipped us to live with a handful of compatriots, in a stable environment with many short-term challenges" (29). Having evolved over several million years with relatively brief life spans, and correspondingly short-term survival skills as the appropriate necessity, we are, from an evolutionary perspective, ill prepared for the long haul before us, in which our problem-solving strategies of the past are increasingly ineffectual.[3] The point is made tellingly in a Gallup poll for Earth Day 2001 in which the American public ranks the environment as number 16 in its list of most pressing concerns at the moment but expects it to rank number 1 in 25 years![4] If the global ice caps are indeed melting, as we are told, in consequence of global warming and could inundate sea-level cities in fifty years, the prevailing attitude appears to be, "That's not my problem." "As long as it doesn't happen on my watch," seems the common rumination among politicians. The moral responsibility to leave our children and their descendants a world as livable as the one we inherited is, so far, a matter of concern only among environmental philosophers.

We have, that is to say, grown accustomed to living with crises by ignoring those that do not affect us personally or by resolving them in some manner or other with comparatively little disturbance to business as usual. But environmental degradation is more than just another crisis. As Eric Ashby reminds us, "A crisis is a situation that will pass; it can be resolved by temporary hardship, temporary adjustment, technological and political expedients. What we are experiencing is not a crisis, it is a climacteric" (quoted in Sheffer 100). For the rest of human history, says Ashby, we will have to live with problems of population, resources, and pollution. Environmentalism and ecological concerns are no fad. More certainly than ever, our history becomes what H. G. Wells described as a race between education and catastrophe.

Wells's "education," in our present circumstances, is clearly related to our understanding and acting sensibly upon the sorts of environmental threats mentioned above. However, C. A. Bowers reminds us that education is not free of its own pockets of vested interest:

> When we consider the power of public education to obfuscate fundamental human/environmental relationships, to delegitimate certain forms of cultural knowledge while conferring high status on other forms, to determine who has access to the credentialing process essential to positions of power within society, and to renew the deepest held mythologies of the dominant culture, the need to develop an educational strategy becomes as important as any challenge now facing the environmental movement. (18)

In addition to these in-house obstructions, education is hamstrung by the widespread refusal to consider the biocultural aspects of human behavior. It has been noted that "the United States is the only developed country where a great many people who consider themselves educated dismiss Darwinian thought" (Stevens 12). If a concern for evolutionary biology seems odd coming from an English teacher, I hope it will seem less so as the book progresses. Darwinian thinking is central to the understanding of human culture, of which literature is a part. Evolutionary theory helps us to realize what makes us cultural creatures. As social scientist Dan Sperber writes, "to characterize 'human' in the phrase 'human culture,' we must draw on biology, hence on evolutionary theory, hence on the Darwinian model of selection" (101).

Postmodernist Frederic Jameson's familiar maxim, "Always historicize," is advice to be followed if the perception of history is also extended—as it seldom is now—to consider not only a recent cultural history, but an evolutionary history, which is increasingly seen as underlying and influencing cultural development, as well as the workings between the two. "The picture of the human mind/brain as a blank slate on which different cultures freely inscribe their own world-view, the picture of world-views as integrated systems wholly determined by socio-cultural history—these pictures, which many still hold, are incompatible with our current understanding of biology and psychology" (Sperber 113). The most thorough discrediting of the blank-slate theory, and a powerful case for the compatibility of modern biology with the social sciences and humanities, is to be found in Steven Pinker's *The Blank Slate: The Modern Denial of Human Nature* (2002).

The notable ignorance or suspicion of science in general, and evolutionary biology in particular, which is evident in higher education, requires examination. Biological evolution and cultural evolution are not independent, but interrelated; hence such scientists' descriptions of the process as "coevolutionary" or "biocultural." Because of the comparative speed with which it is capable of generating change in human behavior, cultural evolution seems our most hopeful avenue for the future. In recognizing this, Ornstein and Ehrlich, in *New World, New Mind*, call for "conscious evolution" to move an environmental ethic to the forefront of the human agenda (12). But this may be blocked, as they point out, not only by the constraints of much slower acting genetic traits, but also by cultural forces that work against needed social change. Among these forces are the walls between departments and divisions in universities and public schools, which often thwart interdisciplinary strategies for addressing the great human problems we face (325).

Environmental thinking within the discipline of English in the decade of the 1990s has seen minor gains of the sort mentioned in the introduction, but much remains to be done. Public awareness of environmental issues and concerns seems ahead of much of the academy, and much of the academy is ahead of English departments. Congressional passage of the Endangered Species Act in 1973 extended legal protection to some species of plants and animals, thus projecting ecological thinking into central public policy. Many young people want to make such thinking a part of their lives.

Environmental studies programs, most emphasizing a strong interdisciplinary science-humanities component, have experienced explosive growth in a number of American colleges and universities. In my college, the University of Oregon, a new undergraduate program in Environmental Studies overflowed with five hundred student majors in its first year. Fields such as psychology, political science, economics, architecture, and urban planning have been strongly influenced by environmental thinking. The question of rights for nonhuman organisms is one of central concern in contemporary philosophy and ethics, as evidenced in Roderick Nash's *The Rights of Nature.* The work of such scholars as Donald Worster, Carolyn Merchant, William Cronon, Roderick Nash, Dan Flores, Stephen Pyne, and Marc Reisner has made environmental history a vital area of study and one with a flourishing controversy, involving, once again, the party of nature-endorsers versus that of nature-skeptics.

That controversy is exemplified in William Cronon's 1995 anthology, *Uncommon Ground: Rethinking the Human Place in Nature.* The nature-constructionist stance represented in that book has been seriously questioned by Michael Soulé and Gary Lease, Donald Worster, George Sessions, Gary Snyder, and others.[5] What remains most strongly etched in my mind after reading *Uncommon Ground,* is the commentary of Anne Whiston Spirn, professor of landscape architecture and one of the book's contributors. Her concluding remarks, part of the round-table discussion in the book's final pages, describe the participants as brought together to live for five months in a "foreign biome and culture—Irvine," and she wonders "how different our conversations might have been if they had not taken place under fluorescent lights, in a windowless room, against the whistling woosh of the building's ventilating system." She regrets that the tangibility of nonhuman nature was inadequately engaged, and, in acknowledging the extent to which her sense of nature as a cultural construct has been furthered, she also affirms that "now more than ever I feel it crucial to reassert the reality of nonhuman features and phenomena. I hope our book doesn't overemphasize the cultural construction of nature to the extent that readers come away with the impression that nature is only a construct" (447–48).

Lawrence Buell similarly finds, in the great body of criticism on art's representation of nature, the presence of a myopic tendency, exacerbated by the interiorized urban environments in which such criticism is usually practiced. "When an author undertakes to imagine someone else's imagination of a tree, while sitting, Bartleby-like, in a cubicle with no view, small wonder that the tree seems to be nothing more than a textual function and one comes to doubt that the author could have fancied otherwise" (*Environmental Imagination* 5).[6]

As nature-endorsers like Gary Snyder, George Sessions, and Donald Worster see it, an unintended but harmful consequence of Cronon's stance in *Uncommon Ground* and other nature-skeptical positions is that they further distance environmental destruction from reality. Like the "Wise Use" movement favored by industry and development interests, the postmodernist skeptics hold that nature constantly changes, that it has changed to the point where there is nothing "natural" left, and so—unspoken or spoken conclusion—there is no reason to consider nature as anything but another venue for doing what we do: control it, change it, use it up. Thus, a cultural-constructionist position—in addition to ignoring biology—plays into the hands of the destroyers.[7] Edward O. Wilson finds that this kind of thinking, in discounting surviving wilderness areas as nothing but part of the human domain, "is specious. It is like flattening the Himalayas to the level of the Ganges Delta by saying that all the planet's surface is but a geometer's plane. Walk from a pasture into a tropical rainforest, sail from a harbor marina to a coral reef, and you will see the difference. The glory of the primeval world is still there to protect and savor" (*The Future of Life* 145).

The controversy over William Cronon's anthology and the dispute among environmental historians and philosphers over a conservation-biology versus postmodernist approach to the topic has its counterpart in the ideological battleground for control of the environmental movement. George Sessions, whose anthology, *Deep Ecology for the Twenty-First Century*, is a record of radical ecological thought from a deep ecology perspective—one which calls for profound changes in human lives and public policy—finds this struggle evidenced in what he describes as the environmental movement's shift since the 1960s from anthropocentric to ecocentric thinking. Sessions describes a tug-of-war developing after the wide public support and success of Earth Day, 1970. At that time, Sessions claims, the Marxist left, which had been little interested or involved in the environmental movement up to that point, attempted to steer it in the direction of its own anthropocentric, urban social agenda. Like Snyder, he sees the core of the environmental movement as thus under attack from both the left and the right in recent times.[8]

Contemporary deep ecologists argue that we must break through our preoccupation with mediating between only human issues—the belief that, as Warwick Fox puts it, "all will become ecologically well with the world if we just put this or that interhuman concern first" (18). Theodore Roszak, in *Person/Planet*, reminds us that

> we have an economic style whose dynamism is too great, too fast, too reckless for the ecological systems that must absorb its impact. It makes no difference to those systems if the oil spills, the pesticides, the radioactive wastes, the industrial toxins they must cleanse are socialist or capitalist in origin; the ecological damage is not mitigated in the least if it is perpetrated by a "good society" that shares its wealth fairly and provides the finest welfare programs for its citizens. The problem the biosphere confronts is the convergence of all urban-industrial economies as they thicken and coagulate into a single planet-wide system everywhere devoted to maximum productivity and the unbridled assertion of human dominance. (33)

The discipline of English has made admirable strides in recognizing important human needs in the conduct of our profession, such as the rights and contributions of women and minorities, as Cheryll Glotfelty has pointed out in her introduction to *The Ecocriticism Reader.* Without denying the importance of these issues to which first priority has been given, however, it seems undeniable that human—including all the subdivisions of human—domination of the biosphere is the overriding problem. It is also undeniable that those of us in the industrially advanced nations bear the greatest responsibility for this domination.

Now that international terrorism has become, among other things, a deadly means of undermining social stability, both the social-justice agenda and the ecocentric, global environmental concerns expressed by Roszak and Sessions can be expected to remain focal points in an emerging ecocriticism.[9] In the days following the September 11, 2001, terrorist attacks on the World Trade Center in New York and the Pentagon in Washington, D.C., prophetic signs of the times, taped in the windows of cars, were American flag posters with the caption, "One Nation Indivisible." Soon a counter-response appeared in other car windows—the familiar picture of planet Earth from space, carrying the message, "One Planet Indivisible." The conflict between national and global-ecological agendas will be increasingly felt in the context of an ever-shrinking, ecologically interconnected earth.

Can Humanism Embrace the Nonhuman?

When we look more closely at the place of our discipline of English in this global-ecological context, what do we see? With some notable exceptions, literary criticism and theory have been slow to respond to environmental considerations, even though the issues involved are engaged implicitly and explicitly in the works of literature to which we devote our professional lives. For the most part English has been, and continues to be, conducted so as to serve as a textbook example of anthropocentrism: divorced from nature and in denial of the biological underpinnings of our humanity and our tenuous connection to the planet.

David Copland Morris reminds us that Robinson Jeffers's "inhumanism"—defined by Jeffers as " 'a shifting of emphasis and significance from man to not-man; the rejection of human solipsism and recognition of the transhuman significance' "—is a continuously repressed counterpoint to humanism in Western history and philosophy. This exclusion is represented by the near-absence of the inhumanist critique in leading contemporary textbooks (Morris 1–2; see also Cokinos). Ornstein and Ehrlich write that from a biological standpoint we live in a world of "caricature" that "simplifies reality so that much of the environment is not registered in the organism's sensory system" (18). Those caricatures may be found as controlling influences in our field of English as well.

It is one of the great mistaken ideas of anthropocentric thinking (and thus one of the cosmic ironies) that society is complex while nature is simple. The publisher's retort in the epigraph for this chapter—"These stories have trees in them"—conveys the assumption that modern readers have outgrown trees. That literature in which nature plays a significant role is, by definition, irrelevant and inconsequential. That nature is dull and uninteresting, while society is sophisticated and interesting. Ignoring for the moment the fact that there is a good deal of human society in Norman Maclean's book, we might examine these assumptions that underlie the editor's put-down.[10] If we have been alive to the revolutionary biological discoveries of recent times, the greatest of all intellectual puzzles is the earth and the myriad systems of life that it encompasses. As W. H. Auden wrote in his introduction to anthropologist-naturalist Loren Eiseley's book, *The Star-Thrower*, "What modern science has profoundly changed is our way of thinking about the nonhuman universe. We have always been aware that human beings are characters in a story in which we can know more or less what has happened but can never predict what is going to happen; what we never realized until recently is that the same is true of the universe. But, of course, its story is even more mysterious than our own" (17).

Adaptive strategies in nature embrace intricacies that boggle our understanding. One of the great challenges of literature, as a creation of human society, is to examine this complexity as it relates—or fails to relate—to the daily work we do as teachers and scholars. Dismissible trees, for example, have received compelling culturally and ecologically informed literary countertreatment in a number of recent works, including Robert Pogue Harrison's *Forests: The Shadow of Civilization*, Michael P. Cohen's *A Garden of Bristlecones: Tales of Change from the Great Basin*, and Simon Schama's *Landscape and Memory*. As Schama says of the tourist-cliché "cathedral grove" of trees, for example,

> Beneath the commonplace is a long, rich, and significant history of associations between the pagan primitive grove and its tree idolatry, and the distinctive forms of Gothic architecture. The evolution from Nordic tree worship through the Christian iconography of the Tree of Life and the wooden cross to images like Caspar David Friedrich's explicit association between the evergreen fir and that architecture of resurrection . . . may seem esoteric. But in fact it goes directly to the heart of one of our most powerful yearnings: the craving to find in nature a consolation for our mortality. It is why groves of trees, with their annual promise of spring awakening, are thought to be a fitting décor for our earthly remains. So the mystery behind this commonplace turns out to be eloquent on the deepest relationships between natural form and human design. (14–15)

The past response from much of the English profession to the rise of ecological consciousness has been that the connection between literature and the conditions of the earth and nonhuman as well as human life is something that we do not talk about. Where the subject has arisen in the past, it has commonly been assigned to a safely negligible category such as "nature writing" or pastoralism or "regionalism." Looking back at the first stirrings of ecocriticism, one might note the nonreception from the English profession of Joseph W. Meeker's seminal 1974 book, *The Comedy of Survival: Studies in Literary Ecology*. Launched by a major publisher at a time of widespread public concern for the environment, with a challenging introduction by the distinguished ethologist Konrad Lorenz, this provocative book offered the first genuinely new reading of literature from a biological/ecological viewpoint. Meeker wrote in his introductory pages,

> Human beings are the earth's only literary creatures. . . . If the creation of literature is an important characteristic of the human species, it should be examined carefully and honestly to discover its influence upon human behavior and the natural environment—to determine what role, if any it plays in the welfare and survival of mankind and what insight it offers into human relationships with other species and with the world around us. Is it an activity which adapts us better to the world or one which estranges us from it? From the unforgiving perspective of evolution and natural selection, does literature contribute more to our survival than it does to our extinction? (3–4)

Meeker's principal contribution in *The Comedy of Survival* is a challenging rereading of literary genres, especially tragedy and comedy, from an ecological viewpoint. Virtually ignored by reviewers in the field of English, though a nominee for the Pulitzer Prize, its interdisciplinary approach seemed to sink it in academic waters. Nature is vexingly interdisciplinary. Annie Dillard's *Pilgrim at Tinker Creek*, another fine and memorable book on nature but one which offered fewer cross-disciplinary challenges, won the Pulitzer that year. But one measure of the significance of Meeker's book is that it confronts essential questions that bear upon us as both informed readers and academic specialists even more strongly today than when it was first published.[11]

The extension of human morality to the nonhuman world, as represented in the passage and widespread public support of the Federal Endangered Species Act, stands as a powerful contrast to our discipline's limited human vision, our narrowly humanistic perception of what is consequential in life. This political widening of the public conception of ethics to encompass the rights of nature calls upon us as academics to redefine our humanistic tradition. Gary Snyder reminds us that we have no word yet for a humanistic inquiry that includes the nonhuman. He adds, "I suggest (in a spirit of pagan play) we call it 'pan-humanism'" ("Rediscovery" 454).[12] The challenge that faces us is to outgrow our notion that human beings are so special that the earth exists for our comfort and disposal alone, to move beyond a narrow ego-consciousness toward a more inclusive eco-consciousness.

As I have suggested, perhaps the most harmful contemporary version of this ego-consciousness is the extreme subjectivism of much postmodernism, a philosophy that Albert Gelpi characterizes as "a deepening sense of the mind's alienation from nature and of the world's alienation from reality; an intensified experience of material randomness and temporal flux, of moral relativity and psychological alienation" (quoted in Murphy, *Farther Afield* 83). Such subjectivism intimates no reality, no nature, beyond what we construct within our own minds. This is a world of human solipsism, denied by the common sense that we live out in our everyday actions and observations. It is denied as well by a widely accepted scientific understanding of our human evolution and of the history of the cosmos and the earth, the real world, which existed long before the presence of humans, and which goes on and will continue to go on, trees continuing to crash to the forest floor even if no human auditors are left on the scene. Of course we humans affect and interpret—"construct"—our earthly environment, inevitably mediating to some degree—culturally and textually—between ourselves and the world. This is perhaps postmodernism's most salient contribution to our thinking. It has done much to raise our awareness of the national, ethnic, racial, gender, and other lenses through which we interpret reality. But it cannot long be ignored that our constructions occur always within the overarching context of an autonomously existing system that we call nature.

Dazzling end runs around the physical world, for all their theoretical and logical ingenuity, have not gone unchallenged. Desert writer Edward Abbey, with a considerable academic background in philosophy, handles them with a typical ask-Abbey comeback: "to refute the solipsist or the metaphysical idealist all that you have to do is take him out and throw a rock at his head. If he ducks, he's a liar. His logic may be airtight, but his argument, far from revealing the delusions of living experience, only exposes the limitations of logic" (111–12).

"Nature" is an abstraction, true, but it is also an imposing material presence in whose highly contested fate we are all deeply implicated, inextricably bound to it through our Darwinian bodies and their equally evolved brains. The great blind spot of postmodernism is its dismissal of nature, and especially human nature. The constructionist nature-skeptics have walled themselves off from the life sciences, often the most reliable source of knowledge of human nature and behavior, which, if acted upon with moral intelligence, offers the best hope of making their humanitarian political goals—shared by nearly all the scientists and nature-endorsers they exclude—more attainable.

A nature-conscious, nature-validating literature and criticism offers a needed corrective in its regard—either implicit or stated—for the nonhuman. Think, in this context, of the example of Joseph Wood Krutch, a twentieth-century intellectual who first achieved a major reputation as a New York literary, dramatic, and cultural critic and scholar. In his later years he moved to New England, and then to Arizona, and became—can it be stated without hearing a snicker from Maclean's dismissive publisher?—a nature writer. In this latter role Krutch authored a book on Thoreau and many further volumes, including *The Twelve Seasons*, *The Desert Year*, *The Voices of the Desert*, *The Great Chain of Life*, and other works on the Grand Canyon, Baja California, and other aspects of the natural world. Having argued in his famous early book, *The Modern Temper* (1929), that contemporary science had sucked modern life dry of its moral and spiritual values, Krutch went on to become something of a scientist himself, but a scientist of a natural world in which he found many of the values that he had presumed to be lost. Not all science murders to dissect. He became a writer of natural history who, under the influence of naturalist authors like Henry David Thoreau, Mary Austin, and Aldo Leopold, came to reassess his dualistic view of human nature.

Describing how his own version of ego-consciousness had gradually shifted toward eco-consciousness, Krutch tells of his growing sense that humankind's ingenuity has outpaced its wisdom: "We have engineered ourselves into a position where, for the first time in history, it has become possible for man to destroy his whole species. May we not at the same time have philosophized ourselves into a position where we are no longer able to manage successfully our mental and spiritual lives?" (*Measure of Man* 28).

Although Krutch remained in many respects a traditional humanist all his life, he found that his investigation of what he called "the paradox of Man, who is a part of nature yet can become what he is only by being something also unique," led him to expand his vision of what is significant (*More Lives Than One* 313). The realization came to be summed up for him in the words with which he found himself responding to the announcement of Spring by a chorus of frogs: "We are all in this together." ("Le grenouille reste.") As he recalls in his autobiography, "This sentence was important to me because it stated for the first time a conviction and an attitude which had come to mean more to me than I realized and, indeed, summmed up a kind of pantheism which was gradually coming to be an essential part of the faith—if you can call it that—which would form the basis of an escape from the pessimism of *The Modern Temper* upon which I had turned my back without ever conquering it" (*More Lives Than One* 284–95).

His growing sense of interconnectedness between the human and nonhuman world led Krutch to risk being labeled with what he calls "the contemptuous epithet, 'nature-lover'" (*More Lives Than One* 338). He might have added that his adoption of the desert Southwest as the subject of his books also left him open to the contemptuous epithet "western writer" or, worse yet, "regionalist."

Krutch's example and his plea for interconnectedness are not likely to be noticed today. The greatest problem ecocriticism presently faces is the inertia of existing literary-critical enterprises. Ecocritic William Howarth has astutely pointed out that disciplines tend to resist new approaches, giving lip service to innovation but remaining largely in their established grooves. "Literary theorists will regard ecocritics as 'insufficiently problematic' if their interests do not clearly match current ideological fashion. An ethical politics is welcome, yet not if it focuses on nonhuman topics such as scenery, animals, or landfill dumps" ("Some Principles" 77).

Part of this resistance derives from the conventional view that humanists study humankind and scientists study such things as the environment, ignoring the irony pointed out by Neil Evernden that studying humankind apart from its environment is a classic example of the reductionism humanists criticize in the sciences. "Indeed, even the suggestion that man is tied to anything but himself, or that he shares biological imperatives with other creatures is seen in some quarters as an affront to humanity," writes Evernden. Humanists must be concerned with environmental matters, he continues, because they involve values, and "values are the coin of the arts. Environmentalism without aesthetics is merely regional planning" (102–3).

"The Whaleness of the Whale"

What shape is the study of literary ecology likely to take in the immediate future? Nature writing, which has been the mainstay of literature-environment studies in the past, will continue to hold a central position. Of nature writing, Barry Lopez has claimed that "this area of writing will not only one day produce a major and lasting body of American literature, but that it might also provide the foundation for a reorganization of American political thought" (297).[13] While such predictions may be considered visionary, one can find some evidence of seeds that have taken root in Aldo Leopold's "Land Ethic," in his *A Sand County Almanac*, or in the widening sphere of obligation described in Roderick Nash's *The Rights of Nature*. The last years of the twentieth century and the first years of the twenty-first have witnessed a plethora of important nature writing and ecocritical studies and anthologies.[14]

Nature writing, continuing and extending its solid achievements with rural and wilderness topics, can be expected to carry on its traditional role while expanding into minority and urban environmental subjects and concerns, as in Michael Bennett and David W. Teague's recent collection, *The Nature of Cities: Ecocriticism and Urban Environments.* The challenge for such studies will be to explore urban, social-justice, and minority concerns from an ecologically conscious point of view that avoids being exclusively anthropocentric.[15] A further expansion of nature-writing study can be expected in the field of what Alison Hawthorne Deming calls "literary science writers" (207). The metaphorical and narrative achievements of scientists such as Loren Eiseley, Rachel Carson, Edward O. Wilson, Richard Dawkins, Stephen Jay Gould, Theodora Stanwell-Fletcher, Gary Paul Nabhan, and many others will repay the interdisciplinary effort of scholars who are interested in extending their literary perspectives. Other critical and thematic areas that will continue to be explored include an increasing response to environmental pollution, as well as writings in ecofeminism, place-centered and bioregional works, reinterpretations of the creations of writers whose canonical position is already established, and an opening of the canon to heretofore silent or silenced voices.

If current critical fashions seem to resist considering humankind as bound to nonhuman contexts, so too do many contemporary writers, says Scott Russell Sanders. "Why is so much recent American fiction so barren?" he asks. Against the encompassing natural world of much past American literature, Sanders finds a contemporary "ever-growing corps of wizards concocting weaker and weaker spells" and asserts that "however accurately it reflects the surface of our times, fiction that never looks beyond the human realm is profoundly false, and therefore pathological" (182, 194). At the present turn of the millennium, unprecedented problems of overpopulation, pollution, global climate change, and accelerating loss of plant and animal species seem to accompany Sanders's judgments. We are the first generation in human history, Jared Diamond reminds us, to question whether our followers will survive or inhabit a planet capable of sustaining healthful human life (*Third Chimpanzee* 313).

Within the emerging themes of literary/environmental studies, the fictional explorations of environmental pollution, bioregionalism, and animal lives seem to claim increased attention and new approaches. Don DeLillo's 1985 National Book Award winner, *White Noise,* cited by Sanders as an example of fiction mired in the human realm, may also be read as a striking new environmental vision, "an ecological novel at the dawn of ecological consciousness," as Frank Lentricchia calls it (7). The novel's narrator, Jack Gladney, and his family are caught in the poisonous fallout from a chemical spill, referred to in the officialese warnings as an "airborne toxic event." This suburbanized and wholly plausible fiction parallels the "toxic events" that killed or fatally contaminated many thousands at Bhopal and Chernobyl and which threatened disaster at Three Mile Island at about the time of the book's publication.

The natural world that Sanders finds missing in *White Noise* turns out to be not so much missing as hiding, a kind of sublimated presence, like Willa Cather's attribution of power to the thing left unsaid, or the seven-eighths of Hemingway's iceberg of meaning that lies beneath the surface. Considering the novel requires what ecocritic Robert Kern calls "reading against the grain," a process he describes as working "to recover the environmental character or orientation of works whose conscious or foregrounded interests lie elsewhere" (11). While not often ostensibly present, nature intrudes in *White Noise* in its apparent absence, even in its commodification, as seen in the garishly lighted vegetables and fruit in the gleaming supermarket where the Gladneys spend their evenings shopping on a trancelike wave of white-noise-bathed acquisition. Nature is the eclipsed farm, now replaced forever by a forest of signs and tour buses and camera-snapping tourists leading up to THE MOST PHOTOGRAPHED BARN IN AMERICA. Nature is behind the spectacular sunsets, technicolored by releases of poisonous gases. Nature drives the fickleness of the wind carrying the airborne toxins. It obtrudes its presence in the fear of death that posseses the main characters, a relentless hold of coporeal mortality upon even their presumably postnatural, postmodern bodies.

The buzzing technological static that encloses the characters in *White Noise*—"CABLE HEALTH, CABLE WEATHER, CABLE NEWS, CABLE NATURE" (231)—lends significance to its silent counterpart: a natural world that watches from the edges, coughs when you would kiss (as in Auden's personification of Time), and sardonically withholds from the thoroughly addled characters its traditional American benisons of pastoral healing and escape.[16] Frederic Jameson's judgment that postmodernism marks the end of the modernization process—when nature is gone for good—may seem to sum up the novel, but reading it Kern-like, against the postmodernist grain, one finds a nature less easily dismissed. Because nature is always "there" in some form or other, and certainly in the evolutionary genetic heritage of our bodies and brains—which are taken up in the following chapters—the reports of nature's death have been greatly exaggerated.

Leslie Marmon Silko also explores threatened human/environment relationships in her 1977 novel *Ceremony*. Here, a spiritually poisoned individual in a technologically threatened landscape finds in the surviving remnants of his Native American heritage the healing detoxifying potentialities of both land and people.[17] Silko's *Almanac of the Dead* also explores this tainted social territory, as do Chickasaw writer Linda Hogan's *Solar Storms* and *Power*. In these novels and in *White Noise*, an economically driven technology may serve as the clear target for an environmental critique. In more muted form such a critique may be found as well in John Updike's last Rabbit Angstrom novel, *Rabbit at Rest* (1990), which Cynthia Deitering has characterized, with *White Noise*, as a "postnatural" novel, a fiction of toxicity, set in an America debased and used up (199–200). In *Rabbit at Rest* Updike's often lyrical sense of nature seems caught up in something like the despoliation and commodification of the physical world that has motivated so much contemporary environmental and nature writing.[18]

Octavia Butler offers a futurist fictional counter to Updike's *Rabbit* realism in her *Parable of the Sower*, depicting urban environmental chaos in post–Big One Los Angeles and following the characters as they flee toward some form of pastoral deliverance. The toxic landscape is also increasingly present in nonfiction works such as Terry Tempest Williams's *Refuge* and in the fields of science fiction and short fiction in recent years, as seen in the works of such writers as Ursula Le Guin, Kurt Vonnegut, Rick DeMarinis, Rudolfo Anaya, Edward Allen, Octavia Butler, John Edgar Wideman, and T. Coraghessan Boyle. The threat of toxicity is seen in current films as well, in *The China Syndrome*, *Silkwood*, *A Civil Action*, and *Erin Brockovich*.[19] The theme of environmental justice is frequently present in such works, as environmental degradation falls most heavily upon the poor and the powerless. The journal *Science* reports that in developing countries one-fourth of the world's population of 6 billion are breathing air below the World Health Organization's level of acceptability, 2 billion have inadequate sanitation, and 1 billion do not have access to clean water (Leshner 897). But toxicity eventually threatens all classes and peoples as an underlying fact of our lives, part of the emerging ecology of being human.[20]

An ascendant and often virulent technology also seems to have revivified concern for place and region—or bioregion, as it would now likely be called to emphasize nonhuman as well as human constituents. Rootedness, says French philosopher Simone Weil, "is perhaps the most important and least recognized need" of the human spirit (quoted in Sale

47). The exploration of this need is evident in the proliferation in recent years of place-centered essayists and fiction writers—Wallace Stegner, Wendell Berry, Gary Snyder, Annie Dillard, Edward Abbey, Sue Hubbell, Barry Lopez, Ann Zwinger, Rick Bass, John Daniel, Ann Ronald, and Terry Tempest Williams, to name a few. Given the long-established American tradition in this field from Bartram, Cooper, and Thoreau to John Muir, Mary Austin, and Aldo Leopold to present-day writers, such an efflorescence in a time of widespread ecological concern is not unexpected.

What is most notable, however, is the number of new books and articles reexamining place and bioregion by scholars from a wide range of disciplines, including philosophers and phenomenologists (Maurice Merleau-Ponty, Edward S. Casey, Maxine Sheets-Johnstone); geographers (Yi-Fu Tuan, Edward Relph, Douglas C. Pocock); anthropologists (Keith Basso); historians (Donald Worster, Dan Flores, William Cronon); and scientists (James Lovelock, Paul Shepard, Edward O. Wilson, Jared Diamond, Gary Paul Nabhan). Their works affirm human connections to place as profoundly important and interesting. What has emerged from these studies is a virtual new science of human emplacement that cries out for attention from literary scholars, who, for the most part, have stayed on their side of the humanist-scientist barrier, limiting their focus to metaphor and language while ignoring the exciting interdisciplinary opportunities that beckon.[21]

Other scientifically related subjects attractive to students of literary ecology are animals and the deep connection between humans and nonhuman animals. These topics recall a long history of mankind in the company of animals, which Darwin's insights first forced us to reconsider. Sociobiological research in the last twenty-five years, as Sarah Blaffer Hrdy notes in her celebrated 1999 book, *Mother Nature: Maternal Instincts and How They Shape the Human Species*, has "looked to the animals to revise and build new theory on both animal behavior and human behavioral ecology" (78). The discovery that reason itself is evolutionary, say George Lakoff and Mark Johnson in *Philosophy in the Flesh* (1999), "utterly changes our relation to other animals and changes our conception of human beings as uniquely rational. Reason is thus not an essence that separates us from other animals; rather, it places us on a continuum with them" (4).

The connection between human and nonhuman animals is strongly made in a work like John Muir's "Stickeen," perhaps the best dog story in our language. Beneath the adventure tale the reader experiences a strong response to the human-dog bond, an emotional attachment formed over the thousands of years in which dogs have been humans' domestic companions. Muir's conception of his little dog as "horizontal philosopher," and his detailed description of Stickeen's emotional responses to the challenges he faces, link him closely to the reader, who must question not only his or her anthropocentrism, but also the extent to which anthropomorphism, applied to animals, is more than a convention of figurative language.[22]

Recent scientific studies and findings complicate our understanding of the subject far beyond the simple categorizations of the past. The traditional reluctance of many scientists and philosophers to attribute consciousness to animals must be questioned in the face of new evidence.[23] This evidence is remarkably consistent with Darwin's extensive argument, in his *The Descent of Man, and Selection in Relation to Sex* (1871) and *The Expression of the Emotions in Man and Animals* (1872), for a psychological and behavioral gradation, a continuum, between humans and other animals. We are increasingly led to the borders of our species, where, for example, we share nearly all of our genetic makeup with the common chimpanzees, and where the ecological fascination with such edges, or ecotones, is increasingly evident.

As the traditional perception of animal otherness is challenged and explored, animal presences assume a larger place in our lives and thinking. This is evidenced in an important recent study by Marian Scholtmeijer of animal victims in modern literature. She argues that animals "contend with the conceptions that seek to subsume them. Their resistance to enculturation influences the nature and profundity of the difficulties literature addresses" (8). Nonhuman animal minds draw the attention of biologically sophisticated nonfiction writers such as Peter Matthiessen, Barry Lopez, David Quammen, and Vicki Hearne, as well as scientists including Paul Shepard, Richard Nelson, Jane Goodall, Edward O. Wilson, Stephen Jay Gould, Bobbi Low, Alison Jolly, Sarah Blaffer Hrdy, Marlene Zuk, and Marc Hauser.

Animal lives are also explored in striking recent poetry by Denise Levertov, Mary Oliver, John Haines, and others. A wave of new nature poetry has been a response to the age of ecology, as the concept of an inexhaustible and constant nature is replaced by one of vulnerability and of recognition that our cultural identity rests uneasily upon deeper responsibilities.[24] Some poets of nature have bridged across to the sciences, including Loren Eiseley, A. R. Ammons, Alison Hawthorne Deming, Pattiann Rogers, James Merrill, Thomas Merton, and W. S. Merwin. The spirit of this new poetry, of relearning a relationship to nature, is expressed by Wendell Berry as "an implicit and essential humility, a reluctance to impose on things as they are, a willingness to relate to the world as student and servant, a wish to be included in the natural order rather than to 'conquer nature,' a wish to discover natural forms rather than to create new forms which would be exclusively human" (quoted in Merrill xviii). As environmental and ecological pressures grow in the century ahead, this new consciousness can be expected to further challenge poets' biotic awareness and linguistic innovativeness.

Revisiting the Canon

Animal presences bring to mind the depiction of animals in past literature, which in turn reminds us of another important function of ecocriticism—to reexamine and reinterpret the depictions of nature in the canonical works of the past. One might note, for example, Joseph Meeker's rereading of Dante's *Comedy* and Shakespeare's *Hamlet* in his *The Comedy of Survival*, or the revisiting of the English Romantic poets in ecocritical books by Jonathan Bate (*Romantic Ecology: Wordsworth and the Environmental Tradition* and *The Song of the Earth*) and Karl Kroeber (*Ecological Literary Criticism: Romantic Imagining and the Biology of Mind*), or Louise Westling's ecofeminist reinterpretation of classic American fiction in *The Green Breast of the New World.* Scott Slovic, first president of the Association for the Study of Literature and Environment, has argued that "there is not a single literary work anywhere that utterly defies ecological interpretation" ("Forum" 1090). Lawrence Buell emphasizes that "there is no site that cannot be startlingly and productively reenvisioned in such a way as to evoke a fuller environmental(ist) sense of it than workaday perception permits" (*Writing* 22–23). Buell's claim is objectified in his book's wide-ranging ecocritical interpretations, especially those dealing with urban and "unloved" environments and subjects.

Of course, memorable literature is not necessarily possessed of environmental correctness or rectitude, or even of any obvious environmental content. But rewarding interpretive opportunities often open up for the student or critic who chooses to read "against the grain" (to repeat Robert Kern's pertinent metaphor) of a text's apparent or primary interests, shifting critical attention from the anthropocentric to the biocentric (18).

Moby-Dick, again, provides a promising opportunity to rethink a classic. The extensive nature-endorsing cetology chapters, traditionally troublesome for scholars and readers, are an obvious point for reentry.

Without questioning the immense complexity of Melville's novel and the multiplicity of his vision, fresh readings exploring what my colleague David Copland Morris calls "The Whaleness of the Whale" will continue to add new convolutions to *Moby-Dick*'s deeply textured depths.[25]

From an evolutionary-biological viewpoint, Moby-Dick may be the most thoroughly realized animal in all literature. Similarly, his narrative interpreter Ishmael ("one of the finest, least-dedicated men in the whole world," Joseph Heller's Yossarian might call him) may be seen not only as a modern survivor, but as an evolutionary step forward, in the terms of Joseph Meeker's *The Comedy of Survival.* Embodying the qualities of accommodation and reconciliation that mark the life force as essentially adaptive and integrative, the biologically open Ishmael outlasts the evolutionarily dead-ended Ahab, who might be seen as the raging tragedian, the ultimate self-absorbed cultural constructionist, fixated with the idea of transforming nature—unsuccessfully, of course—into his own private nemesis, thereby provoking personal and ecological disaster. Eight years before Darwin's monumental work, as one critic points out, *Moby-Dick* reveals Meville's implicit prediction that "humanity will not be able to destroy the Moby-Dicks of the world without psychic and actual damage to itself" (Scholtmeijer 51).

Rethinking the canon along these lines—reading from an ecological rather than a narrowly human-centered perspective—suggests many possibilities. The twentieth century's scientific studies of human and nonhuman animal behavior and genetics have rewritten our conception of much of human nature and the old nature-nurture debate. An obvious candidate for literary reconstruction in this regard is literary naturalism, commonly dismissed as a brief phase of social Darwinism at the turn of the century and beyond. The work of writers as diverse as Jack London, Stephen Crane, Frank Norris, Edith Wharton, Theodore Dreiser, John Dos Passos, Djuna Barnes, Richard Wright, James T. Farrell, Ernest Hemingway, and John Steinbeck—all termed "naturalists" in some context or other—invites reinterpretation from ecocritics, both from informed evolutionary-biological and greened Marxist perspectives.[26]

The similarly unfashionable study of literary realism is also ripe for reconsideration, at a time when reality is increasingly demonstrating that not paying it critical attention does not make it go away. As John Updike reflected recently, "A writer of fiction, a professional liar, is paradoxically obsessed with what is true . . . [and] the unit of truth, at least for a fiction writer, is the human animal, belonging to the species (Homo sapiens) unchanged for at least 100,000 years" (quoted in Pinker 419).

One groundbreaking evolutionarily informed critical study on the influence of Darwin's little-read 1871 volume, *The Descent of Man, and Selection in Relation to Sex*, on American literary realism is Bert Bender's *The Descent of Love: Darwin and the Theory of Sexual Selection in American Fiction, 1871–1926*. Darwin's *The Origin of Species*, published in 1859, makes virtually no mention of *human* evolution. The connection appears in *The Descent of Man* a dozen years later, in 1871, and is continued in *The Expression of the Emotions in Man and Animals* in 1872.

Bender notes that most American literary critics have not read Darwin, especially his 1871 work, and have incorrectly assumed that his theory was simple and unimportant and that its human applications were relevant to only a few literary naturalists like Frank Norris, Theodore Dreiser, and Jack London. Among several other reasons for Darwin's comparative absence in American literary history, Bender observes that the fastidiousness of twentieth-century critics resulted in a general antipathy toward references to evolutionary-biological thought or to our animal heritage.[27] It might be added that many twentieth-century American literary critics, while overcoming fastidiousness in enthusiastically targeting American Puritanism or gentility or hegemony, have nevertheless maintained their own version of this reticence in steering clear of a study of Darwinism and its unrealized applicability to cultural studies.

There is much new territory ahead. The distinguished cell biologist Lewis Thomas has cautioned us that it is time for us as human beings "to grow up as a species." Because of what he considers our unique gift of consciousness, Thomas observes that "it is up to us, if we are to become an evolutionary success, to fit in, to become the consciousness of the whole earth. We are the planet's awareness of itself, and if we do it right we have a very long way to go" (52). As members of a discipline whose defining characteristics are consciousness and language, we in the field of English are particularly involved. We have indeed a very long way to go, and we may have no more than started the journey.

Turning, in our human understanding of nature, from the assumption of simplicity to an awareness of complexity would seem to suggest the need for environmentally concerned humanists to cross over disciplinary lines into the sciences.

2

Ecocriticism and Science

. . . .

> Ten years ago I started teaching about human evolution. I thought it was a one-off effort to tell bemused students in women's studies what any educated person should know about Darwin. A fair number of students hated the idea, to start with. They distrusted a biological straitjacket that might shackle them into traditional gender roles. We had good arguments. Ten years later, I have the opposite problem. A frightening number of people are ready to believe in genes for everything—not just gender but breast cancer, pesticide resistance, homosexuality, extroversion. Is biology omnipotent, and its mysteries solvable?
> —Alison Jolly, *Lucy's Legacy*

Academic borders and interrelationships are shifting as the study of literature and the environment begins to assume an active place in the profession of English. What that place is to be, particularly in its theoretical and methodological base, is still a protean issue. But it seems to me that ecocriticism should, by its very nature, find itself in some new relationship with other relevant disciplines, particularly the life sciences.

Stephen Jay Gould has dryly observed that "common usage now threatens to make 'ecology' a label for anything good that happens far from cities or anything that does not have synthetic chemicals in it" (*Ever Since Darwin* 119). I use the word *ecology* here the way Darwinist Gould would prefer, in its scientific sense, to refer to the study of the relationship between organisms and their living and nonliving environment. Ecocriticism's future is, I believe, encoded in the prefix *eco.* The word *ecology* was coined by German scientist Ernst Haeckel in 1866 (German *Ökologie*, from the Greek *oikos*, house). It is worth noting that Haeckel was a biologist and a zealous follower of Darwin. For Lewis Mumford, Darwin was less notable as the discoverer of evolution—"since others were also engaged in discovering it—but as the 'supreme ecologist,' whose conception of ecology was a combination of science and a sense of responsibility for life."[1]

The new study of literature and nature is connected to the science of ecology—taking from it not only the popular term *ecocriticism* but also the basic premise of the interrelatedness of a human cultural activity like literature and the natural world that encompasses it. Thus ecocritics may have been drawn into the disputes of the 1980s and 1990s over the authority of science, sometimes called the Science Wars. These controversies have been marked by attacks upon science, or the uses to which science has been put (a different issue), primarily by academics from the humanities and the social sciences.

The particular form of antiscience present in these disputes is high intellectual fare, not the sort of popular superstition recorded in Carl Sagan's 1995 book, *The Demon-Haunted World.* Ignorance and warped beliefs—currently exemplified by widespread fascination with conspiracy theories and paranormal wonders like psychics and alien space travelers—have been with us for a long time, though the human need to believe in the unbelievable has reached alarming levels with television's increasing programming of uncontested pseudoscience (see Yam). More alarming is the news that many of the enthusiasts for the paranormal are now drawn from the ranks of the better educated. Whether that new audience includes some of the same antiscience adherents from the academy is unclear. But the broad public support for science is threatened by such assaults, and the scientific community is worried.

As an ecocritic, so am I. Not because I feel compelled to endorse the role of science in the technological engine of perceived prosperity and progress, but because I would affirm the role of *science*—literally *knowledge*—in revealing how we, and nature, function, so that we are better able to think our way through the staggering environmental challenges we face. Furthermore, intellectuals who routinely disparage science weaken their own credibility and provoke a reactive wave of anti-intellectualism that weakens us all.

Antiscience attacks from the academy seem impelled by postmodernist assumptions of the bankruptcy of a scientifically grounded modern civilization. Postmodernism, originally a trend in French philosophy, is often, as a matter of course, opposed to science as authoritarian or oppressive (Segerstråle 474). These attacks have been largely ignored or unnoticed by the scientific community in the past. But in the mid-1990s, a counter-response arose from the scientific community, exemplified by two books, *Higher Superstition: The Academic Left and Science*, by biologist

Paul R. Gross and mathematician Norman Levitt, and *The Flight from Science and Reason*, an anthology edited by Gross, Levitt, and geographer Martin W. Lewis.

A third, and the most devastating, scientific counterattack came from physicist Alan Sokal in 1996, when he parodied cultural constructionist attacks upon science with an article of cleverly disguised scientific gibberish entitled "Transgressing the Boundaries: Toward a Transformational Hermeneutics of Quantum Gravity," submitted to *Social Text*, a journal of cultural constructionist persuasion. The journal's editors quickly accepted the essay as a godsend of antiscience pronouncements from a real physicist and printed it. Sokal than revealed the hoax in a following issue of the journal *Lingua Franca*, after which it made front-page news across North America and Europe.[2] The hoax played out like the plot of Mark Twain's sardonic short story, "The Man That Corrupted Hadleyburg." Satire, in both scenarios, pierced what many apparently saw as the great bubble of presumption. "Against the assault of laughter, nothing can stand," says Philip Traum (Satan), Mark Twain's spokesman in another of his late and dark tales, *The Mysterious Stranger* (360).

What do the Science Wars have to do with ecocriticism and ecocritics? The issues are large and complex, but if ecocriticism is to ground itself in ecology—that is, ecology as a science rather than as a buzzword—it needs to come to terms with questions about the place and worth of science in our lives. I believe that as students of literature and the environment, we have much more to gain than to fear from the company of the sciences, particularly the life sciences.

First, a confession. My experience of scholars in the humanities, myself included, is that they (we) are usually deficient in scientific aptitude and interests. C. P. Snow made this point over forty years ago in *The Two Cultures*, claiming that intellectuals, particularly literary scholars, are typically antiscience. "Natural Luddites" was his phrase, and he urged humanists to wake up and learn something about science (22). Today, the gulf seems even wider. Do nonscientists simply think differently than scientists? This much might be suggested by a certain tentativeness I felt in science courses in high school and college. Also, for the last forty-six years I have been married to a scientist—an ecologist, no less—and I have grown used to being called to account for weak or obscure arguments. As H. L. Mencken said, a man may be a fool and not know it, but not if he is married. Definitely not if he is married to a scientist.

But if I am a little bewildered by science, I am bewildered a lot more by the apparent zeal with which some of my fellow humanists scorn and attack it (Livingston 4). My advice to them is to marry a scientist, or as a less-momentous course of action, befriend one. Take one to lunch, or at least make eye contact when walking across campus. If you do get acquainted with a scientist, you will probably find that he or she knows much more about literature than you know about science. That is the beginning of interdisciplinary awareness.

We nonscientists seem to have three choices when facing up to our basic lack of aptitude for the sciences. First, ignore science. Second, take Snow's advice, pull up our socks, and try to learn something about it. Third, in the current critical fashion and as enthusiastic followers of an often-misunderstood and overgenerously applied Thomas Kuhn, regard and routinely characterize science as no more than another cultural/linguistic construction and thus just as subject to relativistic interpretation and social control as any other human activity.[3] Assuming that the first reponse is an unacceptably craven confession of inadequacy and that the second is considerably daunting, it is not surprising that alternative number three has proven attractive to many in the humanities. A typical judgment runs as follows: "Science is situated in the culture that enables it, thus science should not be exalted over literature, history, philosophy, or other nonscientific cultural expressions" (McRae 1). This attitude has led to a number of attacks from the unexalted, understandably resentful of science's position of power and prestige in the academy over the last half-century.

It is important to acknowledge that some of these attacks have been valid and necessary. Science as taught in the past has often failed to foster a respect for nature. Paul Shepard noted this over thirty years ago in the introduction to his book on ecology, *The Subversive Science.* And one of the most important correctives from the critics of science can be seen in the rise of ecology itself, not only as an important professional field within the sciences but even more as a way of thinking which, as Shepard, Barry Commoner, and others point out, reminds us that everything is connected to everything else and that science cannot be insulated from either the concerns of society or our rootedness in the natural world.

On this point it seems appropriate to question Gross and Levitt's too-easy acceptance of the science and technology-driven engine of economic growth and their tendency to assail what they regard as the excesses of environmentalism rather than taking more seriously than they do the threats to which it is responding. Paul and Anne Ehrlich's recent book, *Betrayal of Science and Reason*, offers an effective response to Gross and Levitt's charges of environmental extremism. So does Peter H.

Raven's 2002 Presidential Address to the American Association for the Advancement of Science. In his address Raven warns against those commentators who ignore science and "pretend to deliver 'good news' about the environment. They win fame by telling people what they want to hear" (955).

Undeniably, the context in which science takes place is a matter of the widest public concern, and much useful and productive criticism has been directed at the structure in which science operates and the technological uses to which it is put. But that does not nullify the force of Gross and Levitt's most telling points. For example, on the qualifications of those who attempt to judge the science itself, they advance one of their most powerful criticisms:

> Thus we encounter books that pontificate about the intellectual crisis of contemporary physics, whose authors have never troubled themselves with a simple problem in statics; essays that make knowing references to chaos theory, from writers who could not recognize, much less solve, a first-order linear differential equation; tirades about the semiotic tyranny of DNA and molecular biology, from scholars who have never been inside a real laboratory, or asked how the drug they take lowers their blood pressure (6).

Gross and Levitt's claim that the detractors of science are usually incompetent to judge the fields they attempt to criticize is particularly telling, especially when followed, as it was, by the Sokal hoax, which made their case more emphatically than they could have made it themselves.

On the Scientific Method

An even more disturbing charge from Gross and Levitt, one repeated by scientists of various political persuasions in *The Flight from Science and Reason*, is that those hostile to science have extended their indictment of science's contextual sins—real enough—to include an attack upon the scientific method itself, which is the heart and center of science.[4] This method of critical thinking through the gathering of data and testing of hypotheses is almost universally defended as the best means humanity has for freeing itself from dogma, prejudice, and error. As anthropologist Sarah Blaffer Hrdy writes in her study, *Mother Nature*, "Unlike superstition or religious faith, a good scientist's underlying assumptions are subject to continuous challenge. Sooner or later in science, wrong assumptions get revised" (xviii). When science is performing its central task, within the strict confines of its method—with its emphasis upon repeatability, weight of evidence, coherent logical progression, falsifiability—it moves eventually in the direction Hrdy describes, toward the revision of wrong assumptions.

On the question, for example, of whether there is a feminist scientific method, even such scientifically knowledgable proponents of feminism as Hrdy, Alison Jolly, Sandra Harding, Evelyn Fox Keller, Helen E. Longino, and Stephen Jay Gould are on record that there is not.[5] Their collective judgment is that, methodologically, there is no masculinist or feminist science, just good science and bad science. In her biography of Nobel Prize–winning geneticist Barbara McClintock, Keller acknowledges that McClintock herself rejected any such feminist methodology and classification (Keller xvii).

Furthermore, it seems clear from McClintock's own accounting that her "feeling for the organism" (the title of Keller's biography of her) is less a biologist's version of the feminine mystique than an example of the careful application of scientific method in which the intimate knowledge of one's subject and close attention to detail might enable a scientist—woman or man—to construct new and testable hypotheses. Keller notes, "I never argued that women would do a different kind of science," but she acknowledges that others have so interpreted her work (Nemecek 100). Doing good science, as McClintock insisted, has nothing to do with one's gender. She was echoing George Eliot (Mary Ann Evans), who had said it over a century earlier: "Science has no sex . . . the more knowing and reasoning faculties, if they act correctly, must go through the same process and arrive at the same result" (quoted in Hrdy xvii).

In the past social barriers to women in science have excluded many of them from scientific careers. The liberation of women to be scientists, or whatever they aspired to be, is some evidence of the improvability of the human condition. The advance of equity feminism in science, and the many women scientists on whose work my argument in this book rests, are evidence that the successful practice of science may draw from the aptitudes of both women and men (Barash and Lipton 188–210).[6] Several of the women scientists cited in these pages describe themselves as both feminists and scientists. Evolutionary biologist Marlene Zuk, in the final pages of her book on sexual selection among animals, voices her agreement with scientist colleague Patricia Gowaty, who has announced that "'Darwinian feminism is an oxymoron no longer'" (200).

To return to McClintock, the question whether the organism can have a feeling for *itself*, a causal role in its own development, a whole that is greater than the sum of its parts, is an interesting one that concerned Darwin and continues to interest many biologists, including Ernst Mayr, Richard Lewontin, and Charles Birch. Mayr calls this mode of thinking "organicism," or thinking in terms of systems (16). This "postmodern challenge to biology," as Birch calls it, is the proposed alternative to what Birch sees as Cartesian mechanistic biology (Griffin 69).[7] But the challenge is hardly postmodern, since Frederick Clements and other ecologists were studying the midwestern American prairies as systems over a century ago. Darwin himself was surely a holistic or systems thinker, enabling him to see and understand the kinds of relationships that led to his great theory. Systems thinking seems to be practiced even by such so-called reductionists as Edward O. Wilson, as is revealed in his *Biophilia* and *The Future of Life.*

Holistic thinking is necessary, even indispensable, but it must also anticipate all the eventualities of a complex system, for which reductionist techniqes may be required. Holistic or top-down thinking may thus depend for its advancement and refinement upon the "tinkering" represented by reductionism and the verifying techniques of the scientific method.[8] As Duke University biology professor Steven Vogel notes, while acknowledging the importance of how whole organisms work, "reductionism may not characterize all science, but it defines most of what we scientists do" (321).

"Scientists always take sides," says postmodernist Birch (76). But allowing that all such ideas as *organicism* or *reductionism* have hypothetical elements does not alter the practice of verification and falsification by which the scientific method works toward the impersonal evaluation of such hypotheses, regardless of which side their proponents are on. It is also important to keep in mind that, contrary to its use as a term of dismissal, reductionism—as Vogel, Wilson, Dan Sperber, and others remind us—is the tool by which science works to understand the constituents of a complex system. "The very word, it is true, has a sterile and invasive ring, like scalpel or catheter," says Wilson in *Consilience.* "Critics of science sometimes portray reductionism as an obsessional disorder. . . . That characterization is an actionable misdiagnosis. . . . It is the search strategy employed to find points of entry into otherwise impenetrably complex systems. Complexity is what interests scientists in the end, not simplicity. Reductionism is the way to understand it. The love of complexity without reductionism makes art; the love of complexity with reductionism makes science" (54).

Without the scientific method, science is indeed nothing but the hopelessly culture-bound activity that its detractors portray. But science has achieved its "exalted" status because it has been successful, through submitting to the rigors of its methodology, in discovering something of how nature works. From an evolutionary perspective, living things have the form that they do, and behave as they do, because that form has worked best for them. It has conferred on them a biological evolutionary advantage. (This is not to say that what once worked best will work best now or in the future, a matter which this book will revisit.) Like literary realism, science is concerned with understanding the system that works.[9] As Theodore M. Porter reminds us,

> Science is supposed to be about nature. It is supposed to yield knowledge that is impersonal, and in some way objective. And, not to persist too stubbornly with these ironic modalities, it succeeds. Knowledge in the sciences is widely shared, to the point that the same textbooks can be used all over the world. This is often taken as decisive evidence of the moral virtues of natural science, and it is real, even if it is often exaggerated. Scientists pride themselves on appealing to nature rather than opinion, and on using a neutral language of facts and laws, numbers and the logic of quantity. The universality of scientific knowledge is by no means complete, but the most skeptical sociology readily concedes that it is impressive. Is it not to the impersonal, objective methods of quantification and experimentation that we owe the universality of science? (219)

In the introduction to his anthology, *Postmodern Environmental Ethics*, nature-endorsing Max Oelschlaeger argues the postmodernist position that "scientific truth exists relative to a community of practitioners who have created a variety of procedures that guide research and criteria by which truth claims are evaluated." Further, he says, "alternative communities exist and therefore alternative descriptions for natural processes can always be offered" (4). Can be offered, yes, but the process of scientific verification, however the various techniques of verification may change or evolve, must still survive worldwide scientific challenge through all the procedures that make up the scientific method and lead eventually, as Hrdy says, to the correction of wrong assumptions. I hope there is room in ecocriticism for accommodation between a nature-endorsing postmodernism and the practice of scientific verification.

The scientific method is that which leads to figuring out something of the system that works, and those of us who fly in airplanes or drive in cars or ride bicycles, or wear glasses or contact lenses, or have our children vaccinated, or go to the hospital for serious surgery, or eat anything we did not grow ourselves, or use any of the million and one products of technology, have already cast our vote on the matter. As biologist Richard Dawkins says, "Show me a cultural relativist at 30,000 feet and I'll show you a hypocrite" (*River* 31–32).

A scientist may overstate or distort his or her data, but the methodology of the discipline is in place to question and refute and correct those misstatements. Unfortunately, in the nonsciences, overstating the evidence or obfuscating reality often enjoys a free ride.[10] When science is put to ill use by society, the social means exist to correct such use. If science has been employed for harmful and destructive purposes, then that needs to be recognized and challenged as bad *policy*, not as an inherent sin of "science." The methodological baby needs rescuing from the contextual bathwater. We require the standards of evidence and rational thought to move us beyond attractive theories of unreality. Ecocriticism, I think, should work in the direction of that spirit of rigorous methodology.

Bertrand Russell once defined the essence of the scientific method as "the refusal to regard our own desires, tastes, and interests as affording a key to the understanding of the world" (108). There is no more demanding test than this. We all, scientists included, want our understanding of the world to be the true one. But we must accept the best means we have to evaluate and weigh our conflicting desires. What uninhibited cultural constructionism grants us is the exact opposite—license to regard our own wishes and desires as the legitimate constructors of that world. Following the lead of Bertrand Russell, philosopher Karl Popper, in his book *Objective Knowledge*, describes the scientific method without actually naming it when he says,

> I am a realist. I admit that an idealism such as Kant's can be defended to the extent that it says *that all our theories are man-made*, and that we try to impose them upon the world of nature. But I am a realist in holding that the question whether our man-made theories are true or not depends upon real facts; real facts which are, with very few exceptions, emphatically not man-made. Our man-made *theories* may clash with these real *facts*, and so, in our search for truth, we may have to adjust our theories or to give them up. (328–29)

Alan Sokal's hoaxing of the social constructionist view espoused in *Social Text* was successful because it told the editors just what they wanted to hear: that physics was nothing more than another field of cultural criticism. If they had followed the scientific method, which would have involved, at a minimum, allowing a physicist—even one of their own political persuasion—to read it, they would have been told that the article was nonsense and that Sokal was pulling their collective leg. Sokal, incidentally, later identified himself as a political leftist who thus might be considered sympathetic to the ideological leanings of *Social Text*, but one who, he claims, continues to believe that the left has been and should continue to be identified with science in its historical role of opposing "obscurantism." He goes on to say,

> The recent turn of many "progressive" or "leftist" academic humanists and social scientists toward one or another form of epistemic relativism betrays this worthy heritage and undermines the already fragile prospects for progressive social critique. Theorizing about "the social construction of reality" won't help us find an effective treatment for AIDS or devise strategies for preventing global warming. Nor can we combat false ideas in history, sociology, economics, and politics if we reject the notions of truth and falsity. (Editors 64)

Former editor of the ecocritical journal *ISLE* Patrick D. Murphy once noted the dearth of scientific contributors to the journal and sensibly invited more participation from scientists ("Centering Connections" v–vi). Their absence may be explained by the fact that the current diehard constructionism of many literary scholars strikes them as absurd. One scientist intervened in the environmental e-mail network dialogue on "constructing nature" with this comment: "The nature discussion is quite delightful. I do think there are people who firmly believe nature is a social construct. These are people who build houses on sandy ocean shores, along fault lines, or on the flood plains of rivers. . . . Nature has a way of correcting such mistakes" (Tiffney). While it is true that our conceptions of nature are to a great extent socially formed and that literature encompasses these perceptions, nature itself is under no compunction to honor them. "Reality," as novelist Philip K. Dick once sardonically defined it, "is that which, when you stop believing in it, doesn't go away" (1).

Antiscience has revealed itself as neither an intellectually defensible nor a politically effective stance. To defend science is not to sanction its corruptions, such as that practiced by "scientists" employed by tobacco companies or by chemical-company house-scientists enlisted to destroy the credibility of Rachel Carson and her book, *Silent Spring*. To defend science is not to endorse the sins of its camp followers—such as a runaway technology—but to affirm its methods of investigation as the best means we have for understanding our world and for finding solutions to the growing problems of pollution, overpopulation, and despoliation.

On Interdisciplinarity and Ecocriticism

With all its pitfalls, serious interdisciplinary work between humanists and the sciences is one of the important tasks that literary ecocriticism must take on in the future. Many scholars of literature and the environment have stressed the need for a cross-pollinating kind of scholarship in ecocriticism. Underscoring this position, Frederick Crews, writing in the introduction to the anthology *After Poststructuralism: Interdisciplinarity and Literary Theory*, notes the yearning he finds in many of the anthology's essays to restore something of the scientific method's empirical spirit: "This, I think, is the real reason why science looms so large here. The point is not that critics should indiscriminately apply recent scientific discoveries to literary interpretation but that they should cultivate the scientist's alertness against doctored evidence, circular reasoning, and willful indifference to counterexample" (x).

The cautions against interdisciplinarity are summed up neatly in Pope's famous couplet about the dangers of a little learning. Still, we can reduce our level of ignorance, particularly in a subject as important as science. William Howarth, in his indispensable article "Some Principles of Ecocriticism" in *The Ecocriticism Reader*, warns us of the need for more extensive ecological literacy than we now possess and presents a wide, basic background library for prospective ecocritics, reaching across a number of disciplines. Lewis Mumford argues for the importance of both special (reductive) and generalized (ecological) knowledge for the educated individual: "[T]here is no such thing as an organism without an environment, just as there is no such thing on earth as an environment without an organism. . . . I never recommend anybody to study things in general. You must know one thing well, and have access to the same kinds of knowledge in other fields. But then combining them together is a habit of life" (Chisholm 4).

Ecocriticism fairly urges its practitioners into interdisciplinarity, into science. Literature involves interrelationships, and ecological awareness enhances and expands our sense of interrelationships to encompass nonhuman as well as human contexts. Ecological thinking about literature requires us to take the nonhuman world as seriously as previous modes of criticism have taken the human realm of society and culture. That would seem to be ecocriticism's greatest challenge and its greatest opportunity.

Taking the world seriously means, among other things, learning something scientific about how the natural world works. Richard Levin, who has perceptively analyzed interdisciplinary misdeeds by literary scholars, offers several proposals for avoiding such errors, including the use of referees from both fields for books or articles claiming to be interdisciplinary, opening up opportunities for students, both graduate and undergraduate, to pursue double majors, and increasing our efforts to end political polarization in the disciplines (33–34). Other useful strategies might include regular reading of a discipline-wide journal such as *Science*, the front sections of which are directed each week to the nonspecialist. The prospective border crosser might attend public lectures and discussion groups (even in cases where one expects to disagree with the conclusions), get acquainted with an actual scientist, and visit a lab. Of course, the main requirement is, as Levin says, to "know enough about the other discipline to use it in ways that will not seem absurd to its own practitioners" (33).

Some humanists have found the field of physics to offer interesting possibilities for interdisciplinary work. However, the hazards of one-drink imbibing from the Pierian spring are sometimes evident in the pursuit of theories of physics involving terms such as *chaos* and *uncertainty*, in cases where the intellectual attraction may be based upon the mistaken notion—so those knowledgeable in the field assert—that such words mean anything goes and freelance constructionism is thereby somehow sanctioned by natural law. On the contrary, chaos theory, as one observer notes, could just as well have been called antichaos theory and would thereby have attracted little attention from outsiders (Turner 66). N. Katherine Hayles, in her *Chaos Bound*, sees significant parallels between the physicist's chaos and deconstruction, but she perceptively notes that "[f]or deconstructionists, chaos repudiates order; for scientists, chaos makes order possible" (317). Gross and Levitt warn outsiders to the scientific fields of chaos and uncertainty that "there is a deep confusion of categories, and a surprisingly naive sense that the use of the same English word in widely separated contexts assures that there are deep thematic similarities" (104). Regarding Heisenberg's uncertainty principle, Gross and Levitt lament that the mere word *uncertainty* has been misappropriated by those like sociological theorist Stanley Aronowitz to suggest a kind of New Age obscurantism, which might have all been avoided "if Heisenberg and company had chosen a less evocative term" (51).

David Lodge, in his latest delightful novel of academic crotchets, *Thinks* (2001), picks up on all this in a conversation recorded in the journal of a humanist, as she speaks with the cognitive scientist to whom she is attracted:

> "Oh I can't stand those people," he said, "postmodernists, or poststructuralists, or whatever they call themselves. They've infiltrated Con-Con lately, caused no end of trouble." I was surprised he was so hostile and asked him why. "Because they're essentially hostile to science. They've picked up some modern scientific ideas without really understanding them and flash them about like a three-card trick. They think Heisenberg's Uncertainty Principle and Schrødinger's Cat and Godel's Theorem licenses them to say that there is no such thing as scientific proof and that science is only one interpretation of the world among others equally valid." "Well, isn't it?" I said, just to be provocative. "Certainly not," he said. "Its explanatory power is of a quite different order from, for example, animism or Zoroastrianism or astrology. . . . These postmodernists are mounting a last-ditch defence of their discipline by saying that everybody is in the same boat, including scientists—that there are no foundations. . . . But it's not true. Science is for real. It has made more changes to the conditions of human life than all the preceding millennia of our history put together. Just think of medicine. Two hundred years ago doctors were still bleeding people for every ailment under the sun." (228–29)

There is satire enough here to touch both sides—the scientist who slips into his lecturing mode and the humanist who opposes "just to be provocative"—but this round seems to go to science. I am disposed to think so because I accept, as the most productive course for ecocriticism, philosopher Maxine Sheets-Johnstone's challenge "to inquire into both the foundations of our humanness and their cultural translations" ("Descriptive Foundations" 165).

Biology and Ecocriticism

If some humanists have been attracted to some of the most difficult and obscure fields of physics, they have for the most part ignored the life sciences, especially evolutionary biology and ecology. Here, I think, is where ecocriticism should find its strongest links to the study of the natural world. When we note that "Evolution and Ecology" is now the standard title for a rapidly growing subarea of biology—and when we realize not only that Charles Darwin was the wellspring of evolutionary thinking, but also that he recognized that ecological principles were inseparably intertwined with evolutionary development—it seems clear that ecocriticism should move toward a better understanding of what one scientist calls "ecolution," the braided record of evolution and ecology.[11]

Historian Carl Degler's important study, *In Search of Human Nature: The Decline and Revival of Darwinism in American Life* (1991), describes how evolutionary biology has come again to command an important place in the social sciences in recent years. And the flow of biologically based research and scholarship has greatly increased since Degler's book was published in 1991. The latest and most notable exploration of recent research on human nature and its scientific, social, and moral implications is Steven Pinker's *The Blank Slate: The Modern Denial of Human Nature* (2002). In the last two decades scientific studies have released a flood of information about genetics, neurobiology, physiology, psychology, and behavior, information that not only rewrites our understanding of human nature but also reignites the never-resolved controversies over Darwin's original insights of nearly a century and a half ago. Unfortunately, as Frederick Turner notes, "just as chaos theory has been wrongly assumed to confirm randomness, evolution has been wrongly assumed to confirm determinism" (66). This is an outworn conception that can grasp only two possibilities: deterministic order and random freedom. Turner and many others emphasize the existence of both deterministic order and free will in describing the creative powers of evolution (68).

But despite the fact that evolution has progressed beyond classification as theory to acceptance as fact by virtually all of the world's reputable scientists, as well as the informed lay community and even some religious leaders (including the current pope, John Paul II), it still strikes fear and loathing into the hearts of many humanists.[12] The record of intellectuals, particularly literary scholars, in misunderstanding and refusing to consider evolution seriously—especially as having any role whatsoever in human behavior—is perhaps sufficient to group many humanists with creationists, backwoods school boards, and others whose efforts are devoted to not wanting to know what is true. Those armed with theories that exclude evolutionary thinking may be counted upon to reject any work that considers such matters. Yet, as philosopher John Searle says of evolution, "like it or not, it is the world view we have. . . . It is not simply up for grabs along with a lot of competing world views" (90). Citing philosopher and noted author on science and morality Mary Midgley, who says pointedly that "no excuse remains for anybody in the humanities and social sciences to evade the challenge of Darwin and treat social man as an isolated miracle," literary critic Robert Storey concludes that evasion may be less to blame in these fields than smug ignorance (36).

Evolution is not popular, because it presents us with evidence that many would rather not hear. But the ultimate verification of scientific ideas is not dependent on their popularity, but on their surviving the demanding tests of authenticity. Evolution has prevailed over more comforting theories because it has repeatedly withstood such challenges. The great geneticist Theodosius Dobzhansky said, "Nothing in biology makes sense except in the light of evolution."[13] Its explanatory capacity has grown to the point where we can say that it is the reality in which we function. Daniel C. Dennett, on the last page of his *Darwin's Dangerous Idea*, characterizes Darwinian natural selection as a universal acid, capable of subsuming all other explanations. That is why it is "dangerous." For us to accept its power—and seductiveness—and "correct each other as we go" from the "second-rate versions" of it, says Dennett, will require vigilance (521).

What seems self-evident is that ecological thinking—insofar as it involves an enlarged sense of what needs to be taken into account in attempting to answer questions about the natural world and our place in it—must include a larger and more vigilant consideration of evolutionary biology and genetics, biocultural evolution, evolutionary psychology, the neurosciences, and other Darwinian-based ideas about human behavior. The rapid explosion of knowledge in these areas is one of the central intellectual and social issues of our times. It has caused significant realignment of thinking in the social sciences, and an evolutionarily based theory may, as one observer predicts, become the dominant viewpoint there within twenty years "in spite of all prejudice and entrenched interests, because of the irresistible force of its explanatory power" (Carroll, *Evolution* 468).

Whether those of us in literary studies are inclined to accept this prediction or not, we need a better scientific understanding of our own and related fields, an ecologically expanded awareness of the social and biological context within which literary acts take place. Evolutionary ideas may be controversial, but they are worth serious consideration, as the opposing idea of creationism is not.[14] Accepting our place in the actual world is a necessary step in divorcing ourselves from such know-nothingism. Questioning this tendency of humanists and social scientists to separate humans from the rest of the animal world, Matt Ridley, in *The Origins of Virtue*, is rankled by the anthropocentrists "preach[ing] the same old defensive sermon of human uniqueness that theologians clung to when Darwin first shook their tree" (155).

As interdisciplinarians, ecocritics will rely primarily upon expert testimony from those scientists in the field, but this need not preclude self-immersion in the scientific element. As Gaston Bachelard has said, "Modern science takes man into a new world. If man thinks science, he is renewed as a thinking being. He accedes to an undeniable hierarchy of thought" (Jones 174). Mary McAllester Jones, Bachelard's translator and critic, comments,

> Bachelard believes that any one of us can enter science by reading. . . . Failure to understand is unimportant, though; what matters is the work of the mind as it encounters the close pattern of reference points that constitutes scientific argument. Reading modern science is hard but very productive work, which allows us to experience, more than ordinary life ever can, a precise, ordered coherence which because it is constantly being rectified is always reordered, the coherence of ordered possibility and coordinated discontinuity, an open pattern of difference (174).

Social scientist Dan Sperber urges his colleagues in this direction when he writes, "The sciences are capable of giving us a special kind of intellectual pleasure: that of seeing the world in a light that at first disconcerts, but then forces reflection, and deepens our knowledge while relativizing it. I wish the social sciences would, more often, give us pleasure of this kind" (155).[15]

The humanist might find a literary pattern paralleling Bachelard's and Sperber's in Melville's *Moby-Dick* and Steinbeck's *The Grapes of Wrath*, in which the scientific interchapters and sections are alternately laced with the human-centered narrative. Melville, for example, virtually overwhelms the reader with natural science in the whale-centered cetology chapters only to question science's capacity to reveal—or the human mind's to encompass—the limitless dynamism of nature. And the biologically trained Steinbeck explores strongly conflicted humanistic and scientific allegiances in the part-whole rhythm of his story. In these profoundly moving ways, we undergo a compelling reading experience, a needful counterpoise, a version of the powerful oscillating movement that Bachelard describes. Here are common instances of the subtle interconnections between science and art that affirm the possibilities of deeply rewarding unities between them. One might think of Bachelard's "reader's prayer": "Give us this day our daily need" (Jones 176).

Melville's myriad explorations of cetology and the natural sciences serve to reprove Ahabian anthropocentrism. Similarly, Steinbeck's ecological vision enclosing the Joads' personal odyssey suggests a point from

C. P. Snow's 1964 retrospective essay about his original 1959 lecture on the two cultures. In the later 1964 essay Snow argued that, among the natural sciences, biology may offer humanists the best and most available means of taking nature seriously through significant and valid interdisciplinary effort (72–75). Biologist Ernst Mayr has made the point more bluntly: "There is simply no pathway from physics to ethics, culture, mind, free will, and other humanistic concerns. The absence in physics of these important topics contributed to the alienation of scientists and humanists that Snow decried. Yet all these concerns have substantial relationships with the life sciences" (37).

Aldous Huxley's *Literature and Science*, published in 1963, shortly before his death, was another response to the original Snow lecture and the controversy that it kindled. Huxley made a similar claim for public knowledge of biology: "Biology, it is obvious, is more immediately relevant to human experience than are the exacter fields of physics and chemistry." He called for the scholar to offer humanity the interconnections that only "'a heart that watches and receives' and a bird's eye knowledge of science can provide" (79). If the proper study of mankind is Man, says Huxley, echoing Pope, then the next most proper study is Nature, and the connections between them, the concerns of ecology, are matters of the greatest importance:

> In the light of what we now know about the relationships of living things to one another and to their inorganic environment—and also of what, to our cost, we know about overpopulation, ruinous farming, senseless forestry and destructive grazing, about water pollution, air pollution and the sterilization or total loss of once productive soils, it has now become abundantly clear that the Golden Rule applies not only to the dealings of human individuals and human societies with one another, but also to their dealings with other living creatures and the planet upon which we are all traveling through space and time. (108–9)

Huxley's prescient 1963 statement not only outlines the impending environmental crisis but also calls for the kind of bridge between the scientific and literary communities, "traditionally regarded as completely disparate," upon which will be discovered "the raw materials for a new kind of Nature literature" (Huxley 110). And, presumably, a new kind of criticism.

Huxley's ominous overview almost certainly was influenced by Rachel Carson's best-seller, *Silent Spring*, published in 1962. Carson's book, as Lawrence Buell points out, owes as much to the author's novelistic and imaginative skills as it does to its carefully supported scientific argument (*Environmental Imagination* 290–93). As a professional biologist, but one whose first ambition was to be a creative writer, Carson shares important affinities with Aldous Huxley and with the biology-literature connection. Indeed, one might regard *Silent Spring* as an ecological *Brave New World* in its dark prophecies of the diminishment of life. As the opening salvo in modern activist environmentalism, Carson's book came to have an enormous effect, bringing scientific biology and the possibilities for eco-catastrophe into widespread public awareness.

The roots of ecocriticism, as has been noted, lie in this developing awareness during the remainder of the 1960s and the 1970s. The biological-environmental-literary connection reached its first major critical expression in 1974 with the publication of Joseph W. Meeker's *The Comedy of Survival: Studies in Literary Ecology*. Employing a comparatist approach—comparative literature, he maintained, is to the humanities what ecology is to the natural sciences—Meeker argued the inseparability of literature from nature and the ecological whole.

Thus a skein of biological thinking was an early accompaniment to the study of literature and the environment. Biologically verified evidence of environmental destruction, made known largely by Carson's *Silent Spring*, brought the obscure biological discipline of ecology out of the field and the science lab and into public consciousness, acting eventually upon the academy as a catalyst for new and interdisciplinary thinking. Biology was the natural connecting point, as the most accessible of the natural sciences, and the one—as Huxley had emphasized—that can claim a permanent and important relationship to human life.

While most border-crossing literary scholars during recent decades have been attracted to theories from the discipline of physics like chaos and uncertainty, the life sciences, especially the knitted biological fields of ecology and evolution, remained, after Meeker, strangely untouched until the 1990s. One reason for this was that scholars from the humanities were frightened away by reactions to the final chapter of Edward O. Wilson's *Sociobiology: The New Synthesis* (1975), which I will discuss later. All of this changed during the decade of the 1990s and at the turn of the millennium, when a number of ecologically informed books on literature, a few with strong evolutionary and environmental connections, were published, including Jonathan Bate's *Romantic Ecology* (1991), Alexander J. Argyros's *A Blessed Rage for Order* (1991), Karl Kroeber's *Ecological Literary Criticism* (1994), Lawrence Buell's *The Environmental Imagination* (1995), Frederick Turner's *The Culture of Hope* (1995), Joseph

Carroll's *Evolution and Literary Theory* (1995), Robert Storey's *Mimesis and the Human Animal* (1996), Brett Cooke and Frederick Turner's *Biopoetics: Evolutionary Explorations in the Arts* (1999), James C. McKusick's *Green Writing: Romanticism and Ecology* (2000), Eric Wilson's *Romantic Turbulence* (2000), and Jonathan Bate's most recent book, *The Song of the Earth* (2000). Several of the essays in *The Ecocriticism Reader* (1996), edited by Cheryll Glotfelty and Harold Fromm, also fall within this context.[16]

Of these books, Joseph Carroll's *Evolution and Literary Theory* is the most extensive and ambitious attempt thus far to apply evolutionary biological ideas to the construction of an overarching literary theory. The work of Carroll, Storey, Cooke, Turner, and other recent critics in this field is strongly influenced by John Tooby and Leda Cosmides's "The Psychological Foundations of Culture," the opening article in the groundbreaking anthology, *The Adapted Mind.* The Tooby-Cosmides essay has been widely recognized as successfully challenging the old, nature-skeptical "Standard Social Science Model" (SSSM) of the mind as "a social product, a blank slate or an externally programmed general-purpose computer" with a new paradigm, that of culture as the "product of evolved psychological mechanisms situated in individuals living in groups" (24).

Proceeding from such an evolutionary-adaptive basis, Carroll's book includes a formidable argument to dismantle poststructuralism, finding it based upon unsound principles that oppose "the total structure of scientific knowledge, especially biological knowledge." His case against the poststructuralist paradigm, yet to be answered, is summarized in terms that the student of ecocriticism might find most telling: "the rich world of experience within reality has been emptied out, and in its place we have been given a thin and hectic play of self-reflexive linguistic functions. This is a dreary and impoverished vision of life and literature; worse, it is a gratuitous and false vision. It depletes the world, and in order to accomplish its depletion it gives a false account of our experience in the world" (466).[17]

In place of poststructuralism Carroll argues, in his *Evolution and Literary Theory*, for the validity of the evolutionary explanation of human experience as the most adequate and complete theory of life, including human life, available to us. As he says, "It thus necessarily provides the basis for any adequate account of culture and of literature" (467). One feature of Carroll's book that is of particular interest to ecocritics is its implicit answer to the charge that ecocriticism, like the discipline of ecology with which it allies itself, has no widely accepted underlying theory.

The uniting theory, in both Carroll's study and the scientific field of ecology, is evolutionary biology. In my argument for a biologically based ecocriticism, I follow Carroll's assertion that "only a Darwinian conception of the evolved and adapted character of the human mind can provide an understanding of human nature that is sufficiently profound and incisive to correspond with the intuitive understanding embodied in the literary tradition" ("Deep Structure of Literary Representation" 165).

Carroll concludes his book in both hope and disappointment, confident that the evolutionary paradigm will prevail in the social sciences within twenty years because of its explanatory power but resigned to the expectation that its presence will not be welcomed in English departments for a long time. Robert Storey, another author of evolutionary-literary critical persuasion, reviews Carroll's book enthusiastically but also predicts a cold reception in heavily politicized English departments. Storey invokes the earlier experience of Edward O. Wilson, whose publication of *Sociobiology: The New Synthesis* in 1975, with a final chapter positing genetic influences on human behavior, met with a furious resistance from Marxists and others.

But just as Wilson's early proposal of a biocultural basis for human behavior is now fairly standard thinking in the sciences and some of the social sciences and even among some humanists, Carroll's important work seems to be finding more open minds among his literary peers, and more quickly, than he anticipated. A steadily growing body of evidence gives increasing corroboration to the idea that human behavior and nature reflect the complex workings of the evolved and adapted human mind, all of which lends support to Carroll's position. As Steven Pinker reminds us, our attention to a work of art is not based on sensory experience alone but also on its emotional pull to our common biological experience and fate. "Today, we may be seeing a new convergence of explorations of the human condition by artists and scientists—not because scientists are trying to take over the humanities, but because artists and humanists are beginning to look to the sciences, or at least to the scientific mindset that sees us as a species with a complex psychological endowment" (418).

The Example of Edward O. Wilson

The work of Wilson deserves special attention at this point. By virtue of their author's stature as a world-famous evolutionary biologist and theorist and a writer of memorable prose, Wilson's books over the last few decades, I believe, comprise the most important and challenging interdisciplinary research and writing relating to ecocriticism available to us.[18] Two of his books, *On Human Nature* (1978) and *The Ants*, with Bert Höll-dobler (1990), have won Pulitzer Prizes, and he has received numerous national and international awards and honors for his work in science. In addition he is a leading conservationist and a world-recognized proponent in the movement to preserve biological diversity, emphasizing that biodiversity is the necessary ingredient to the continuance of the world as we know it.[19] This aspect of his career is represented in his *The Diversity of Life* (1992), *Naturalist* (1994), and *The Future of Life* (2002).

Wilson's *Biophilia* (1984), which argues for our innate affinity, as humans, with other forms of life, was followed by *The Biophilia Hypothesis* (ed. Stephen R. Kellert and Wilson 1993), in which Wilson submitted his biophilia thesis to the scrutiny of an interdisciplinary group of scholars whose essays comprise the volume. Although findings of contributors to *The Biophilia Hypothesis* on this large and complex issue fell short of any conclusive verification, they are immensely interesting and important. And Wilson's willingness to submit his hypothesis to testing and evaluation by experts from other disciplines was an example of the scientific method at work that interdisciplinarians from outside the sciences might well emulate.

At the same time Wilson's attention to literary and humanistic themes and ideas—as revealed, for example, in *Biophilia*, in his autobiography, *Naturalist*, and in *Consilience* (1998)—mark him as a notable presence in the humanities. He has been called America's most famous scientist and one of its greatest writers (Cooke 98). It can be argued that Wilson deserves attention from literary scholars as a unique nature writer, one whose personal and philosophical reflections may resonate more strongly with his readers because of his extensive scientific achievements. Thus, the alternating rhythm of description and reflection, the underlying structural movement of nature writing, takes on an added layer of significance in his work, exemplifying the experience of scientific reading—as Bachelard describes it, the ordered coherence constantly being reordered through reflection and rethinking. The prologue to Wilson's newest book, *The Future of Life*, offers a brilliant example of this process.

It is unfortunate that, as Storey and others have observed, Wilson remains little known in the humanities or, worse, misrepresented or demonized for ideas that have steadily grown in influence and become accepted in his own and other fields across the social sciences.[20] Robert Wright finds that "sociobiology seems to prosper in everything but the name" (180). Biologist Alison Jolly notes that "[o]ne of my colleagues in the humanities recently told me that sociobiology had been 'worsted,' by which she means that the argument is twenty years old and not a current problem for feminists. It's not a problem in biology, either. It's normal science that we accept and use" (125).

Wilson, it needs emphasizing, was not the first sociobiologist. It all began, as John Alcock reminds us, with Darwin, whose work was sociobiological because it encompassed social behavior and evolutionary thinking. "Without Darwin," Alcock writes, "there could be no sociobiology" (*Triumph of Sociobiology* 17). One of Wilson's most significant contributions in *Sociobiology*, says Alcock, was to synthesize a great accumulation of earlier biological research on social behavior (16).

Under the influence of Wilson and others, Tooby and Cosmides's understanding of the place of heritable influences upon human behavior has become a central corrective to the SSSM conception of the human mind as a blank slate to be inscribed only by culture. Wilson and Charles J. Lumsden, in their 1983 book, *Promethean Fire*, were leaders in disputing the social sciences' model of a human mind as separate from the physiology of the brain and the view that culture therefore encompasses a unique function of the brain, to be explained only by unique procedures. Wilson and Lumsden saw this nonbiological conception of mind as "the ultimate source of the troubling gap between the two cultures, between the hard sciences and the humanities" (19). They went on to take a very different view, which they called gene-culture coevolution, "a complicated, fascinating interaction in which culture is generated and shaped by biological imperatives while biological traits are simultaneously altered by genetic evolution in response to cultural innovation. We believe that gene-culture coevolution, alone and unaided, has created man and that the manner in which the mechanism works can be solved by a combination of techniques from the natural and social sciences" (19–20).

The scientific study of gene-culture coevolution, just beginning in 1983 when Wilson and Lumsden wrote this, has attracted study from many other biologists, including, most recently, Paul R. Ehrlich in *Human Natures: Genes, Cultures, and the Human Prospect*, and Sarah Blaffer Hrdy in *Mother Nature*. Hrdy, a distinguished anthropologist who calls herself a sociobiologist but who also makes wide use of historical and cultural evidence in her research, writes, "Instead of old dichotomies about nature versus nurture, attention needs to be focused on the complicated interactions among genes, tissue, glands, past experiences, and environmental cues" (174). The study of the interconnection between biological and cultural influences on human behavior, pioneered by Wilson over twenty-five years ago, is now a widely accepted practice.[21] Like many pioneering efforts, Wilson's early work in sociobiology had questionable aspects, as Hrdy points out (406), but these have been addressed in the normal progress of the scientific methodology as it works toward verification.

The opposition to sociobiology (now often called "evolutionary psychology") has quieted down as the evidence for an evolutionary component in human nature and culture has steadily increased. The return of biology to the study of human behavior, as historian Carl Degler reminds us, "has no place for the reintroduction of discredited practices like racism and sexism and eugenics."[22] Rather, the return of biology "is to place once again the study of human nature within evolution, to ask how human beings fit into that framework which Darwin laid down over a century ago" (ix). And, as biologist Alison Jolly has recently noted, Wilson's opponents have moved on to other things: "It no longer seems obvious that proposing biological bases for human behavior leads straight to justifying the gas chambers" (126). Ullica Segerstråle's detailed study of the history of the sociobiology debate, *Defenders of the Truth*, finds Wilson something of a moral winner in the long controversy (311–12, 404).

Wilson's 1998 book, *Consilience: The Unity of Knowledge*, is his most wide-reaching prediction of synthesis between the disciplines thus far, extending interdisciplinarity to its limits. A work of impressive scope and learning, it takes its title from an 1840 synthesis of the sciences by William Whewell. For Wilson, consilience is the linking of causal explanations across all disciplines. He finds such a theory validated in the natural sciences, where disciplinary boundaries have disappeared or are disappearing as chemistry, physics, and the various fields of biology—witness biophysics, biochemistry, biogenetics or bioinformatics, organic chemistry, and so forth—are rendered consilient. He posits that the study of culture, assuming consilience is a correct description of the direction of world knowledge, will divide itself between the natural sciences and the humanities. "These domains will be the two great branches of learning in the twenty-first century. The social sciences will continue to split within each of its disciplines, a process already rancorously begun, with one part folding into or becoming continuous with biology, the other fusing with the humanities. Its disciplines will continue to exist but in radically altered form. In the process the humanities . . . will draw closer to the sciences and partly fuse with them" (12).

A striking example of Wilson's predicted synthesis and its methodology is seen in Jared Diamond's Pulitzer Prize–winning *Guns, Germs, and*

Steel (1997), in which the author studies the influence of environment on the history of different human societies from the perspective of the sciences, particularly evolutionary biology. Diamond writes,

> Naturally, the notion that environmental geography and biogeography influenced societal development is an old idea. Nowadays, though, the view is not held in esteem by historians; it is considered wrong or simplistic, or it is caricatured as environmental determinism and dismissed. . . . Yet geography obviously has some effect on history; the open question concerns how much effect, and whether geography can account for history's broad pattern.
>
> The time is now ripe for a fresh look at these questions, because of new information from scientific disciplines seemingly remote from human history. Those disciplines include, above all, genetics, molecular biology, and biogeography as applied to crops and their wild ancestors; the same disciplines plus behavioral ecology, as applied to domestic animals and their wild ancestors; molecular biology of human germs and related germs of animals; epidemiology of human diseases; human genetics; linguistics; archaeological studies on all continents and major islands; and studies of the histories of technology, writing, and political organization. (25–26)

Diamond's multidisciplinary background helps him toward the challenging synthesis that he describes, which closely resembles Wilson's conception of consilience. Acknowledging the "overweening" confidence of his predictions, Wilson, in *Consilience*, still argues the case for science as "the boldest metaphysics of the age" and anticipates its leading role in the consilience of knowledge (12). His chapters on the arts and their interpretation and on ethics and religion, both of which are evidence of his strong attraction to the humanities, should be of primary interest to humanists. And his framing of the need for consilience in confronting the foremost global problems of the twenty-first century—overpopulation and environmental destruction, resulting particularly in mass extinction of species—should resonate strongly with all readers, not merely those who practice the study of literature and the environment.

With their attraction to the grand, overarching synthesis, Wilson's positions have often been resisted by fellow-academics who are likely to resent what they see as alien invasion of their home turf, and by others such as Wendell Berry, in *Life Is A Miracle*, who sees in *Consilience* an attack upon spirituality.[23] But in a world where the earth's peoples are increasingly joined by economic and population pressures into uneasy interdependence, the sort of border-crossing, ecologically sensitive work that Wilson has undertaken should continue to prove necessary and important. The spirit of Wilson's major contributions to science and literature is well described in Rachel Carson's words: "[T]he aim of science is to discover and illuminate truth. And that, I take it is the aim of literature, whether biography or history or fiction. It seems to me, then, that there can be no separate literature of science" (Lear 219).

A New Synthesis? A Third Culture?

While making the case for at least a limited consilience between biology and ecocriticism, one must recognize—as Snow, Huxley, and others have noted—that biology can be seen as the least exact of the hard sciences, hence the most open to conflicting interpretations. The wide range of reactions to the tenets of sociobiology, like those to Darwin's conceptions more than a century earlier, illustrate the potentiality for conflict and the need for continuing good science and informed debate. But at the same time, we are not quite at biological ground zero. "Nature" is a social construct, but merely to repeat this ignores the need for better scientific understanding of our place within the biosphere. All cultural constructions of nature are not equally valid. In celebration of diversity, we have ignored how much alike we humans all are. We may ponder whether human nature is inherently good or bad, but, as Mary Midgley reminds us, "this is quite a different position from the official line that there is no such thing as human nature at all" (68).

On this issue it is useful to note the work of philosopher Maxine Sheets-Johnstone's *The Roots of Thinking* (1990), *The Roots of Power* (1994), and *The Primacy of Movement* (1999), all of which present a challenging evolutionary corrective, through their analysis of the human body as the primal model of thinking, to the current political emphasis on cultural difference. In what might be an admirable summary of many of the arguments made in support of the biological-literary connections described in this book, she writes in *The Roots of Power:*

> This inordinate bewitchment by culture results in a reductionism that is as pernicious and costly as its biological corollary. Cultural reductionism keeps us from taking evolution seriously. It in fact quickens the passing of natural history. It precludes our recognizing that, our individual and great historico-cultural diversities notwithstanding, we humans are basically the same. Though we speak in different tongues, speaking tongues are part of our evolutionary heritage; though we explain the world in

> different ways, explaining the world is part of our evolutionary heritage; though we dance, sing, tell stories, and paint differently, such creations are part of our evolutionary heritage. . . . When we ignore these ties that bind us in a common humanity . . . we put ourselves out of reach of our own history, insulating ourselves from corporeal matters of fact and the archetypal forms within them. We proportionately distance ourselves from our own human nature. (328–29)

Sheets-Johnstone's work, like Ellen Dissanayake's studies of the evolutionary basis of human art, has literally vital possibilities for connections to the interdisciplinarity that is the future of ecocriticism.

Philosopher Alexander Rosenberg, in his *Instrumental Biology, or The Disunity of Science*, offers a recent reminder of the potential for slippage in biological theorizing. While he, like Snow and Huxley, sees biology as a more variable and somewhat less predictable account of reality than is found in physics and chemistry, he also allows that it may have great importance "as a collection of useful instruments for organizing our interaction with the biocosm" (1). Since human interaction with the biosphere is widely perceived as the defining issue of the coming century, as well as the center of ecocriticism's claim to a role in literary study, biology seems positioned for an increasingly important place in our lives.

"Biology promises to be the leading science of this [twenty-first] century," claim the editors of a new series on theoretical biology.[24] Their prediction is based upon the dramatic recent achievements in biological research and the growing integration of biological findings into related areas of the sciences and the social sciences. It is reasonable to expect that ecocriticism and the humanities will also be challenged by these new formulations. Also challenged, and increasingly vulnerable, are the assumptions of the "Standard Social Science Model," whose empirical foundations are steadily eroding in the flow of new evidence. "The result," claims Steven Pinker, "is a rearguard effort to salvage the Blank Slate by disfiguring science and intellectual life: denying the possibility of objectivity and truth, dumbing down issues into dichotomies, replacing facts and logic with political posturing" (421–22).

C. P. Snow's closing appeal in his 1964 retrospective look at *The Two Cultures* is for a "third culture," a body of intellectuals from various fields who are all conversant with the sciences (70–71). What are the prospects for the larger involvement of humanists in applying, say, ecological concepts to the writing, reading, teaching, and criticism of literature?

Unfortunately, literature may be the last of the humanistic disciplines to take evolution/ecology seriously, since, as Joseph Carroll, Robert Storey, Maxine Sheets-Johnstone, and many others point out, the radical edge of the reigning poststructuralist explanation of things is incompatible with the Darwinian/ecological paradigm. Still, the Darwinian views are gaining in ascendancy, cracks in the nature-skeptical edifice are increasingly evident, and a number of ecocritics and others are working in these fissures to good advantage. And whether or not evolutionary biology becomes the theoretical bridge between the two cultures, those of us who practice ecocriticism have increasing opportunities for exciting new scholarship by deepening our interaction with the natural sciences.

Some of us may find little opportunity to use scientific information in the sort of criticism that we do, but for those whose work bears significant relationships to contemporary science, and for all of us concerned with refining our knowledge of human nature and its relationship to literary study, these are interesting times. And we might all, as Frederick Crews says, emulate the scientific regard for unbiased evidence and logical reasoning, whatever our critical approach. Indeed, we are actually *doing* science, Carl Sagan reminds us, when we regard our own work critically and subject our ideas to the test of the outside world (39).[25]

Looking ahead, biologist Jane Lubchenko, recent president of the 144,000-member American Association for the Advancement of Science, has called the environment the defining issue of the twenty-first century, underlying the economy, health, the threat of war. "It's not economy versus the environment," says Lubchenko. "It's short-term versus long-term" ("OSU biologist" D-5). Those interested in the field of literary ecology may rightly respond that the study and teaching of literature is an underlying and long-term environmental issue as well.

Environmental studies, particularly ecology, began in the life sciences and broadened to include the humanities. But most of us have yet to become scientifically literate, and the two cultures are as largely incommunicado as Snow described them over forty years ago: "The clashing point of two subjects, two disciplines, two cultures—of two galaxies, so far as that goes—ought to produce creative chances. In the history of mental activity that has been where some of the breakthroughs came. The chances are there now. But they are there, as it were, in a vacuum, because those in the two cultures can't talk to each other" (16). Given the urgency of our environmental concerns and the many opportunities for emerging synthesis, it is time to outgrow the stereotypes of the two cultures. It is time for humanists and scientists to start talking to each other.

The social implications of biological thinking and research offer one of the great intellectual engagements of our time, sufficient to draw the attention and interest of all who are concerned with the place of humankind on the planet. As participants in something like Snow's third culture, scientifically informed ecocritics have an opportunity to reinvigorate the teaching and study of literature and to help redirect literary criticism into a more consequential social and public role.

A reasonable starting point in the construction of a biologically informed ecocriticism is a revisit to the ancient and tenacious genre of pastoral. A fresh consideration of the pastoral tradition may reveal whether pastoral theory and practice can maintain its significance in an age of increasing environmental anxiety.

3

Et in Arcadia Ego: Pastoral Meets Ecocriticism

• • • • • • • • • • • • • •

> However frenetically we get and spend, an attachment to the natural life of the planet remains fixed in our system. . . . One cannot think of a single composer, painter or writer who has not tracked at least one major inspiration to a bird, a tree, a rose. People automatically lose themselves in wordless reverence at the sight of a curlew or a silver cloud of anchovies or at the mournful wail of howler monkeys. Or they stare dumbly out at oceans, as if longing for their microbial past.
> —Roger Rosenblatt, "All the Days of the Earth"

"'So,' say the parable-makers, 'is your pastoral life whirled past and away.'" In this spirit of elegy, Leo Marx concludes *The Machine in the Garden*, his 1964 landmark study of pastoralism in American literature and culture (354). But reports of pastoralism's demise proved premature, as Marx himself notes in a retrospective 1986 essay, "Pastoralism in America."[1] Besides Marx, a number of other recent commentators, such as Lawrence Buell, Andrew Ettin, William Howarth, and Terry Gifford, join in reasserting pastoral's continuing relevance. "Like the terms tragedy and comedy," says Ettin, "the term pastoral denotes experiences and ideas that are permanently parts of our thinking and writing" (1).

The eighteenth century's Dr. Johnson held that pastoral was vulgar and escapist, hence dismissible. The escapist label has been reapplied to the genre in the twentieth century by some class-oriented and Marxist critics. Disparagement of the genre, however, has been countered since Johnson's time by generations of subsequent scholarship, much of which explores the idea that pastoral can be a serious and complex criticism of life, involved not merely with country scenes and natural life but with a significant commentary on the explicit or implicit contrast between such settings and the lives of an urban and sophisticated audience. The 2001 MLA Bibliography lists nearly 1,400 article and book titles on pastoral published in recent years. Nature, in the pastoral equation, continues to be an embodiment of nobility, a trusted value against which we are invited to weigh our experiences of culture and society.

Evidence of pastoral's continuing—even increasing—significance is forced upon us constantly by events that have thrust the natural world into the forefront of contemporary public and social life. As Robert Finch and John Elder write in the introduction to the *Norton Book of Nature Writing*, "All literature, by illuminating the full nature of human existence, asks a single question: how shall we live? In our age that question has taken its most urgent form in relation to the natural environment" (28).

The interconnections between human beings and nature—the concern of pastoral from ancient times to the present—take on a heretofore unprecedented significance at a period when the comfortably mythopoeic green world of pastoral is beset by profound threats of pollution, despoliation, and diminishment. From the earth-centered context in which we now find ourselves, the study of pastoral is thrown open to new interpretation.

A central problem of pastoral in present-day contexts is that it reflects the same sort of anthropocentric assumptions that an ecocritical viewpoint would presume to reassess. Literary pastoral traditionally posits a natural world, a green world, to which sophisticated dwellers of court or city withdraw in search of the lessons of simplicity that only nature can teach, as exemplified in the lines from Shakespeare's *As You Like It:*

> And this our life, exempt from public haunt,
> Finds tongues in trees, books in the running brooks,
> Sermons in stones, and good in everything
> (2:1, lines 41–43)

In the pastoral world, amid sylvan groves and rural characters—idealized images of country existence—the sophisticates attain a critical vision of the salutary, simple life that will presumably sustain them as they return at the end to the great world on the horizon.

While the impetus, the motivation, for pastoral may be no less relevant and understandable today than it was in its earliest recorded appearance in the work of the Greek poet Theocritus 2,300 years ago, the terms by which its contrastive worlds are defined do, from an ecological viewpoint, distort the actuality of each. Pastoral's green world becomes a highly stylized and simplified creation of the humanistic assumptions of the writer and his audience. Arcadia has no identity of its own. It is but a temporary and ephemeral release from court or city, which still manifests its dominance by its linguistic control and manipulation of the generic form itself and by its imposition of its human-centered values upon both city and country.

Pastoral's continuing capacity to demonstrate the potentialities for human renewal remains rooted in the local, the specific, the regional, at the same time that it speaks to the larger world. As Gaston Cleric, Jim Burden's teacher in Willa Cather's *My Ántonia*, explains to his young student, Virgil's "patria" in the Latin phrase "'*Primus ego in patriam mecum . . . deducam Musas*'; 'for I shall be the first, if I live, to bring the Muse into my country'. . . . meant, not a nation or even a province, but the little rural neighbourhood on the Mincio where the poet was born. . . . to his own little 'country'; to his father's fields, 'sloping down to the river and to the old beech trees with broken tops'" (171).

Still, Virgil's little neighborhood reached out to grace a hitherto unstoried Nebraska frontier for Jim Burden and his creator. In a similar spirit of connectedness, we must now consider that the beeches of Virgil's homeland may be the victims of acid rains drifting from far cities, and the poet's river polluted from industrial wastes dumped somewhere upstream. Pastoral's ancient and universal appeal—to come away—requires new examination in an age in which there is no away. Pastoral, rightly understood, has always been a serious criticism of life. Ecocriticism, I think, can give us a serious criticism of pastoral. It is time for pastoral theory and ecocriticism to meet.

Pastoral and Ideology

To better understand the present state of pastoral criticism, it is helpful to review the important survey of the genre by Lawrence Buell in his *The Environmental Imagination*, an overview that clarifies not only the literary-historical, but also the ideological, position of American pastoral scholarship in recent years. Buell locates American pastoral's ideological origins in D. H. Lawrence's *Studies in Classic American Literature* (1923) and in Lawrence's claim that classic American writing revealed the American male in retreat from civilization. This assertion was refined and enlarged by Leslie Fiedler in *Love and Death in the American Novel* (1960), wherein male self-fulfillment in nature is seen as an immature rejection of the woman-defined social sphere of the towns and cities. Leo Marx's *The Machine in the Garden* (1964), to this point the definitive work on American pastoral, made explicit the connections between the old

European dream of Arcadia and the pastoral experience encompassed in the works of major American writers from Jefferson, through the nineteenth-century transcendentalists, up to the 1920s and the tragic vision of loss at the end of Fitzgerald's *The Great Gatsby* (1925).

During the last few decades, feminist readings of American pastoral such as those by Annette Kolodny and Nina Baym, Buell notes, have challenged the view that the wilderness flight or the traditional frontier narrative represents the definitive tradition in the American novel, these approaches tending to ignore women's literature and history. Kenneth Lynn and Bernard Rosenthal have further questioned the radical credentials of Marx's figures, and Myra Jehlen has sought to implicate the American reverence for nature as a conservative force rather than a basis for radical dissent (*Environmental Imagination* 33–35).

These and other revisionist interpretations, Buell concludes, have in common a tendency to see American pastoralism as "conservative and hegemonic, rather than as a form of dissent from an urbanizing social mainstream" (35). He sees two very significant points in this diagnosis:

> First, it bespeaks a shift from the hermeneutics of empathy that by and large marks pre-1970 new critical and myth-symbol American scholarship to a hermeneutics of skepticism that appraises texts more in terms of what they exclude or suppress. Second, and related, the newer scholarship stresses even more than the older scholarship did nature's function as an ideological theater for acting out desires that have very little to do with bonding to nature as such and that subtly or not so subtly valorize its unrepresented opposite (complex society): as the true direction of the pastoral impulse (Lynn, Rosenthal), as the provider of necessary legal protection and communal support (Kolodny), as the institutional grid in terms of which the "natural" is seen (Jehlen). (35–36)

While acknowledging the corrective contribution of these recent developments, Buell goes on to question the prevailing assessment of American pastoral as a locus of establishment sentiments. He argues, through a number of revealing texts—including not only works by such familiar figures as Thoreau, Burroughs, and Leopold but also, for example, the work of American women nature writers and writing representing the African diaspora—for pastoral in America, and in the new literatures of the Third World, as a complex, important, and continuingly relevant model for social and literary interpretation. Buell also makes the point that pastoral's form remains constant despite changes in ideological content. A new sense of ecocentrism tends to move the conception of pastoral away from mere ideological theater for human concerns to nature advocacy for its own sake (51–52).

In his well-known study of English rural-urban life, *The Country and the City*, Raymond Williams's class-centered Marxist perspective parallels socioeconomic challenges to pastoral from the above-mentioned American critics. What these arguments have in common, Buell notes, is "the implication that the biota itself is not likely to be anyone's primary concern" (14). While recognizing that environmental issues must be seen as connected to other matters, he notes that the environment as a public concern has assumed such proportions that it is no longer dismissable as only a mask for other agendas.

From England, pastoral critic Terry Gifford, in his 1995 book on British nature poetry, *Green Voices*, reaches a similar conclusion, arguing that the best contemporary nature poetry "outflanks" the old polarizations of pastoral and antipastoral, just as it questions—indeed, refutes—fashionable postmodern constructs (19). According to Gifford,

> When my students say, "But there are no 'grand narratives' possible any more," I say, "We are living them. We call them 'growth and decay,' 'the seasons,' 'a river.'" I point to my balding head as a not-so-grand narrative, in flux, capable of many representations and demanding constant questioning, but following a natural pattern of decay. Daily, postmodernists have to use an active, if tentative, concept of aging, or of justice, or of environmentalism, however these concepts have been socially constructed. (15)

Gifford, in a new book continuing his study of pastoral, reemphasizes the significance of, and the need for a "post-pastoral" literature that explores, within today's responsibilities, pastoral's traditional pattern of retreat and return.

The age of environmental anxiety has projected nature into the forefront of social and intellectual concerns, and pastoralism, we can reasonably conclude, is destined to engage us increasingly in the time ahead. Ecological threats unsparingly force our recognition of a natural reality beyond postmodernist constructions. The ungreening world insistently intrudes as natural fact, as cultural locus, and—so pastoral reminds us—as literary tradition. Retrospective considerations of pastoral, heightened in significance by the headlong alteration of the physical universe, leave us poised to consider new directions for present and future pastoral scholarship.

When Lawrence Buell notes in his review of late twentieth-century pastoral scholarship the widespread if unspoken implication that "the biota is not likely to be anyone's primary concern," he intimates the direction for an ecological approach to pastoral which, I think, deserves to be widened beyond a primary concern for ideology. Buell's two or three insightful references to a biological biota, as presented in Edward O. Wilson's *Biophilia*, seem to invite, even require, more attention to the biocultural approach that I advocate in these pages. Even Raymond Williams's influential Marxist analysis of the pastoral tradition in Britain, in which pastoral gloved the iron hand of city exploitation of country workers, did not prevent Williams from recognizing the permanence and value of country life itself. The lasting appeal of pastoral can, I think, be related to Wilson's *biophilia*—reverence for life, our instinctive sense of ourselves as creatures of natural origins. My aim is once again to risk valorizing, rather than expunging, the natural world by questioning the disjunction between text and world that, as Buell wryly notes, is commonly accepted as the proper opening point for sophisticated literary discussion.

Building upon the recent ecologically informed pastoral studies mentioned above and impelled by the tenacious and long human history of pastoral, I believe that a plausible argument can and should be made for examining pastoral's evolutionary-biological, not simply cultural, history and sources. Roger Rosenblatt's gentle nature-endorsing epigraph at the beginning of this chapter would evoke little opposition from the general reader (his essay appeared in *Time Magazine*). Similarly, in his new book, *The Nature of Generosity*, writer William Kittredge reflects without trepidation that "The yearnings built into our DNA, which evolved in wilderness, are for us the imperishable world" (244). But Rosenblatt's and Kittredge's mild assumptions that nature is part of human nature, that there *is* such a thing as human nature, that we are creatures who are continually reminded of what we did not know we knew about what is "fixed in our system" by our encounters with natural life—these would raise a red flag with culturally predisposed nature-skeptics. It is their hostility to this nature-connected human nature that needs to be addressed.

"Just-So Stories"

First, it is necessary to consider the meaning and status of so-called just-so stories. The term, taken from Kipling's *Just-So Stories*, was coined in its present use by Stephen Jay Gould in his 1978 article, "Sociobiology: The Art of Storytelling." The epithet is often applied to discredit evolutionary explanations of behavior, that is, explanations that certain behaviors exist because they provided adaptive advantages (those that confer survival and reproductive benefit) in evolutionary development. The Kipling just-so stories are merely clever stories for children, giving fanciful accounts of how, for example, the leopard got his spots. They have nothing to do with evolution. Applying the just-so-story label to accounts that *do* have to do with evolution and that *may* be true, or false, is misleading and unfair, since such a label announces *all* such stories to be false beforehand. Biologist John Alcock, in *The Triumph of Sociobiology*, calls the just-so-story epithet "one of the most successful derogatory labels ever invented, having entered common parlance as a name for any explanation about behavior, especially human behavior, that someone wishes to dispute" (64). Gould has had a wide public following owing to his skills as a writer, which have deservedly made his columns in the *Natural History* journal well known over the years. His books and essays are broadly influential.

As a result, the just-so-story label often serves as a journalistic cliché, eclipsing the sort of careful thought that the subject of an evolutionary component in behavior deserves.[2] Since Gould's (and his colleague Richard Lewontin's) antiadaptationist stance in deriding just-so stories corresponds to the Standard Social Science Model (SSSM) and the blank-slate theory of human behavior—culture alone determines our behavior, and no evolutionary explanations need apply—it has proved ideologically appealing. Now that the SSSM is under major attack from a rising tide of evidence to the contrary, the just-so-story epithet is also receiving renewed scrutiny.

Philosopher of science Daniel C. Dennett, the most astute examiner of Gould and Lewontin and the just-so story, notes in his *Darwin's Dangerous Idea* that anyone who wishes to ask and answer "why" questions about human behavior has no choice but to participate in the just-so game and be an adaptationist (247). As Dennett points out, Gould himself is an endorser of just-so stories, even though he also takes an antiadaptationist stance. Robert Storey, in *Mimesis and the Human Animal*, claims that "Gould enthusiastically embraces those 'just-so stories' about human adaptation that accord with his Marxist politics (see, for example, *Ever Since Darwin* 260–67), while dismissing all others as sociobiological *ignes fatui*" (212). Joseph Carroll, in *Evolution and Literary Theory*, notes a similar tendency in Richard Lewontin's "characteristic strategy . . . to surround sociobiological theses with a skepticism that renders all knowledge of human nature indeterminate, but then simultaneously to presuppose that Marxist views of human nature are simply and self-evidently true" (269).[3]

What might best serve the cause of informed debate is to throw out the term *just-so story*, since it stigmatizes all evolutionary hypotheses relating to human behavior and since, as Dennett points out, "*some story or other* must be true" (245). We are ill served by a term whose only meaning is pejorative. Its employment is akin to the practice of creationists who believe they are refuting the arguments of speakers on evolution by shouting, "Were you there?" No, none of us was there, but the "why" questions in human behavior are still amenable to hypotheses based upon strong evidence and sound reasoning. "In science," say Tooby and Cosmides in criticizing Gould and Lewontin's routine disparagement of adaptationism or an evolutionary contribution in human behavior, "this is usually called 'explanation'" (77). Dennett cautions that such explanations, to be credible, must meet the rules of thumb that he lays out for the prospective "reverse engineer" (247). Dennett concludes,

> Adaptationism is both ubiquitous and powerful in biology. Like any other idea, it can be misused, but it is not a mistaken idea: it is in fact the irreplaceable core of Darwiniam thinking. Gould and Lewontin's fabled refutation of adaptationism is an illusion, but they have raised everybody's consciousness about the risks of incautious thinking. Good adaptationist thinking is always on the lookout for hidden constraints, and in fact is the best method for uncovering them (261).

Cautious Thinking about Biophilia and the Roots of Pastoral

A hypothesis for the evolutionary roots of pastoral literature should, I would argue, relate to Wilson's conception of biophilia, the human affinity for life. He devotes his 1984 book by that title to making the case for a universal human propensity to respond positively to natural life. Until recently an argument for biophilia, or any other argument leading in the direction of human nature or human universals—that is, a biological component to human behavior—would have been rejected out of hand as "essentialist" or "reductionist" or worse by the social/cultural constructivist nature-skeptics. Commenting upon this situation, Brian Boyd writes, "Those reluctant to read outside Theory's approved reading lists may not be aware of it, but evidence has been accumulating for more than thirty years, and with steadily mounting momentum, that not only is it not the case that biology is a product of culture, but that culture is a product and a part of biology, and that it is impossible to explain cultural difference without appreciating the complex architecture of the human mind, of a 'human nature [that] is everywhere the same'" (38).

A recent anthology entitled *Human/Nature: Biology, Culture, and Environmental History* exemplifies the conflicted thinking presently taking place within the social sciences on the part of those who sense a growing challenge to the Standard Social Science Model. In the opening lines of their introduction, the editors of this volume write: "Human nature is a dead idea. Efforts to uncover a fundamental biological component of human behavior are based on an unsophisticated understanding of both culture and science and contribute little to our exploration of human society. This is an assertion that many scholars would readily agree with, but is it true?" (Herron and Kirk 1) Though the editors go on to affirm that the idea of human nature "is very much alive and well," the contents of their volume indicate that few of their contributors are ready to agree with them.[4]

The lone outspoken advocate is University of Montana environmental historian Dan Flores, whose essay "Nature's Children: Environmental History as Human Natural History" opens the anthology. Flores proceeds from a Wilsonian sociobiological perspective, despite what he notes as the "venomous hostility" that has greeted Wilson's work from the culturalists and their commitment to the "bottomless plasticity" of human behavior (20). Flores argues that we need to reconsider sociobiology because of its greater explanatory power than any social constructivism has provided. Flores's biocultural perspective yields a modern environmental history that is

> manifestly not a history of a godlike creature gone over the edge of sanity, but the story of a wildly successful species that has been doing the same things, and for the same reasons, for three million years. It's the history of a species that late in its evolution has stepped outside the external limits nature usually imposes on efflorescence and now doesn't recognize the ancient imperatives, doesn't believe it should be chary of them, or can't muster a resolve to resist their darker implications. (25)

Although few of Flores's co-contributors follow his lead, the debate over human nature, a subject of "unspeakable importance," has advanced far beyond the rejection prescribed by the Standard Social Science Model.[5] The perceived overstatements of Wilson's final chapter in his

1975 textbook, *Sociobiology*, which transferred certain principles of animal-related behavior in previous chapters to the study of human behavior, led to the virulent and what are today commonly recognized as often unfair and erroneous early attacks upon Wilson. What historian Carl Degler called "The Return of Human Nature" in his 1991 book by that title was hastened forward by Wilson's 1978 Pulitzer Prize–winning *On Human Nature*. Not a book "of science," Wilson called it, but a book "about science, and about how far the natural sciences can penetrate into human behavior before they will be transformed into something new. It examines the reciprocal impact that a truly evolutionary explanation of human behavior must have on the social sciences and humanities" (x).

Now, as described in the preceding chapter, there is a sense abroad that Wilson's ideas about human nature and behavior, modified and developed in his and others' subsequent books and articles, have steadily gained influence and acceptance. Wilson has been careful to explain and defuse the misunderstandings that attended his early work, as when he writes more recently,

> In sociobiology, there is a heavy emphasis on the comparison of societies of different kinds of animals and man, not so much to draw analogies (these have often been dangerously misleading, as when aggression is compared directly in wolves and in human beings) but to devise and to test theories about the underlying hereditary basis of social behavior. With genetic evolution always in mind, sociobiologists search for the ways in which the myriad forms of social organization adapt particular species to the special opportunities and dangers encountered in their environment. (*In Search of Nature* 76)

A broadening collection of books and studies, many of which have been or will be discussed in these pages, offers evidence of this growing influence and acceptance. It seems plausible to extend the parameters of these studies and apply their findings to address the possible origins of literary pastoral.

The myth of the pastoral garden, including the Genesis story of the Garden of Eden, is one of the most powerful and richly textured visions in human history, from its folkloric beginnings in Persian, Greek, and Roman history, through the Middle Ages, as in "The Romance of the Rose," and the Renaissance, as in Sidney's "Arcadia," to the New World connections described in Leo Marx's *The Machine in the Garden*, and down to its present conflicted state in the age of ecology.[6]

But for the direct origins of the literary pastoral, one turns first to the mythology of Arcadia, the region of ancient Greece that is pastoral's home ground. Phillipe Borgeaud points out in his fascinating study, *The Cult of Pan in Ancient Greece*, that the Greek god Pan is an Arcadian and, for the Greeks, Arcadia symbolized the original life. The ancient Arcadians were seen in Greek mythology as rough, bestial, wild primitives who occupied their barren and forbidding region as "Pre-Selenians," that is, older than the time when the moon rose for the first time. "The Arcadians are autochthons, earth-born . . . integrally connected with the earth from which they were born" (8–9). They were identified with animals, herding, and hunting, and their chief divinity, Pan, was half animal, half man, copulating with animals as well as humans.

Borgeaud points out that the Arcadians of the pastoral poets, "that happy, free Arcadia caressed by zephyrs, where the love songs of the goatherds waft—is a Roman invention, part and parcel of a meditation on the theme of the origins of Rome. The bucolic landscape of Vergil, set in Arcadia, is a kind of stage set" (5–6).[7]

Paul Shepard, in books like *Nature and Madness* and *Back to the Pleistocene*, and Gary Snyder, in *The Practice of the Wild*, find in our hunter-gatherer Pleistocene heritage the deep-rooted need for wildness and connection with nature that Rosenblatt and Kittredge have also noted. The ancient myths of the wild Arcadians, with their half-animal god Pan, suggest this more Darwinian link to the idea of the literary pastoral than the sanitized and sweetened Roman version provides. (Could these wild Arcadians have been a folkloric memory of the time when Homo sapiens first encountered the Neandertals?[8]) Simon Schama notes in *Landscape and Memory* that "In an unexpected way, then, the Greek myth of Arcadian origins anticipated the theory of evolution in its assumption of continuities between animals and men" (526–27).

Although Schama's observation is his only mention of evolutionary theory in his magisterial study of 3,000 years of human interrelationships with landscape, his references—as in his explanation of the cathedral grove, to "the richness, antiquity and complexity of our landscape tradition," to "our most powerful yearnings," to "the deepest relationships between natural form and human design" (14–15)—all bespeak the sort of elemental aspects of human nature that evolutionary psychology addresses. As Carlo Ginsburg writes in his *Clues, Myths and the Historical Method*, "In the absence of verbal documentation to supplement rock paintings and artifacts, we can turn to folklore, which transmits an echo, though dim and distorted, of the knowledge accumulated by those remote hunters" (102).

On the question of whether these are universal or culture-bound relationships, Schama writes that he leaves this to the reader to judge. As a historian (that is, avoiding the unrecorded prehistorical territory that is being explored here), he admits to being "necessarily" tied to cultural perspectives rather than universal manifestations of human nature. Still, he cites Carl Jung's belief that the universality of nature myths is evidence of their ubiquitous psychological role in responding to human fears and longings. Schama observes that Mircea Eliade also assumed these nature myths have survived in all contemporary cultures. And Schama concludes, "it is clear the inherited landscape myths and memories share two common characteristics: their surprising endurance through the centuries and their power to shape institutions that we still live with" (15). All of these points are consistent with the case for evolutionary history and adaptation as a plausible explanation of the origins of literary pastoral.

Returning to Wilson's texts—scientifically significant as well as unusually rich and sensitive in their literary nuances and relevance—one may find in them explicit points of connection to the origins of pastoral.[9] *Biophilia*, an outgrowth of Wilson's longstanding devotion to worldwide environmental conservation issues, focuses, as I have said, on the question of a partly genetic "sociobiological" affiliation with other life and life processes. Wilson proposes not so much a hardwired response for a human attraction to nature—*hardwired* is an extreme term, not much in favor with biologists, since so many other cultural, historical, and situational factors are often involved—but a biological bias, or an innate propensity or orientation, within which there is considerable room for cultural and other variability.[10] "From infancy we concentrate happily on ourselves and other organisms. We learn to distinguish life from the inanimate and move toward it like moths to a porch light." But he goes on to claim much more: "I will make the case that to explore and affiliate with life is a deep and complicated process in mental development. To an extent undervalued in philosophy and religion, our existence depends on this propensity, our spirit is woven from it, hope rises on its currents" (*Biophilia* 1). He concludes that sociobiology provides a way of seeing the world that is "incidentally congenial to the inner direction of biophilia. In other words, instinct is in this rare instance aligned with reason," a pairing that leads him to a hopeful conclusion: "to the degree that we come to understand other organisms, we will place a greater value on them, and on ourselves" (*Biophilia* 2).

At this point it is useful to consider, even briefly, that pastoral's eventual emergence as an art form 2,300 years ago can also be implicated in

Ellen Dissanayake's important pioneering work in the biobehavioral origins of human art. Her books, especially *What Is Art For?* (1988) and *Homo Aestheticus: Where Art Comes From and Why* (1995), emplace the origin and appeal of art within the evolutionary perspective of a universal human nature. Thus, she consider art's origins as precultural and its practice as a behavior whose tendencies proved to be of evolutionary advantage. Questioning the contemporary view of most humanists and social scientists that art can only be seen as an individual or cultural production, Dissanayake builds an impressive case for a biocultural origin for art. Her argument, like that of other investigators proceeding from a biological view, finds a genetic universal, not an immutable and determined "essence" but a certain range of tendencies underlying the grafting on of, admittedly, vitally important cultural differences.

Although she does not deal specifically with an acquired art form such as written literature (writing is less than 10,000 years old), her work relates to the storytelling, dramatic, and religious ceremonies out of which so venerable a literary form as pastoral may reasonably be assumed to have arisen. For Dissanayake, a Darwinian, species-centered examination of art "reveals that the aesthetic is not something added to us—learned or acquired like speaking a second language or riding a horse—but in large measure is the way we are, Homo aestheticus, stained through and through." She argues that a biological understanding of the arts does not necessarily rule out other perspectives but precedes and underlies them, providing a broader justification for their continuing relevance in human life (*Homo Aestheticus* xix, xvii).[11]

Dissanake's hypothesis on the origins of art in human nature is that at some point in evolution, art became a means of what she calls "making special," recognizing and enhancing important events and activities, making them distinctive and significant—as in ritual and play—perhaps so as to exert influence or control over them. A recent article in *Lingua Franca* on her iconoclastic work and the growing influence of sociobiology's successor, evolutionary psychology, emphasizes the common interests of its practitioners with Darwinian precepts "that the arts are rooted in human nature inflected by age and gender and that the variations among the human races are trivial" (Crain 36).[12] With Dissananke's work in mind, the investigation of biophilia's claim to the attention of pastoral scholars can be rejoined.

Given his propensity for bold hypothesizing, Edward O. Wilson's enthusiasm for his own biophilia thesis is a scientific caveat. Wilson, who was aware of this, submitted his idea to a number of scholars in various related fields for examination and for research on it as it applies to their own fields—a model of the scientific method at work. The result is *The Biophilia Hypothesis* (1993), edited by Stephen R. Kellert and Wilson. Of particular relevance to the study of literary pastoral is part two of *The Biophilia Hypothesis*, "Affect and Aesthetics," which includes two essays that address pastoral concerns, "Biophilia, Biophobia, and Natural Landscapes," by Roger S. Ulrich, a geographer and environmental psychologist, and "Humans, Habitats, and Aesthetics," by Judith H. Heerwagen, a psychologist in behavioral ecology, and Gordon H. Orians, a zoologist and environmental studies scholar. Both studies test ideas raised by Wilson's *Biophilia* chapter, "The Right Place." Both seem to relate directly to the question of a biosocial basis for pastoral's long history and its characteristic praise for a human return to natural settings as the site of emotional and physical health and regeneration.

Ulrich reminds us of the Darwinian axiom that "if biophilia is represented in the gene pool it is because a predisposition in early humans for biophilic responses to certain natural elements and settings contributed to fitness or chances for survival" (75). Ulrich argues that theoretical proposals for biophilia gain credence if they consider as well the adaptive counterevidence for biophobic (negative) responses. He examines biophobic responses involving dangers and fears of natural settings during evolution, such as threats from predatory animals, as well as biophilic (positive) responses.

He concludes that the study of biophilia is still at an early stage, and although he summarizes some evidence favorable to the biophilia hypothesis, he finds no conclusive evidence as yet that positive responses to nature have a partly genetic basis. But he calls attention to the deep cultural shift of the last two decades, in which genetic factors, previously derided and dismissed by scientific investigators in such areas as alcoholism and infants' innate capacity for mathematics, have been seen as important determiners. "Recently . . . the mainstream theoretical orientation of the behavioral and brain sciences has been altered by a cascade of studies showing convincingly that biological or genetic factors play a role not only in alcoholism and math skills but in numerous other aspects of human behavior and response" (126). The debate, he says, is no longer along polarized nature/nurture lines. Mainstream science increasingly accepts the role of genetics in human behavior but debates its contribution in such a role (125–26). Ulrich ends his essay with an urgent call for more study on biophilia.

In the other pastoral-place-relevant study, "Humans, Habitats, and Aesthetics," Judith Heerwagen and Gordon H. Orians proceed from the evolutionary psychology perspective set forth by Tooby and Cosmides in their influential essay, "The Psychological Foundations of Culture," to question not whether biophilia exists (since, as Ulrich also notes, there are both joy and loathing in human experiences with the natural world) but rather what form biophilia takes. Their reseach centers upon habitat selection and an examination of Wilson's claim in his *Biophilia* chapter on "The Right Place" that "If you get to the right place, everything else is likely to be easier" (106). Wilson had further noted that "whenever people are given a free choice, they move to open tree-studded land on prominences overlooking water. This worldwide tendency is no longer dictated by the hard necessities of hunter-gatherer life. It has become largely aesthetic" (110). If this claim is supported convincingly, I believe it offers a provocative insight into the pastoral impulse and may be a further indication of the relevance of biophysical responses to aesthetic issues—issues that until very recently were adjudged the province of only culturally based criticism.

Heerwagen and Orians hypothesized that, given the 99 percent of human evolutionary history spent in hunting-gathering cultures, environmental preferences today should be consistent with subsistence roles and enhanced evolutionary fitness. In this essay, in their earlier related research, and in the works of other investigators in this field, they provide evidence for what might be considered the psychological appeal of pastoral environments. Landscapes of the African savannas, for example, in which early humans evolved, offered advantages that were appropriate to both hunting and gathering, as well as visual surveillance for predators, enemies, and competitors. Such landscapes, with their views of wide prospects, mosaics of open grassland with gatherings of trees and other vegetation, and water sources, provide material for testing today's human subjects—through visual representations in paintings, drawings, and photographs—for their preferences in landscapes and landscape components.

Although responses to these natural environments are wide and variable, Heerwagen and Orians provide considerable evidence that modern humans prefer and seek out environments with wide, sunlit vistas, climbable trees, grazing animals, water, flowers, and grass. Conversely, in reflecting upon biophobic responses it is revealing, as the two investigators point out, "that the real hazards of modern life—guns, bombs, drugs, polluted water—do not generate nightmares or intense fears as frequently as do hazards from our evolutionary past (snakes, predators, darkness)" (164).

Results of the limited number of studies done so far suggest the influence of nature on our emotional and physical health. Witness the existence of national, state, city, and neighborhood parks. Even pictures and posters and slides and views from windows seem to be beneficial. We see the widespread use of nature posters in public buildings, especially medical offices and hospitals, and the addition of flowers and plants and aquariums to places where people work and gather (166–67). The presence of parks in neighborhoods, cities, counties, states, and national scenic treasures should also be noted. The evidence for our natured dispositions is regularly a part of our lives, as can be seen in the report that hospital patients whose rooms look out upon a tree require less medication and are discharged earlier than those whose windows face a blank wall (Gifford, *Pastoral* 156; Wilson, *Future* 139–41). In *Biophilia* Wilson anticipates a counter-response:

> The practical-minded will argue that certain environments are just "nice" and there's an end to it. So why dilate on the obvious? The answer is that the obvious is usually profoundly significant. Some environments are indeed pleasant, for the same general reason that sugar is sweet, incest and cannibalism repugnant, and team sports exhilarating. Each response has its peculiar meaning rooted in the distant genetic past. To understand why we have one particular set of ingrained preferences, and not another, out of the vast number possible remains a central question in the study of man. (113)

Another way of measuring the strength of biophilia has to do with our relationship with animals, especially the first domesticated animals, dogs. The role of animals in improving the mental health of hospital patients, hyperactive or autistic children, persons with chronic organic brain disorders, and ordinary citizens offers further material for speculation upon pastoral's continuing appeal. The word *pastoral* derives from the Latin *pastor*, for shepherd, and the original meaning refers to shepherds, herdsmen, and others directly involved in animal husbandry. In another chapter in *The Biophilia Hypothesis*, "Dialogue with Animals: Its Nature and Culture," medical doctors and research investigators Aaron Katcher and Gregory Wilkins explore our relationship with animals and caution us to consider the power of culture to "reduce the complex roles played by animals to simple images defined by human interest or need. Coyotes and wolves are always bad; sheep and cattle are always good. . . . To complete the circle, it is necessary to consider how culture and human nature interact and reintroduce the moral or political agenda for the preservation of biodiversity" (190). Katcher and Wilkins find cultural instruction powerful enough to overcome biophilia, if it exists, but believe that posing the existence of biophilia and employing it as a part of science pedagogy will probably have beneficial effects in protecting biodiversity and slowing global environmental degradation (194).

Two anthropologically and biologically based essays in *The Biophilia Hypothesis* offer additional evidence on these issues. In his chapter, "Searching for the Lost Arrow: Physical and Spiritual Ecology in the Hunter's World," Richard Nelson, Alaska anthropologist and author, sees biophilia at the heart of traditional hunting-fishing-gathering cultures such as those he has studied. Their connectedness with nonhuman life is interfused with all their thinking, spiritual belief, and behavior. Such people, he speculates, might be unable to get far enough outside themselves to imagine a separation from nonhuman life:

> Yet an affinity for other life may be as vital to us as water, food, and breath; may be so deep in us that only by a centuries-old malaise of drifting away have we come to the point of thinking about it. At the conclusion of *Biophilia*, Wilson . . . asks: "Is it possible that humanity will love life enough to save it?" Surely there is no more important question in the latter twentieth century. But it seems nearly certain that throughout most of [evolutionary] history, humans did love life. Every aspect of culture and mind was permeated with biophilia. (225)

A biologist whose research relates to people of India, Madhav Gadgil, points out in his essay that kinship and reciprocity, which hold human societies together, was, in hunter-gatherer and subsistence-agricultural peoples, extended to include nonhumans as well: "For them rivers and streams could be mothers, antelopes and bears brothers." Nonhuman members of the fellowship provided humans with food, water, and shelter. Humans reciprocated by protecting them from excessive destruction and by offering them gifts. So a length of river might never be fished, or protection could be offered to sacred mountains, groves, streams, or individual animals:

> A whole range of genuinely effective conservation measures was implemented through such practices. Thus on the hill chain of Western Ghats in South India, as much as 6 percent of the land was covered by a

> dispersed network of sacred groves covering all habitat types from swamps and gallery forests to stunted scrub on wind-swept hilltops. Even today, when the network is greatly reduced, sacred groves protect the northernmost stands of *Dipterocarpus* and rare habitats like *Myristica* swamps. In the same region all trees of the genus *Ficus*, now recognized to be keystone resources, are given nearly total protection against felling, as are all primate species protected against being hunted. (371–72)

Now, Gadgil speculates, the ever-growing role of artifacts in our lives has resulted in the former human veneration for sacred places and animals being transferred to these artifacts, increasing the necessity for nurturing the necessary natural diversity, even as artifacts continue to evolve (376).

Gary Paul Nabhan and Sara St. Antoine, in their *Biophilia Hypothesis* study of Native American children in the desert Southwest, found that these children's learning environment, where television and classroom had usurped time and importance formerly given to direct experience, storytelling, and personal instruction by elders, had resulted in a "whittling away" of the childrens' affinity for plants and animals and thus their expression of a genetic basis for biophilia.[13]

From a more familiar perspective to those of us in English, David W. Orr, chair of Environmental Studies at Oberlin College, adopts a values-oriented stance in one of the closing essays in *The Biophilia Hypothesis.* Orr concludes that "whatever is in our genes, the affinity for life is now a *choice* we must make" ("Love It or Lose It" 416). Looking back across the divide from earlier cultures who lacked the power or knowledge that we have, Orr writes that we cannot claim their ecological innocence, and now we "must choose between biophobia and biophilia because science and technology have given us to power to destroy so completely as well as the knowledge to understand the consequences of doing so" (417).

Orr notes the unlikelihood that the human brain could have evolved in a moonscape devoid of biological diversity. He touches upon Dissanayake's research in positing a sense of awe before the natural world as related to the origin of language and the desire to talk, sing, and create art in the first place. "Elemental things like flowing water, wind, trees, clouds, rain, mist, mountains, landscape, animals, changing seasons, the night sky, and the mysteries of the life cycle gave birth to thought and language. They continue to do so, but perhaps less exuberantly than they once did" (425).

"Do we, with all our technology, still retain a built-in affinity for nature?" asks Orr. "I think so, but I know of no proof that would satisfy skeptics" (423–24). Are the longevity and the continuing and widespread appeal of literary manifestations of pastoral attributable to a human nature formed in our hunter-gatherer past or even before? Like Orr, I think so but doubt that the doubters do, despite the considerable supporting evidence. Were we there? No. Just-so stories? Probably not, but no ironclad guarantees for the skeptical. The note of apprehension is sounded again in editor Stephen R. Kellert's "Coda" to *The Biophilia Hypothesis.* Kellert observes that the idea of biophilia casts back upon us all its own note of deep skepticism regarding "the human capacity to thrive in a biologically depaupered world that has countenanced and abetted in the massive destruction of life" (457). Like Richard Nelson and others, Kellert wonders whether we can survive in the absence of biophilia. In this case, ironically, the nature-endorsers may also be the nature-skeptics.

Et in Arcadia Ego

These dark references to a stricken biosphere, increasingly posited, as we have seen, in contemporary art and discourse, return us to the subject of traditional pastoral and its characteristic pairing of those grand narratives, nature and death. We are back with the deep human yearning, as Simon Schama describes it, "to find in nature a consolation for our mortality." (Or perhaps, in contemporary environmental terms, to find in ourselves a consolation for nature's mortality.) The nature-death pairing is observed in several Renaissance paintings, including pastoral landscapes by the Italian artist Guercino (Francisco Giovanni Barbieri), and the French painter Nicolas Poussin.[14] In these pictures the Latin phrase, *Et in Arcadia Ego*, was found as an inscription, accompanied by a human skull (in Guercino) and a tomb (in Poussin). Erwin Panofsky, in a classic essay published in 1936, explicated the ambiguous meaning of the motto and traced the popular acceptance of the elegiac and assuaging interpretation, "I, too, lived in Arcadia," which is attributed to a departed shepherd. Largely forgotten over time was the original meaning, "Even in Arcadia there is death." Panofsky's analysis reveals what he calls the "discrepancy . . . between the supernatural perfection of an imaginary environment and the natural limitations of human life as it is" (300).

Seen from the vantage point of our own times, we might cite this preference for "soft" pastoral over "hard" as another example of human avoidance of unpleasantness. But from an ecological perspective, we find in this historical triumph of the celebratory appeal of idyllic nature something of our present environmental dilemma. Despite the temporary comforts of denial, death has reentered the picture. The figurative death's head of the Renaissance pastoral, a traditional Christian memento mori, has emerged as a more universal and implacable corrective to human evasion. Until recently, the fate of the individual human soul was played out against a seemingly permanent setting of natural grandeur and certainty. Now, in a new and totally unanticipated global environment of degradation, loss, extinction, it is the death of that old conception of nature itself that disturbs our pastoral dreams.

Of course, there is a long tradition of death as a subject within pastoral literature. The mourning elegy, as Andrew Ettin reminds us, is the most noteworthy and distinguished of all forms of pastoral poetry (116). Because death is a universal experience, it invites reflection, causing us to ponder our relationships to the human and natural world. "Death, the great leveler," writes Ettin, "makes us all pastoral characters, and therefore the knowledge that death must come should make our earthly pastoral world that much more precious to us. . . . Against the marmoreal chill of death, life on this bountiful earth, filled with moments of small yet important pleasures, is itself pastoral" (144–45).

What has changed profoundly in present-day writing is the conception of the bountiful earth and its assumed otherness and permanence. Not only may many fashionable contemporary writers slight the natural world, as Scott Russell Sanders has argued, but where nature does appear in our discourse, it is often less a bountiful than a baleful or threatened presence. In modern invocations of pastoral, then, nature has been transformed from a model of certainty to one of uncertainty, tainted, as Bill McKibben asserts in *The End of Nature*, by evidence that we are capable of altering—and have indeed irrevocably altered—nature, and for the worse: "We have changed the atmosphere, and thus we are changing the weather. By changing the weather, we make every spot on earth man-made and artificial. We have deprived nature of its independence, and that is fatal to its meaning. Nature's independence is its meaning; without it there is nothing but us" (58).

McKibben is, like most of us, operating from anthropocentric assumptions. Humanity is and always has been a part of nature. Though our position is ambiguous, we cannot withdraw from nature nor ever wholly subsume it. Nature has not "ended," nor will it, as McKibben acknowledges, but human actions may have begun a process that, ironically, ends humankind's place on this planet. The earth has gone through such periodic changes before: extreme climate changes caused by variations in radiation from the sun; cataclysmic collisions with asteroids;

changes in soil nutrients; the evolution of photosynthesis, which brought oxygen into the earth's atmosphere about 2 billion years ago and allowed the evolution of aerobic forms of life, including the higher plants and animals such as humans (McKibben 63–64).

There is, admittedly, scant human comfort in such lengthened, (Robinson) Jeffersian perspectives, and human comfort is the province of pastoral.[15] Pastoral as a genre works upon the principles of harmony and reconciliation. It emphasizes resemblances and points of accommodation, often drawing the opposing worlds of nature and society into that characteristic meeting point of cultured or humanized nature, the garden. Implicit in this strategy of reconciliation, however, is a factor that has diminished the relevance of pastoral in contemporary thinking. That factor, which must be addressed if pastoral theory is to retain its critical authority for the present and the future, is its tendency to devalue wild nature, wilderness, the old, wild Arcadia, which, from the time of the softened pastorals of the Roman poets until very recently, has been seen as an untenable extreme.[16]

Standing at the opposite pole from the cacophonous, machine-driven city, wilderness is, at least in the traditional pastoral equation, the heretofore disregardable alternative. The city, by virtue of its sanctioning as a wholly ubiquitous human creation, was never disregardable. The attributes of wilderness, in such a dialectic as traditional pastoral represents, become those of doctrinaire primitivism and escapism, that is, a total rejection of civilization and a mindless immersion into the appeals of sensory life and apparent simplicity. The tension between the extremist values of primitivism and urbanism have, in the past, allowed pastoral the normative and conciliatory territory between the two. The pastoral garden, then, has functioned in traditional pastoral as a comforting point of synthesis.

But what has emerged in response to the last few decades of environmental concern is a revolutionary reconsideration of wilderness. Max Oelschlaeger, for example, in his *The Idea of Wilderness*, attempts to reclaim wilderness from the outer edges of our worldview, arguing that the alchemy of modernism transmuted wilderness into nature—that is, into "a stockpile of resources, lifeless matter-in-motion, a standing reserve for human appropriation" (24). If the key terms for relatively untrammeled nature in the past were *simplicity* and *permanence*, those terms have shifted in an ecologically concerned present to *complexity* and *change*. Instead of seeing wilderness as an appealing but ultimately impossible alternative, it is now increasingly studied and interpreted as the model of a complex diversity and a new pattern for survival. "[N]o man's garden, but the unhandseled globe," as Thoreau said of the wild and forbidding heights of Mount Ktaadn (Ronald 33–34). Like Thoreau, we seek further contact with the inhuman, with wildness, contact from which we have somehow become insulated by the comforting familiarities of pastoral landscapes and conventions.

Wild nature has replaced the traditional middle state of the garden and the rural landscape as the locus of stability and value, the seat of instruction. The old pastoral artists kept nature at a distance, standing outside the green world. Their depiction of nature softened and stylized its coarse realities, and their call to return to it was not to be taken entirely seriously. All that has now changed. The rough beast-men from their wild land of ancient Arcadia, evolutionary reminders of our Pleistocene beginnings, call to mind the radical significance of wilderness and lead us to look behind its conversion by the unexamined pastoral tradition into the benevolent swains and maidens and the comfortable landscapes of the garden. Under the influence of ecological thought, wilderness has radicalized the pastoral experience.

Wilderness today is, of course, still the region of the world's tropical rain forests and evergreen conifer forests; the polar regions, the deserts, and the open oceans; and the territory of grizzly and polar bears, mountain lions, wolves, and whales. But we can increasingly respond to Gary Snyder's argument that wilderness surrounds us, in the spiders in our house corners and the bacteria in our yogurt and our bodies (*Practice* 14–16). Kneeling to examine a rotting log near Walden Pond, Edward O. Wilson finds a naturalist's gratification in the worlds it encompasses. "Untrammeled nature exists in the dirt and rotting vegetation beneath our shoes. The wilderness of ordinary vision may have vanished—wolf, puma, and wolverine no longer exist in the tamed forests of Massachusetts. But another, even more ancient wilderness lives on. The microscope can take you there." Still, as Wilson reminds us, we will always require the large reserves of wilderness where large animals continue to live "life on the large scale to which the human intellect and emotion more naturally respond" (*Future* xvi, 146).

The impetus for a radicalized pastoral has come principally through the burgeoning influence of this sort of natural-history and nature writing, which John Tallmadge has called "arguably the most exciting realm of American literature" ("Rev. of *Norton*" 64). Many ecologically conscious readers have apparently turned to nature writing as the clearest and most direct antidote to the presumption of total human dominance and control, a presumption that has fueled not only the myriad environmental crises, but the unquestioned and unquestioning anthropocentrism of most academic discourse as well. Looking at, listening to, the natural world seems an act of sanity, of deference to natural systems and communities that work and survive—in a world context of momentous human mismanagement.

Insofar as much contemporary literature and criticism has insulated itself from the biological and the natural world, nature writing seems to have responded to that lack and to have provided a growing contemporary audience with that sense of an ecological reality check that they do not find elsewhere.[17] Pastoral is, of course, a cultural construct, an idea. But that observation does not consume its significance. As Neil Evernden writes, "The inclination to tell the story of 'how the world is' seems basic to being human. . . . We can only hope that when the story turns out to be too far removed from actual experience to be reliable, we still have the skill to return to the world beneath the categories and re-establish connections with it" (quoted in Oelschlaeger, *The Idea of Wilderness* 134). Such an evolutionary story as accompanies the history of the pastoral impulse may prove to be more valid and meaningful than those stories "too far removed" from the hard actualities beneath the social constructions.

James Applewhite has argued that postmodernist society, and the art that it produces, "seems to have lost the capacity to think in terms of environmental fact, as it has lost the capacity to deal with other essential relationships: to history, to character, to the cause-and-effect sequences of real human emotions" (15). For a postmodern "thinking" primitivist like Max Oelschlaeger, "wildness is not just the preservation of the world, it is the world—self-organizing order out of chaos" (*The Idea of Wilderness* 285).

It is in this context that a redefined pastoral might emerge. Our social construction of reality takes us only so far in understanding ourselves or the world. Reality, as Thoreau reminded us in *Walden*, is what we crave, despite our tendency to delude ourselves with "Arabian Nights' Entertainments" (65). From our perspective today, perhaps the new pastoral exemplified in contemporary nature writing and scientific ecology has the capacity to reel us in when we have gone too far, insisting upon our implacable connection to a nature finally resistant to our controlling and ideologizing tendencies. This contemporary perspective is powerfully revealed in a work like Richard Nelson's *The Island Within*, in which the complexity of the wild world and the physicality of the writer's experience within it expand our sense of nature-consciousness.

To summarize, the traditional pastoral middle landscape, in contemporary times, finds itself bearing the stigma of a human-caused despoliation. Bright visions of progress through a humanized and mechanized natural world have been erased by the reality of population bombs and the rape of the fair land and the mass extinction of species. "What the pastoral tradition calls 'nature,'" as Joseph Meeker points out, "is merely simplified civilization" (*Comedy*, 1974, 90). As the awareness of this fact settles upon us, it is not hard to understand why pastoral theory seems tied to narrowly humanist assumptions and in need of contemporary redefinition and application.

Et in Arcadia Ego. The motto explicated by Panofsky, whether a lament for a lost golden past or a reminder of death's ineluctable chill, suggests the inevitability of change. In terms of our environmental afflictions, casting ourselves out of the garden and into the wilderness, Snyder-fashion, along with the rest of evolved life, may prove to be less an exile than a necessity. A viable pastoral for the future might well find its healing vision not in the simplicity of the garden but in the complexity of the old-growth forest or of the microwilderness in the ground beneath our feet.

"I bequeath myself to the dirt to grow from the grass I love," says Whitman's speaker, a voice for the life force whether great or small, at the conclusion of *Song of Myself*. "If you want me again look for me under your boot-soles."

In the chapters that follow I pursue the potential lines of connection between literary criticism and biology/ecology as elements of literary analysis, addressing some canonical works of American fiction. Is a productive "consilience," a joining of the fields of knowledge, possible or likely between the disciplines of literary study and biology, which apparently exemplify the conflicts of the two cultures?

4

Place, Style, and Human Nature in Willa Cather's *The Professor's House*

• • • • • • • • • • • • • •

> Our habits of environmental perception, while they are invariably modified and shaped by cultural, social, historical, and personal experiences, are not created out of nothing by those influences; rather they are the derivatives of mechanisms of survival behavior which were already there, elements of our innate make-up. Aesthetic pleasure is the pleasure of *perception*. Environmental perception is the key to environmental adaptation which is in turn the basis of the survival of individual organisms and a central theme in the Darwinian theory of evolution by natural selection, while pleasure emerges both as the driving force of the whole biological system and as the criterion of excellence in a hedonistic aesthetics.—Jay Appleton, *The Symbolism of Habitat*

Willa Cather's *The Professor's House* is, on the face of it, another version of pastoral, with its famous and often troublesome southwestern desert tale, "Tom Outland's Story," inserted into the middle of a novel about the complex social strains in the life and family of a midwestern history professor approaching his later years. Outland's story, however—patterned after the account of the actual discovery of the ancient Mesa Verde cliff dwellings in southwestern Colorado that was told to Cather by cowboy Dick Wetherill—provides much more than a pastoral interlude in the lives of urban subjects and readers. It is also the center of the novel's fascinating stylistic experiment and the catalyst for an examination of the work's deeply experienced human relationships with place and habitation.

These relationships refer us again to the pioneering literary criticism of Joseph Carroll, who argues that biology is presenting us with an increasingly convincing and coherent explanation of the human place in nature. Cultures are diverse, but they also reveal, across cultural lines, an underlying universal set of evolved features—formed during our long evolutionary period of development of body and brain but most crucially and fully in the Pleistocene hunter-gatherer stage—which we call human nature. Impinging upon this universal pattern of orientations or predispositions, and capable of modifying them in significant ways, are the aspects of cultural difference.

Literary artists have long been aware of the elements of human nature, as Carroll notes, and have provided us with an enormous body of information about it. Their intuitive understanding of human experience and of the shared interchange of these experiences among author, characters, and audience has always been at the center of literary experience. A sense of these universals drives the literary tradition as it must have driven the oral traditions that are its ancestors (Carroll, "Deep Structures" 165). Ellen Dissanayake's similarly groundbreaking research on the biological origins of art and its function as a universal human characteristic supports this conception of art, not as something laid on by culture or acquired, but as part of the range of tendencies and orientations that are encompassed by the term human nature. Although Dissanayake's work is confined to the evolutionary period preceding written literature, its application to storytelling and other aspects of language-based arts undergirds the sense that literature, like all art, is a record of our common humanity.

The Place of Place in Art

For prospective interdisciplinarians, the cluster of ideas surrounding the terms *human nature* and *place* increasingly offer literary scholars cross-field entry into interesting territory. To begin with place, Aristotle announced in his *Physics* that "the power of place will be remarkable."[1] Many writers—George Eliot, Mark Twain, Hamlin Garland, Sherwood Anderson, Willa Cather, Sinclair Lewis, D. H. Lawrence, Eudora Welty, Ernest Hemingway, Laurence Durrell, N. Scott Momaday, Leslie Marmon Silko, bell hooks, Scott Russell Sanders, to name a few—have directly asserted the importance of place, often attributing to it the role of indispensable participant, even leading character, in their work. "Call it what you like," D. H. Lawrence said, "[b]ut the spirit of place is a great reality" (16).[2] Literary criticism in the past has not studied this connection assiduously.[3] But under the impetus of sociobiological and ecological thinking, scholars may find suggestively relevant approaches to the interpretation of place in literature in related areas of evolutionary biology and psychology, geography, phenomenology, anthropology, cognitive studies, and other fields in the natural and social sciences.

Robert Kern's conception of ecocritical reading—against the traditional anthropocentric grain of other forms of criticism—can be extended beyond theme and substance, I believe, to embrace also the means by which the author's emotional grasp of the narrative is given the rhetorical and stylistic form that appropriately conveys the emotional charge to the reader. "How does narrative commend itself to the reader?" asks sociobiological literary critic Robert Storey. "As much else does to the human animal: through his or her emotions. When it is operating most efficiently, it engages the body in a powerfully affective embrace. What psychologist Victor Nell calls the 'ludic reader' feels rapt before narrative—fiction, non-fiction, the tug of the imaginative current is what matters—the effects of which on the nervous system are clearly measurable" (Storey 104). While I leave to Storey and later literary scholars the use of physiological measurements in criticism, there is, I think, ample room for reconsideration of the thematic and rhetorical features of this affective condition in the territory already opened up to us by recent advances in those biologically oriented fields increasingly related to our own.

According to Willa Cather, an understanding of this aura of emotional attachment, working in the mind of the writer as the communicative agent, is at the heart of it all. As Cather once explained: "An artist has an emotion and the first thing he wants to do with it is to find some form to put it in, a design. It reacts on him exactly as food makes a hungry person want to eat. It may tease him for years until he gets the right form for the emotion" (*Willa Cather in Person* 79). In what may be Willa Cather's most intriguing and challenging novel, *The Professor's House*, the emotional qualities and implications suggested by the place-bound title should repay study from interdisciplinary perspectives.

As might be expected, it is the eclectic field of geography that has done most to bring place and nature-centered insights of writers and thinkers into the purview of scholarly investigation. Geography has been called the Mother of the Sciences, since it distills and concentrates questions about the nature of our physical surroundings, questions that have been common to all people, everywhere. Throughout human history a regional geographic sense has been a given in all cultures. "Beyond that of any other discipline," geographer David Lowenthal writes, "the subject matter of geography approximates the world of general discourse; the palpable present, the everyday life of man on earth, is seldom far from our professional concerns." More than any other subject, Lowenthal argues, geography studies aspects of human surroundings on the scale and within the contexts in which they are usually encountered in everyday life (241).

Such broad-gauge interests and claims have not gone unchallenged by those who find in them evidence of theoretical and methodological fuzziness. Even while defending his field's interests in and dependence upon many allied disciplines in the natural and social sciences, geographer N. Peter Haggett allows that his subject "is unusual (perhaps promiscuous) in the range of its trading partners" (12). The wide-reaching concepts of place and region came under particular questioning in the middle and late years of the twentieth century as outmoded and diminished perceptions, no longer relevant to a world of interchangeable, media-fed urban settings and ubiquitous shopping-mall experiences. Academics of various disciplines regularly announced the end of nature, place, and region, and a fiction writer like Don DeLillo, in *White Noise,* provided (as has been noted) ominous evidence of an apparent postmodern erasure of place.

Still, even during this recent history in which place has been threatened with displacement, it has proved resistant to efforts to dismiss it. With the growing emphasis upon ecological thinking, the rapid joining of interdisciplinary fields in the sciences and social sciences, and the rise of new approaches in the humanities such as ecocriticism, place would seem poised to resume its position as a vital human concept. The work of contemporary human geographers Yi Fu Tuan, Edward Relph, and Robert David Sack, for example, has kept the place of place before us. Sack reminds us of the importance of holding together concepts that other fields take apart:

> We cannot live without places, and yet modernity is so quietly efficient at creating and maintaining them that whatever the mix and whatever the thickness, thinness, or porosity of places, their existence and effects often seem to be invisible. We run the risk of becoming geographically unaware at the very moment we have to be most aware. . . . A geographical awareness helps reveal how the segments of our lives fit together. It shows how we are cultural and natural, autonomous and independent. Most important, it focuses our will on our common purpose as geographic agents—transforming the earth and making it into a home. (257)

Important arguments for the revaluation of place have also been provided by philosophers of place, from early proponents such as Gaston Bachelard and Simone Weil to recent contributors such as Edward S.

Casey, J. E. Malpas, and David Abram. Their line of reasoning is increasingly influenced by the allying of place to body, in the phenomenological tradition of Edmund Husserl and Maurice Merleau-Ponty, in which the primacy of the lived world of bodily experience is the foundation for all human thinking, meaning, and communication. "Just as there is no place without a body," writes Edward S. Casey, "so *there is no body without place*. . . . [W]e are embodied-in-place. . . ." (*Getting Back Into Place* 104). This echoes the ecological observation that there is no organism without an an environment, no environment without an organism. From now on, as Lewis Mumford said, all thinking must be ecological—an assertion with which phenomenologists and other contemporary scholars of place would seem to agree.

Phenomenology confronts a narrowly reductionist cultural constructionism with the lived body, the source of our place in the world, and, as Casey describes it, the common but unrealized root of our thought (*Getting Back Into Place* 50).[4] Phenomenology can be seen to intersect literary analysis in the provocative rhetorical criticism of Kenneth Burke and his perception of poetry, or any verbal act, as "symbolic action" or "the dancing of an attitude," which has at its base level a bodily or biological expression.[5]

Phenomenologists George Lakoff and Mark Johnson, in their *Philosophy in the Flesh: The Embodied Mind and Its Challenge to Western Thought* (1999), employ the findings of the cognitive sciences to argue for the authenticity of the embodied mind and reason. Lakoff and Johnson recognize that if all human reasoning is embodied, then a valid theory of human meaning will have to be based in that science for which there is "broad and deep converging evidence," namely evolutionary-ecological Darwinism, which holds that human rationality is not unique but builds upon forms and inferences present in so-called "lower" animals (4, 92). In looking to evolutionary biology as the basis for their theory of a human nature, Lakoff and Johnson join literary critics such as Joseph Carroll, Robert Storey, and Joseph Meeker in demonstrating the growing movement toward an interdisciplinary blending of humanistic interests with the intertwined scientific concepts of evolution and ecology.

Place itself, through the influence of humanistic geographers, has been revivified as a field of study and positioned for collaborative inquiry. Phenomenology, the study of the experiential core of our lives, has added the working of the body and brain to the power of place, bringing philosophy and the cognitive and life sciences into the mix. The rise of an ecocritical viewpoint in the discipline of English has led literary critics to begin considering these issues from a fresh, new perspective. Even the academic left, long resistant to evidence of biological influences on human behavior and hostile to even the concept of a human nature, may be moving toward a rapprochement with such ideas, as is suggested in renowned ethicist Peter Singer's recent book, *A Darwinian Left: Politics, Evolution and Cooperation* (1999). Noam Chomsky has stated in an interview that he considered it "*important* for political radicals to postulate a relatively fixed human nature in order to be able to struggle for a better society" (Segerstråle 205). Such realignment can be expected to continue as evidence steadily increases in the natural and social sciences that inherited factors common to Homo sapiens have a major role in human behavior.

Anthropologically trained Gary Snyder offers a comfortable commonsense stance for spanning the spatial divide between the humanists and the evolutionary-based sciences when he writes,

> Recollecting that we once lived in places is part of our contemporary self-discovery. It grounds what it means to be "human" (etymologically something like "earthling"). . . . How could we *be* were it not for this planet that provided our very shape? Two conditions—gravity and a liveable temperature range between freezing and boiling—have given us fluids and flesh. The trees we climb and the ground we walk on have given us five fingers and toes. The "place" (from the root *plat*, broad, spreading, flat) gave us far-seeing eyes, the streams and breezes gave us versatile tongues and whorly ears. The land gave us a stride, and the lake a dive. The amazement gave us our kind of mind. We should be thankful for that, and take nature's stricter lessons with some grace. ("The Place, The Region" 29)

If, as I believe, we are edging toward a better understanding of place, embodiment, and human nature that will undergird our reading and criticism of literature, the work of writers like Willa Cather, for whom these concepts have been of defining significance, will invite new interpretations. Notable scholarship on Cather and place already can be found in Leonard Lutwack's groundbreaking *The Role of Place in Literature* (1984), Judith Fryer's *Felicitous Space* (1986), Laura Winters's *Willa Cather: Landscape and Exile* (1993), and Diane Dufva Quantic's *The Nature of the Place* (1995), as well as in numerous chapters and articles from Cather scholars through the years.[6]

Susan J. Rosowski has called attention in her 1995 article, "Willa Cather's Ecology of Place," to "a Cather we have scarcely met" (37), whose emplaced ideas were formed in the intellectual excitement of University of Nebraska pioneering botanists and ecologists Charles Bessey and Frederic Clements, whom Cather knew and admired in her student days and long after.[7] Citing Michael Kowalewski's "Writing in Place: The New American Regionalism," Rosowski finds in Cather's fiction and its relationship to the discipline of scientific ecology a proper response to Kowalewski's call for "'something challengingly new'" in place studies (48). In what follows, I pursue this direction with a consideration of Cather's *The Professor's House* from an interdisciplinary perspective, one which looks to the biological and geographical sciences for their contributions to literary analysis.

Archetypes and the Place of Human Nature

My admiration for *The Professor's House* goes back some thirty-five years to the time I first read it. It has been an often-chosen text for my classes in American literature at the University of Oregon, and enthusiastic student responses to the novel, along with a substantial body of critical commentary, give evidence of the work's fairly wide appeal to readers. Cather has written approvingly of Sarah Orne Jewett's observation that "[t]he thing that teases the mind over and over for years, and at last gets itself put down rightly on paper—whether little or great, it belongs to Literature" (*On Writing* 47). If such things become literature, it must be because they come to tease the minds of readers as they did the mind of the writer. We recognize the description of an archetype here. But what is the archetypal or mythic appeal of *The Professor's House*, and why should it draw author and reader as it does? I believe that the answer lies in what a recent conference has entitled "Willa Cather's Environmental Imagination"—which is, I would claim, a biological and topographical imagination—and in what is one of its most intriguing and suggestive manifestations, "Tom Outland's Story," and the secret of the Blue Mesa.[8]

Putting it that way makes Cather's story of Tom Outland and the Blue Mesa, curiously inserted into *The Professor's House*, sound like a Nancy Drew mystery. But that is how archetypes work. For all of our acculturated subtlety, we are drawn in memorable literature by appeals that may be shaped by culture but whose origins are often subcultural, epigenetic, in the language of evolutionary biology.[9] Great writers often draw from such primal sources, as Constance Rourke pointed out in her classic study of American humor: "inevitably genius embraces popular moods and formulations even when it seems to range furthest afield. From them literature gains immensely; without them it can hardly be said to exist at all" (130).

Terms such as *epigenetic* and *evolutionary biology*, or even *nature*, may, as we have seen, still raise what philosopher of science Mary Midgley has called "the fear of biology" that continues to haunt the social sciences and humanities. Writing of this phobia, Midgley says,

> This is not a denial of evolutionary theory itself, which is usually conceded as correct in its own sphere, but a steady rejection of any attempt to use it in the interpretation of human affairs. A sanitary cordon is erected at the frontier between the physical and social sciences, at which biological explanations generally and evolutionary ones in particular still tend to be turned back, marked with an official stamp which may read "Fascist," "Racist," "Galtonist," "Innatist," "Biological Determinist," or at times most grimly of all, merely "biological."
>
> This habit is fortunately on the way out, and a modest two-way traffic now does go on, to the general advantage. But a good deal of work is still needed to explain—as is always necessary in these cases—the distortions which gave rise to the prejudice in the first place, and just why they are not actually a part of biological science. (*Evolution* 7)

Since Midgley published these words in 1985, a great deal of such explaining has gone on and a considerable amount of cross-disciplinary work has arisen in the natural and social sciences and even in some of the humanities.[10] The increasing scientific verification of a universal human nature has, as I have noted in previous chapters, increasingly challenged and replaced the misconception that human nature is a dead idea and that all human behavior is the product of social conditioning.[11]

Although there are behaviors and beliefs particular to specific cultures, there are also many—and these are of the deepest significance—that are common across all cultures, as anthropologists Donald E. Brown, George Murdoch, Ellen Dissanayake, and others have established. Included in the category of human universals are our similarities in the following: living in social groups rather than alone; our tendency to form cooperative relationships and to accept reciprocal obligations; the underlying structure and semantics of human languages; human facial, hand, and arm gestures; our use of fire; our territoriality (including our attraction to specific places); the play of children; our propensity to create art; our distinctions between close and distant kin; age grading and age distinction; division of labor; dominance relationships between men, women, and children; rules of social-unit membership; mistrust of "others" and associated conflicts structured around in-group and out-group relationships; reasoning; distinguishing right from wrong; religious or supernatural beliefs, and so on.[12]

If human universals tend to confirm the presence of an evolved level of psychological human orientations that are involved in the creation of what we call human nature or the human condition, archetypes of wide-reaching significance take on an importance that has been ignored in recent decades and is deserving of much greater attention.[13] In an important recent essay, "Literary Universals," Patrick Colm Hogan argues convincingly for the need to rethink "the neglected and misunderstood topic of literary universals" (227). Noting that universalism in no way excludes cultural and historical specificity, Hogan urges a broad empirical research program that recognizes the value of studying these universals.

It is necessary to stress—as does virtually every commentator on the issue of human universals—that such classifications carry no evaluative judgments. As bioethicist Peter Singer writes, "I am not saying that because something like hierarchy, or male dominance, is characteristic of almost all human societies, that therefore it is good, or acceptable, or that we should not attempt to change it. . . . My point is not about deducing an 'ought' from and 'is' but about gaining a better understanding of what it may take to achieve the goals we seek" (38). Steven Pinker, like many others who have investigated the clash of human nature with moral issues, identifies as a widespread fallacy the belief that "whatever happens in nature is good. . . . As soon as we recognize that there is nothing morally commendable about the products of evolution, we can describe human psychology honestly, without the fear that identifying a 'natural' trait is the same as condoning it" (162–63).

That Cather found the story of the Blue Mesa archetypal is clear. She understood that a place may be informed by a powerful coalescence of personal, cultural, and natural features, affirming Kim Stafford's observation that a place is a story happening many times. Cather's topographical fascination with the southwestern mesas and their hidden cliff dwellings and lost civilizations led her to make them the emotional catalyst and center of two of her novels, *The Song of the Lark* and *The Professor's House*,[14] and of her 1909 short story, "The Enchanted Bluff"; and elements of it, as David Harrell points out in his *From Mesa Verde to The Professor's House*, are found in many of her other works. Cather admitted in a 1925 interview that "[w]hen I was a little girl nothing in the world gave me such a moment as the idea of the cliff dwellers, of whole civilizations before ours linking me to the soil." Edith Lewis, Cather's longtime companion, identifies the mythic elements of this early enchantment when she says of Cather's visit to Walnut Canyon in 1912, "She had never seen any cliff-dwellings before; but she and her brothers had thought and speculated about them since they were children. The cliff-dwellers were one of the native myths of the American West; children knew about them before they were conscious of them" (quoted in Harrell 8).

Harrell's book details revealing differences between "Tom Outland's Story" and the factual history of Mesa Verde's discovery, as well as the scientific archaeology and anthropology subsequently carried on there. In noting these discrepancies, Harrell's study underscores many of the elements by which Cather sets aside historical reality in order to heighten the mythic and emotional power of her story. The Blue Mesa carries a particularly packed texture of meaning for Cather. A closer look into her treatment of human nature and embodied place in Tom's relationship to the Cliff City reveals something of her keenly archetypal and place-centered imagination.

Geographically, the mesa's height as a natural feature of the landscape lifts it to a metaphorical level that Cather reserves for her characters' moments of greatest emotional awareness and inspiration.[15] More significantly, within the mesa's heart is the hidden Cliff City, enclosing a cluster of incipient meanings central to the novel. "Tom Outland's Story," like the novel as a whole, is engrossed with the human need to find one's place, literally and figuratively. The Blue Mesa not only draws Tom Outland into his search for the right place, but also offers in the Cliff City the opportunity to ponder the human significance represented by the stunning record of a civilization that has been built into it. "Carving out places," writes geographer Robert David Sack, "and creating a world occurs in the simplest preliterate societies. Identifying parts of the landscape, clearing sites, erecting shelter, bounding areas, establishing rules about what should or should not be in the place, knowing where to be and when, where to find this or that resource, and conveying all this through an oral tradition is world-building" (7). So is it in a written tradition, not only in "Tom Outland's Story," but in its enclosing books one and three of *The Professor's House*, where the characters in modern setting are also uneasily experiencing the necessity of coming to terms with the implications of place.

Within these similar place-huntings, Cather foregrounds the nascent archetypal potentialities of the Cliff City, which lies waiting for what Tom's consciousness can make of it, a "lost" civilization that was the product of the long ages of evolutionary development, during all of which time, place, and geography were life-and-death matters, and the ability to read the landscape correctly amounted to a survival factor. Yet the cliff dwellers' evolutionary step forward, a literal leap from earth into a fixed habitation and an agricultural rather than a wandering way of life, could not, in Cather's perception of it, survive the aggressiveness of surrounding hunter-gatherers who, unlike the cliff dwellers, suffered no decline in the arts of war as the price of high cultural attainment. All of this in the parallel context of the Professor's contemporary world, in which ideals continue to fall victim to a reigning aggressive materialism.[16]

Cather calls up the perception of a shared human condition not only through her own commentary, but also through the statements of characters she admires, such as Tom Outland and his friend from the Southwest, the scholar-priest Father Duchene. It is significant that Cather puts into Father Duchene's words what she calls, in her 1916 Mesa Verde essay, the most plausible explanation of the cliff dwellers' extinction (Rosowski and Slote 85).

Duchene feels reverence for Tom's Cliff City because it represents the desire of "*humanity*" for a home, "some *natural* yearning for order and security. They built themselves into this mesa and *humanized* it" (221). To Tom, Father Duchene calls the cliff dwellers "*your people*" (221), a characterization that Tom accepts when he later upbraids his friend Roddy for selling the artifacts that belonged "to *all the people* . . . , to boys like you and me that have no other *ancestors* to inherit from. . . . I'm not so poor that I have to sell the pots and pans that belonged to *my poor grandmothers* a thousand years ago" (242–43). Later, in book three, Professor St. Peter longs to "look off at those long, rugged, untamed vistas dear to the American heart. Dear to *all hearts*, probably—at least calling to *all*" (270). My italics in these passages underscore Cather's implicit argument for a deeper human unity than unexamined assumptions of total cultural uniqueness might find acceptable.[17] Cather's position anticipates that of many of today's evolutionary biologists and psychologists who find in all human cultures the expression of a heritage of commonly evolved tendencies. As Matt Ridley writes in *The Origins of Virtue*,

> That is why the same themes crop up in all cultures—themes such as family, ritual, bargain, love, hierarchy, friendship, jealousy, group loyalty and superstition. That is why, for all their superficial differences of language and custom, foreign cultures are still immediately comprehensible at the deeper level of motives, emotions, and social habits. Instincts, in a species like the human one, are not immutable genetic programmes; they

> are predispositions to learn. And to believe that human beings have instincts is no more determinist than to believe they are the products of their upbringing (6).

Joan Acocella, in her recent book on Willa Cather and academic politics, describes Cather as the victim of "political critics' revenge on the 'liberal humanism' of the fifties and sixties" (64). Acocella cites the "wearying . . . tone of recent political criticism of Cather," aggressively and self-righteously calling her to judgment for failing the political litmus tests of a later age (68). For Acocella, Cather's view of life is that it is unfair, and the unfairness "happens all the time. . . . Such a view does not accord with any program of political reform, for it gives implicit assent to life's unfairness, the very unfairness that political reform seeks to banish. And that is why Cather has given her political critics so much trouble" (89). Tom's actions as an amateur archaeologist and his attempting to preserve the ancient remains of the Cliff City as a national treasure may be the target of such criticism, a "cultural appropriation" that offers another slant on his story.[18] Here, and in other race-, class-, and gender-based criticism, recent readings have done much to increase our understanding of Cather's implication in the dominant white settlement perspective of her time.

Still, it is also important to remember that Tom's efforts are consistent with his deep sense of his own human bonds with the lost inhabitants of the Cliff City and his efforts to do the right thing by them and the relics of their civilization. For their time, these actions would have been perceived largely as Cather depicted them, as noble and self-sacrificing. Moreover, Tom's perception of a shared humanity takes on added significance in the light of new genetic research that leads most scientists to discount the idea of separate and distinct human races. Steve Olson, in *Mapping Human History: Discovering the Past Through Our Genes* (2002), notes that established racial classifications ignore the overwhelming genetic similarity of all human individuals. "One need go back only a couple of millennia to connect everyone alive to a common pool of ancestors" (Olson 47). Tom's universalist sentiments are now verified by the DNA in our Darwinian bodies.

In the same context, Tom's reverential naming of the mummified body of the woman among the ruins as "Mother Eve" proves remarkably prescient. A recent genetic discovery finds that all of the mitochondrial DNA sequences that exist in all 6 billion of us alive in the world today come from the mitochondrial DNA of one single woman who lived about 200,000 years ago, our common ancestor, the so-termed "mitochondrial Eve" (Olson 23–27, 237).

Cather dramatizes the presence of the heritage of our mortality as a further human universal when she depicts, in book three, a weary Professor St. Peter who has reverted to a preintellectual state and has become a virtually wordless and elemental self. It is as if Cather were anticipating, and undercutting, the assumption that culture and language have somehow lifted us above our biology and rendered our bodies and their elemental emplacement inconsequential. Such invocations of a deeply felt presymbolic existence are frequently encountered in Cather, and to note them is to memorialize many of her most powerful scenes: the children on the river sandbar, glimpsed from the window of a passing train, recalling to Bartley Alexander of *Alexander's Bridge* the dreams of his youth; young Jim Burden feeling himself melting into the slow fecundity and self-sufficiency of the pumpkin patch; Ántonia's children swarming up out of the root cellar in a kind of evolutionary fast-forward, an explosion of the victory of the life force over the underground world of the dugout that claimed the Shimerdas in their early days on the Divide and still holds the father in his suicide's grave; Thea Kronborg of *The Song of the Lark* lying on the floor of her bedroom, bathed in moonlight that seems to pour its essence into her young body, thirsting with creative desire.

Cather's art is, of course, complex enough to embrace other influences than the archetypal. But with the return of human nature to serious consideration, we might reconsider what Dorothy Van Ghent described years ago as a quality of Cather that "allowed the back door of her mind to keep open" to archaic and instinctive influences. For Van Ghent, Cather's best fiction is characterized by "a sense of the past not as an irrecoverable quality of events, wasted in history, but as persistent human truth repossessed—salvaged, redeemed—by virtue of memory and art" (5).

One such line of reexamination is presented by Edward O. Wilson in his *Consilience: The Unity of Knowledge* (1998). There Wilson suggests the applicability of his theory of gene-culture coevolution to an intepretation of the arts. "We know that virtually all human behavior is transmitted by culture. We also know that biology has an important effect on the origin of culture and its transmission. The question remaining is how biology and culture interact, and in particular how they interact across all societies to create the commonalities of human nature" (126). Briefly summarized, "culture is created by the communal mind, and each mind in turn is the product of the genetically structured human brain" (127). (Steven Pinker correspondingly reminds us that "culture, for all its importance, is not some miasma that seeps into people through their skin. Culture relies on neural circuitry that accomplishes the feat we call learning" [60]).

In *Consilience* and in his earlier book, *Biophilia*, Wilson employs, to illustrate the creation of an archetype, the example of human reactions of fear and fascination toward snakes—a human behavior spread across many different cultures of the world—as the genetic component, formed out of hundreds of thousands of years of human evolution in proximity to snakes. "Poisonous snakes have been an important source of mortality in almost all societies throughout human evolution. Close attention to them, enhanced by dream serpents and the symbols of culture, undoubtedly improves the chances of survival" (127). The culture draws upon those reactions of fear and fascination to create art, thereby transforming the natural snake into the archetypal serpent of art.[19]

Cather depicts corresponding versions of zero at the bone on the matter of snakes: the ominous dread of the snake-serpent expressed in the "Snake Root" chapter of *Death Comes for the Archbishop*, or Jim Burden's battle with the giant rattlesnake in *My Ántonia*, a creature presented in unmistakeably prototypical terms who "seemed like the ancient, eldest Evil. Certainly his kind have left unconscious memories in all warm-blooded life" (45–6). Such primal memories also manifest themselves in *The Professor's House* with the intrusion of the snake-serpent into the relationship between Professor St. Peter's two daughters, Kathleen and Rosamond: "'When she comes toward me, I feel hate coming toward me, like a snake's hate,'" Kathleen confides to her father, whose response is described as an anguished suffering in which he replies "'We can't, dear, we can't, in this world, let ourselves think of things—of comparisons—like that" (85). Then there is the rattlesnake that strikes old Henry Atkins, Tom and Roddy's cook and companion, as they are exploring the Blue Mesa ruins, killing the old man almost instantly. Although, as David Harrell reports, snakes were not a problem in the actual Mesa Verde-Wetherill excavations (126), the "terrible" (216) death of old Henry seems another example of Cather's heightening the mythic trials of Tom's quest.

Traditional Freudian interpretations of snakes as phallic representations and dreams as forbidden wishes that evade the brain's censorship have recently been seriously questioned or replaced by biological explanations.[20] As Wilson says, "If brain and mind are at base biological phenomena, it follows that the biological sciences are essential to achieving coherence among all the branches of learning, from the humanities on down to the physical sciences" (*Consilience* 81). What is interdisciplinarily new, then, in such literary criticism (as can also be seen in the books of Joseph Carroll and Robert Storey) may invite us to reconsider something resembling the archetypal criticism of Northrop Frye in his 1957 *Anatomy of Criticism.* Frank Kermode has called Frye "the major figure in literary criticsm of our century." For M. H. Abrams, Frye "has proved himself to be the most innovative, learned, and important literary theorist of my generation," and Harold Bloom called Frye "the foremost living student of Western Literature" (quoted in Carroll, *Evolution* 117).

As Carroll proposes, Frye's innovative work with archtypes may today be separated from its questionable mysticism and obsolete science and revised with a strong new underpinning drawn from recent research in the cognitive and behavioral sciences (*Evolution and Literary Theory* 382–90). Robert Storey adds that "given the current degradation of literary studies into mere tub-thumping for this or that special interest group, one feels the force of Frye's chief complaint: 'Criticism seems to be badly in need of a coordinating principle, a central hypothesis which, like the theory of evolution in biology, will see the phenomena it deals with as parts of a whole'" (Storey xvii).[21]

In explaining the fear and veneration of the snake/serpent as an outgrowth of human nature then acted upon by culture, Wilson emphasizes how our perceptions yield many images with specific connotations while remaining consonant with the underlying forces of natural selection:

> How could it be otherwise? The brain evolved into its present form over a period of about two million years, from the time of *Homo habilis* to the late stone age of *Homo sapiens,* during which people existed in hunter-gatherer bands in intimate contact with the natural environment. Snakes mattered. The smell of water, the hum of a bee, the directional bend of a plant stalk mattered. The naturalist's trance was adaptive: the glimpse of one small animal hidden in the grass could make the difference between eating and going hungry in the evening. And a sweet sense of horror, the shivery fascination with monsters and creeping forms that so delight us today even in the sterile hearts of cities, could see you through to the next morning. Organisms are the natural stuff of metaphor and ritual. Although the evidence is far from all in, the brain appears to have kept its old capacities, its channeled quickness. We stay alert and alive in the vanished forests of the world. (*Biophilia* 101)

Wilson emphasizes that a theory of the biological origin of the arts is only a working hypothesis, vulnerable and meant to be tested, but that it offers the humanities the attraction of a reinvigoration of interpretation, just as science would benefit from the interpretive and intuitional power of the arts.[22] A scientific theory that is consistent with what we know from the recent and rapidly unifying sciences of neurobiology and cognitive psychology—the brain and the mind—is worth our attention as literary scholars in reconsidering the interpretation of archetypes as defining elements of art.

Such a rapproachment with science squares with the existing evidence and with the work of Ellen Dissanayake, and it may offer exciting new possibilities for productive interconnections. For example, a recent essay in the journal *Science* by noted neurobiologist Semir Zeki describes his research on the neurological basis of art. "By probing into the neural basis of art," Zeki writes, "neurological studies can help us to understand why our creative abilities and experiences vary so widely. But it can only do so by first charting the common neural organization that makes the creation and appreciation of all art possible" (51). (Note the characteristic pulls of holistic and reductive scientific techniques, described in chapter 2 of this book, in Zeki's description.) Robert Storey's book, *Mimesis and the Human Animal*, marks an important beginning for the consideration of similar biogenetic bases of literary representation and response.

If the sciences have a role to play in interpretation, they cannot replace interpretation. As Nobel laureate and codiscoverer of the structure of DNA James D. Watson explains, "The brain is the last and grandest biological frontier, the most complex thing we have discovered in the universe. It contains hundreds of billions of cells interlinked through trillions of connections. The brain boggles the mind" (iii). Thus the variety and intensity of responses and connections as they play back and forth between artist, subject, and critic are virtually infinite. There will always remain work for the critic to do. Further, as Wilson notes, "Science can hope to explain artists, and artistic genius, and even art, and it will increasingly use art to investigate human behavior, but it is not designed to transmit experience on a personal level or to reconstitute the full richness of the experience from the laws and principles which are its first concern by definition" (*On Human Nature* 206). Biology will not replace literature but will help make us more understanding readers and critics by linking the two aspects of human experience that these fields represent.

The Professor's House, particularly "Tom Outland's Story," is rich in archetypal elements whose interpretation has been central to several critical treatments, especially in David Harrell's book; in Susan Rosowski and

Bernice Slote's 1984 article, "Willa Cather's 1916 Mesa Verde Essay: The Genesis of *The Professor's House*"; and in John N. Swift's 1986 essay, "Memory, Myth, and *The Professor's House.*" It seems likely to me that the reprinting of "Tom Outland's Story," as reported by Cather, in French, Polish, and Dutch as a short narrative for school students learning English may owe something to the appeal of Tom Outland as a version of the code western hero.[23] "Tom Outland's Story" reminds us that "The Western" in fiction and film is a clear example of the appeal of archetypes across cultural lines, leading to The Western's position by the mid-twentieth century as what was called at the time the only contemporary worldwide myth.

Tom Outland's short life, taken in summary, is more mythic than real. A western orphan, he discovers the Cliff City, comes to Professor St. Peter's college, becomes a physicist, inventing a device that revolutionizes airplane engines, then rushes off to die nobly in war, leaving others to deal with his ambiguous legacy. But though he seems a "glittering idea," as one of the characters describes him, his spoken narrative anchors him to the commonality of human experience and to the everyday magic of sensory life.

"Tom Outland's Story," centered as it is upon the discovery and archaeological investigation of the Blue Mesa cliff dwellings, is a particularly packed meditation on biological-cultural coevolution. In the story Cather recreates a complex pattern of human history incidentally including a deadly serpent and a Mother Eve, but most importantly, a hidden lost Eden that sprang from its hunter-gatherer origins on the plain into a fixed habitation—a Catherian city in the sky, named for the sky's color.

Along with these thematic elements, an interdisciplinarily aware reading of the novel would note its sensitive response to the often-ignored phenomenological base of our directly felt bodily experience. Cather affirmed such experience as a kind of fundamental archetype when she claimed that "art appeals primarily to the senses" (*Willa Cather in Person* 146). Tom's life on the Blue Mesa is one of heightened physical attunement to his surroundings: a keenly sharpened sense of colors, sights, tastes, textures, sounds, silences, and especially the feel and smell and taste of the air itself. These prereflective sensations, like Shakespeare's bites and blows of weather, "are counsellors / That feelingly persuade me what I am." They suggest Maurice Merleau-Ponty's claim of "our primordial inherence in the world."[24] The frequently noted array of houses and dwellings in the novel seems related to the sense of bodily emplacement that such structures arouse, returning us, as Edward Casey suggests, to our bodily emplacement "immeasureably enriched" (*Getting Back Into Place* 178).

Like the phenomenologists, Cather never loses the sense of normative significance that characterizes subjective physical experience. As Maxine Sheets-Johnstone notes, "however diverse their perspectives, and whether explicitly or implicitly, phenomenology, Darwinian evolutionary biology, and ecocriticism all insistently refuse a world without experience. They thereby insistently authenticate a world of living subjects—a world of Darwinian bodies" ("Descriptive Foundations" 177).

The Place of Style

If the thing that teases the mind is the archetypal element, it does not become literature, as Jewett and Cather affirm, until it is put down rightly on paper. As Nancy L. Easterlin observes, the mere presence of archetypal or evolutionary universals in a text are not sufficient to guarantee literary worth ("Do Cognitive" 246). If art appeals, as Cather says, primarily to the senses and the emotions, that appeal finds its form in language: "what was any art but an effort to make a sheath, a mould in which to imprison for a moment the shining, elusive element which is life itself," muses the young heroine among the cliff-dweller ruins in *The Song of the Lark* (378). The quality of place and character is subtly established in any written work by its style, or—as Monroe Beardsley defines "good" style—the compatibility of explicit and implicit meaning within the work (13).

It is worth considering the style of *The Professor's House* as a means of triangulating the work's thematic universals of human embodiment and emplacement with our understanding of the work as a text, a palimpsest of denotative and connotative meanings imposed upon these earlier bodily and emotional inscriptions. With the concept of style we are again in ecological territory, where everything is connected to everything else and the commingling of organism and environment can be foregrounded for closer study.

In considering the novel's style as an ecological conception, one notes that the three sections, or "books," into which the work is divided are each focused—as the novel's title alerts us—upon a house, either a literal physical dwelling or an emblem of human emplacement. "Book One: The Family" centers upon Professor Godfrey St. Peter's well-worn old house, the locus of his familial and professional life. "Book Two: Tom Outland's Story" reaches its culmination in Outland's discovery of the

Cliff City, the ancient Anasazi dwellings in the Blue Mesa of the desert Southwest. "Book Three: The Professor," reduces the idealized home of Tom's Cliff City to St. Peter's old study and to his anticipation of his fateful emplacement in the grave, a progression that Cather underscores in St. Peter's recollection of a Longfellow translation of an Anglo-Saxon poem:

> For thee a house was built,
> Ere thou wast born;
> For thee a mould was made
> Ere thou of woman camest.[25]

"Lying on his old couch he could almost believe himself in that house already" (272). For St. Peter, in his final estrangement from his wife and family, the grave seems indeed a fine and private place. That none do there embrace does not, in Cather's characteristic sense of sex as invasive, lessen the pull of this final house upon him.

The three emplaced books of *The Professor's House* are also stylistic representations of the unfurnishing and omitting process that Cather had set forth in her essays "On the Art of Fiction" and "The Novel Démeublé." In the latter she concludes with a writer's injunction to "throw all the furniture out of the window . . . and leave the room as bare as the stage of a Greek theater."[26] The relative lengths of the novel's three sections parallel this process. "Book One: The Family" is 166 pages long; "Book Two: Tom Outland's Story" is 75 pages; "Book Three: The Professor" is only 27 pages.

It is important to keep this radical diminution in mind when weighing Cather's external comments upon the form of *The Professor's House.* She called attention to her formal experimentation by providing four metaphors or analogies, all acknowledging the structural audacity of inserting Tom Outland's story within the story of Professor Godfrey St. Peter's life. The first of these four figurative expressions is the reference, in the novel's title-page epigraph, to "a turquoise set in dull silver." The remaining comparisons are found in Cather's 1938 letter, "On *The Professor's House*," published in her collection of essays addressing the craft of composition, *On Writing.* There, the book is first described as a *Nouvelle* placed within a *Roman.* Then it is compared to the form of a musical sonata, with its ABA structure. Finally, in what has become a kind of archetypal fenestration in Cather criticism, she compares the novel's form to paintings of crowded Dutch kitchen interiors, in which a square window looks out upon a seascape.

Insofar as all four of these comparisons emphasize the novel's three-part structure with its intrusive middle element, they are figuratively appropriate but at the same time somewhat misleading in their suggestion of a triptych, or a balanced three-part construction. The sheer brevity of book three leaves the novel curiously lopsided if the reader is led to expect symmetry. But Cather perhaps offers a corrective in the last and most famous of her analogies, her compelling depiction of Tom Outland's story as an opening of the square window in the stuffy domestic interior to "let in the fresh air that blew off the Blue Mesa" (*On Writing* 31–32). In this image of sensory release from constraint, Cather shifts attention away from the static concept of symmetry and balance and toward the phenomenological counterforce of lived sensations, dynamism, and process as the key to the novel's form. It is this notion of physically felt experience that most appropriately expresses Cather's formal experimentation in the work and that calls attention to the text's deconstructing of itself.

Tom Outland's story provides the cleansing, eradicating wind—sweeping aside the propensity to frame the world as a succession of human cultural constructs—that begins the novel's progressive diminution. The cluttered and stuffy interior is reduced at last in book three to a nearly empty—which is to say, wordless—room, the bare stage, the one passion and four walls of Dumas's minimalist pronouncement, which Cather had posited as her ideal prose architecture.

Tom Outland's "style" itself becomes a thematic concern before the young man actually begins his monologue in book two. Throughout book one, Tom, dead in the war, still exists most meaningfully as a pattern of fugitive reverberations in the lives of Professor St. Peter and his family. Book one establishes the realistic setting of the traditional "overfurnished" novel, doing so stylistically by means of longer than normal sentences, often grammatically complex, employing involved hierarchies of value and relationship (Weaver 120–24).

As a result of this linguistic overstuffing, book one also subtly creates within the reader's mind a hunger for the spare directness of Tom's own words and story. " 'Always very different from the other college boys, wasn't he?' " says the Professor, underscoring this anticipation: " 'Always something in his voice, in his eyes' "; "that singularly individual voice of Tom's—mature, confident, seldom varying in pitch, but full of slight, very moving modulations" (132, 125). In the hands of Louie Marsellus, the Professor's elder son-in-law, married to his daughter Rosamond, who had been engaged to Tom before his death, Tom's meaning has been smothered under the Marselluses' displays of conspicuous consumption, fueled from the profits of Tom's scientific work.[27]

In the Professor's eyes, both of his sons-in-law are the fools of words, set in opposition to the rhetoric of understatement associated with Tom. Scott, married to the younger St. Peter daughter, is a Chum Frink of the newspapers, a syndicated prose-rhymer whose column is a small success but whose mind is shallow and uninteresting. Louie Marsellus is loquaciously charming, but, as the Professor says, "one likes the florid style or one doesn't." Cather intimates her own preference when she disparages her own early writing as "my florid, exaggerated, foamy-at-the-mouth period" (*Willa Cather in Person* 12).

St. Peter also prefers holding back, which he praises as a knightly trait: "a man should do fine deeds and not speak of them. . . . It's a nice idea, reserve about one's deepest feelings: keeps them fresh" (47–48). These same qualities are those that the Professor finds in Tom's diary, a work which, we are told, characteristically says almost nothing about Tom himself. "If words had cost money, Tom couldn't have used them more sparingly. The adjectives were purely descriptive, relating to form and colour, and were used to present the objects under consideration, not the young explorer's emotions." There, "one felt the kindling imagination . . . like the vibration in a voice when the speaker strives to conceal his emotion by using only conventional phrases" (262–63). For Tom, too, the most important things are not to be talked about directly.

In several senses "reading" Tom Outland, both before and after Tom narrates his own story in book two, becomes the principal concern of the Professor's life. Reading Tom is important to the other members of the Professor's family as well, although they are not privileged to receive the crucial text, "Tom Outland's Story," for it was orally told and its only auditor was the Professor. But it seems clear that in book one the novel takes on richness and complexity as the reader joins the characters in attempting to fix Tom's meaning. Though he is not part of book one's title grouping, he is the controlling presence there, and we are led to anticipate reading him more fully. The novel takes shape following Kenneth Burke's conception of dramatic form: the arousing of an expectation in the mind of the audience and the satisfying of that expectation ("Psychology and Form" 31). The closely rendered, overfurnished place of "The Family" whets our appetite for the understated ardor of Outland's Blue Mesa, which becomes its own sort of outdoor rebuke to its cluttered and strident predecessor.

The "unfurnished" quality of Tom's story is its primary stylistic feature, as Cather employs the technique, set forth in her earlier essays on style, of emphasis through suppression. Formally, several characteristic features of book one are immediately altered in book two as Tom begins his monologue. One notices the shorter, simpler sentences. Cather's decision to employ first-person oral narration—letting Tom tell his story rather than write it—permits her to radicalize the unfurnishing even more sharply, as we leave book one's conventional third-person point of view, with the Professor as the sentient central consciousness. In Tom's narrative another filter is removed between tale and reader, and a corresponding sensory and environmental immediacy is achieved.

The most noticeable stylistic features of "Tom Outland's Story" are those that emphasize Cather's sense of the charged simplicity and resonance characteristic of the unfurnished novel. Tom's narrative contains less than half the pages of text in book one. Its sentences average ten fewer words than those in book one and are much less likely to employ grammatical subordination and complexity. Words are more likely to be monosyllabic. Yet within this unpacking, there is the sense of the mythopoeic latency that many readers have noted. These reductions mark Cather's sense of the most significant creation, that which accompanies "whatever is felt upon the page without being specifically named there" ("The Novel Démeublé" 41–42). It is worth noting the attention Cather gives to bodily emplacement and sensation in the climactic moment of "Tom Outland's Story." Cather has carefully prepared her readers for this moment.

Style and the Darwinian Body

The Blue Mesa, high and intriguing, has occupied Tom's thoughts and hopes of exploration since he had first seen it—perhaps even before, as it had teased the imagination of prairie children, who, as Edith Lewis said, had an archetypal sense of the presence of the cliff dwellings. Now, several strayed cattle from the herd in Tom and Roddy's care over the winter have swum the river and disappeared in the canyon winding into the mesa. Tom, alone on duty, quickly decides to follow them. He swims the river with his horse and, at first running beside the horse to keep warm, begins trailing the cattle into the canyon as it twists back into the mesa. Cather's keen sense of place and the lived sensations of the body in place are immediately evident in Tom's description:

> The bluish rock and the sun-tanned grass under the unusual purple-grey of the sky, gave the whole valley a very soft colour, lavender and pale gold, so that the occasional cedars growing beside the boulders looked black

> that morning. It may have been the hint of snow in the air, but it seemed to me that I had never breathed in anything that tasted so pure as the air in that valley. It made my mouth and nostrils smart like charged water, seemed to go to my head a little and produce a kind of exaltation. I kept telling myself that it was very different from the air on the other side of the river, though that was pure and uncontaminated enough. (200)

Cather here exemplifies the bodily phenomenological immediacy of the opening window in the crowded interior of the Dutch paintings, which she later cast as the metaphor for "Tom Outland's Story": "Then I wanted to open the square window and let in the fresh air that blew off the Blue Mesa, and the fine disregard of trivialities which was in Tom Outland's face and in his behaviour" ("On *The Professor's House*" 31–32).

At this point in Tom's story, the ground becomes so rough that he hobbles his horse and goes on alone. His eyes are steadily on the ground, mindful of the dangerous footing (201). The act of coming into the country calls to mind Leonard Lutwack's observation that "[t]he quality of a place in literature is subtly determined by the manner in which a character arrives at it, moves within it, and departs from it" (59).[28] Hemingway, whose style and manner had something to learn from Cather, was also deeply engrossed at this same time with writing about coming into a place, walking into the country. "Some days, " he wrote, "it went so well that you could make the country so that you could walk into it" (quoted in Tanner 82). As Stephen L. Tanner points out, for Hemingway, "[m]aking country—that is, creating place—was the real challenge. 'The people were easy to do.' He [Hemingway] thinks of a number of writers who do people well and concludes, 'They weren't after what he was after.' People were easy to do, he reasons, because 'nobody knew anything about them. If it sounded good they took your word for it.' . . . Implied here," Tanner suggests, "is that everybody knows what a sense of place is; they won't take your word for it—you must satisfy their sensuous and emotive apprehension of *topos* or physical location" (85).

Cather anticipates Hemingway's topographical imagination, making the most of the excitement of coming into the country, walking into the country. Nick Adams, walking into the country of the Big Two-Hearted River, has much in common with Tom Outland, walking into the canyon of the Blue Mesa. Basic to Tom's experience is the primacy of bodily movement—swimming the river, running, walking, and scrambling over stony ground, finally stopping to catch his breath, a moment of physical repose after strenuous action, which will find its counterpart in what he is to see.

Cather's sensitivity to the significance of human movement is a novelist's corroboration of Maxine Sheets-Johnstone's claim that "[p]rimal animation and tactile-kinesthetic experience are at the core of our infancy and remain the unsurpassed core of our adult being. Indeed, the wonder of being lies in aliveneness and the wonder of aliveness originates in movement. Human being, and the being of all who must learn to move themselves, is foundationally and essentially kinetic" (*The Primacy of Movement* 271). Biologist Steven Vogel, international authority in the field of biomechanics, affirms this in his book *Prime Mover* when he writes, "We're animals. Whether we're more than animals turns on one's theology, but at least we're animals. It would be strange, indeed, if our animal nature made no difference to history, culture, technology. Nothing is more animal than movement—animation, in a word—and underlying our every movement are our muscles" (3).

Cather at this point heightens our eventual gratification of fulfilled expectations by purposefully misdirecting our attention for the moment to the ground under Tom's feet, with its hazardous footing, a jumble of stones fallen from above:

> It was such rough scrambling that I was soon in a warm sweat under my damp clothes. In stopping to take breath, I happened to glance up at the canyon wall. I wish I could tell you what I saw there, just as I saw it, on that first morning, through a veil of lightly falling snow. Far up above me, a thousand feet or so, set in a great cavern in the face of the cliff, I saw a little city of stone asleep. It was as still as sculpture—and something like that. It all hung together, seemed to have a kind of composition: pale little houses of stone nestling close to one another, perched on top of each other, with flat roofs, narrow windows, straight walls, and in the middle of the group, a round tower. (201)

Tom happens to look up. From his ground-held scrutiny of the dangerously rock-strewn canyon floor at his feet, his eyes lift in an involuntary glance, and he *beholds*—in a Burkean surprise, just when he and we least expect it—the secret of the Blue Mesa: a revelation of composition overhanging formlessness, confusion topped by proportioned human meaning, both the country and what can be fashioned out of the country. The sight suggests what might have been an actualized creation myth of the early people of this place, in which chaos was magically transformed into ordered home place. The climactic sentence beginning "Far up above me" may be one of the great sentences in Cather, in literature. Periodic, dramatic, a string of parallel phrases serving to heighten the significance of the very simple main clause that follows: "I saw . . . ," and all rounded off by the single suggestive modifier, "asleep." In this climactic moment Tom lifts up his eyes to the hills, and the teased authorial mind gets it all down rightly on paper.[29]

The quality of the moment is thickened by the many associations it encloses: the sense of human participation in, and obligation to, natural setting; the aesthetic clarity with which the stone city expresses the timeless human need for prospect and shelter and protection from hazard;[30] the dramatization of the topographical hypothesis that "cognition, personality, creativity, and maturity—all are in some way tied to particular gestalts of space";[31] and the feeling of authorial excitement, the pleasure of perception, which accompanies the realization of the original emotion that inspired the work in the first place—in this case, through the recovery of a childhood possession, a communal myth of the American West.

"Book Three: The Professor" is starkly short, only a few pages. Its dominant thematic note is that of a deterministic corporeality of human life, conveyed in a stylistic devaluation of language and dispensability of words. The progressively inward quality that Richard Giannone has noted (46–47) in the novel's movement—from third person (book one) to first person (book two) to interior monologue (most of book three)—is also a progression toward a prelinguistic and prehuman muteness. Tom Outland's physical presence in guiding St. Peter through the southwestern country of his historical researches, we are told, caused the last four volumes of the Professor's historical series on the Spanish explorers to be "more simple and inevitable than those that went before" (258). Tom's book two seems to exercise a corresponding stylistic influence upon its follower.

Professor St. Peter, in book three's pages, regresses into a Jungian primitive dream state. This condition is conveyed stylistically in a series of extremely short sentences and clauses, devoid of sequentiality or the logic of subordination: "He was a primitive. He was only interested in earth and woods and water. Wherever sun sunned and rain rained and snow snowed. . . . Desire under all desires, Truth under all truths. . . . He was earth, and would return to earth" (265). From an ecological perspective, the style here suggests a uniquely conscious, once-flourishing social organism, capable—unlike, perhaps, all other species in its awareness of its own mortality—of anticipating and beginning to adapt to the more restricted environment into which it is moving. The Professor's utterances seem drawn from a kind of primal language. The repetitions suggest incantation. They reveal a kind of denial of style, a refusal to reach out for graceful synonyms, as if these would somehow be a false attempt to muffle the hard reality with which the Professor must contend. When he speaks, it is to himself and in virtual grunts: "That is right," he says. "That is it. . . . That is true; it is time" (265–66).

Book three presents an interesting paradox in two senses. From the perspective of the reader Cather withholds more and more, thus requiring more and more of the reader, radically pressing her theory in "On the Art of Fiction" that what has been suppressed contributes to the reader's consciousness as though it were there on the page. Book three cuts away perhaps more than the reader can provide or be asked to provide. It is a notable phenomenological test for the reader, something akin to a Hemingway game: How much can you take, dear reader? From the perspective of the writer, Cather has carried her unfurnishing process almost to the point of having to renounce her medium. She gives us at the last not only "the original, unmodified Godfrey St. Peter" (263) of a wordless sensory existence, but also a kind of rhetoric of obliteration, a paring down of place and action and style to the vanishing point. If Tom's diary is almost beautiful because of the things it did not say, Cather's conclusion subversively intimates the final attraction of silence.

Cather's unusual richness of mind and imagination repays study from the many ecocritical approaches that are currently developing in response to individual and collective environmental imaginations. Tom Outland's story is both a powerful bioregional study of a human adaptation to place over a long period of time and a complex contemporary human response to that adaptation. Cather's version of the cliff-dwellers' history questions any romanticizing of the hunter-gatherer past as an ecological paradise, yet she recognizes in it our common evolutionary development.[32] She sees the promise of the stunning architecture and the ordered agriculture of the early mesa people, "growing strict fields of corn and beans" in the words of Gary Snyder's suggestive poem of revery, "Anasazi" (*Turtle Island* 3), but she understands the cliff dwellers' vulnerability to human and natural-based catastrophe. She looks beneath culture to its roots in human animality, as is suggested in the mummified figure of Mother Eve, with its broken skull, its pierced side, and its face frozen in a scream of agony. The mummy's silent scream is the wordless embodiment of the human potentiality for destructiveness or sexual aggression, a potentiality that reaches far back to a time before the European presence in the New World.[33] The emptiness of the Cliff City, whether one attributes it to murdering marauders or prolonged drought or other ecological change, is a lesson in stone that biology counts, that past human life has been almost unbearably hard, and that any progress has been dearly bought.

In this sense "Tom Outland's Story" and *The Professor's House* remain intensely contemporary, calling upon us to face our own nature. Ecological consciousness seems to be an inevitable consequence of place consciousness. Whether we read the Blue Mesa as another scene of the ordinary agonies of human history or an ecological violation of the local carrying capacity, the silence of the abandoned Cliff City reminds us that we cannot culturally construct the world any way we choose.

Cather's best work demonstrates that it is not the minor differences that divide humans culturally but the major similarities that unite us as a species which provide the basis for memorable communication and human understanding. Without the universals of human experience, the sense of which strikes Tom when he first beholds the Cliff City, there would be no communication, no art, nor learning or teaching, nor the need or wish for any, beyond those internally required by disparate and isolated cultural enclaves.

For "Tom Outland's Story" as for all stories, the medium is the message. Stories are one thing that has made us human, and their origins are at the heart of our evolutionary development.[34] Tom's story is the opening window letting in the disregarding wind that sweeps away pettiness and disorder and joins us to reverberating human experience. Narration serves the ancient and literally humanizing function of lining out a meaningful structure from the confused and confusing mess of ordinary existence.

That this particular story contains its own questioning of the cathartic power of such narrative—as seen, for example, in Tom's guilt over his dismissal of his friend Roddy Blake and in Professor St. Peter's virtual withdrawal from his family and from life itself under the near-suffocating influence of Tom's heroic idealism—these are ironies that nevertheless depend for their effect upon the continuing appeal of the underlying archetypal structure. Like the drawings in the Lascaux cave, "Tom Outland's Story" reminds us of the timelessness, the antiquity of human aspirations as they reach for meaning and coherence through artistic expression.

"Tom Outland's Story" and the Professor's characterization of Tom's style and literary voice in Cather's 1925 novel describe and predict the style of Ernest Hemingway, then an almost unknown young writer. Cather's central theories of style anticipate and closely resemble Hemingway's celebrated theory of omission, or "iceberg principle" (Plimpton 34), through which he was to carry the sort of minimalist experiments we see in *The Professor's House* to brilliant new heights. Hemingway was to become the best proof that Cather's new stylistic ventures were valid. But he was to fashion a theory of tragic individual conflict with the natural world that would be his alone.

5

Hemingway among the Animals

Do you know the sin it would be to ruffle the arrangement of the feathers on a hawk's neck if they could never be replaced as they were?—Ernest Hemingway, *Death in the Afternoon*

Watch how a man plays a game, says the regimental folklore, and you'll see what sort of man he is. For Ernest Hemingway, whose regimental credentials are second to none, the connection between sports and life has always been central to both the writer and the man. From even a cursory examination of the Hemingway canon and its critical commentary, one is sure to learn that Hemingway's fictional sports are stages for ritualized conflict wherein the hero is tested for his behavior under extreme physical and psychological pressure.

The blood sports, such as hunting and fishing and boxing and bullfighting, are to be preferred. Their violence takes one to the confrontive edge. They resemble warfare rather than play and are, as such, fit metaphors for the ultimate warfare of life, whose purpose is, after all, to kill you. "They threw you in and told you the rules and the first time they caught you off base they killed you. . . . You could count on that. Stay around and they would kill you" (*A Farewell to Arms* 327). Sooner or later you lose, but what matters, as Philip Young first made clear to us, is how you play the game (*Ernest Hemingway: A Reconsideration* 55–78).

To invert a line by Robert Frost in "Two Tramps in Mud Time," the play is work for mortal stakes in Hemingway. And if, as Frost's speaker claims, the object in living is to unite one's avocation and one's vocation, then Hemingway darkly succeeded where Frost's woodchopper did not, his code resolve wavering before the obligation to his fellow creatures, the two rough tramps who need the work of chopping that he merely loves.

Love and need for Hemingway are made of grimmer stuff. An early and justly famous Hemingway story, "Big Two-Hearted River," illustrates not only the carefully prescribed code of streamside behavior, but also the peculiar drive toward conflict and deathful adventure in what most readers would surely, on the face of it, regard as a restorative pastoral experience—camping beside, and fishing, a lovingly remembered river. "God never did make a more calm, quiet, innocent recreation than angling," said Isaac Walton in *The Compleat Angler* (262), but Hemingway's Nick Adams is looking for something more. At first the experience is restorative for Nick, back from the war and regaining his hold on his nerves. Still, there is only the barest mention of mental conflict in the story, and Nick is repeatedly described as cheerful and content.[1] Near the end of his first day, he crawls into his little tent, happy, the form of the sentences themselves suggesting Nick's tired but satisfied sense of rightness and control over things: "He had made his camp. He was settled. Nothing could touch him. It was a good place to camp. He was there, in the good place" (215).

In the second half of the story, Nick's fishing experiences the next day on the stream continue his pattern of deliberate and pleasurable behavior. Fishing intensifies the sense of simplicity and control that Nick seeks: he with his rod on one end; nature, alive, in the form of a fish, on the other; and a taut line joining the two. Thus far, the story has followed a simple pastoral line, the hero having withdrawn from some threatening scene on the horizon into the green world. Here the beauty and order of the setting permeate the young man's spirit and act to restore his inner equilibrium. The story might well end at this point, but it will not end until Hemingway has given it his inevitable twist toward darkness. The twist presents itself as a swamp that Nick approaches as he fishes his way down the river. It is a place where at first Nick does not want to go. "He felt a reaction against deep wading with the water deepening up under his armpits, to hook big trout in places impossible to land them. In the swamp the banks were bare, the big cedars came together overhead, the sun did not come through, except in patches; in the fast deep water, in the half light, the fishing would be tragic. In the swamp fishing was a tragic adventure. Nick did not want it" (231).

"So startling is the word 'tragic' here," writes critic Richard Hovey, "that we wonder what must be the matter with Nick."[2] Exactly. This brown study astonishes us all. Even more startling is our realization, by the end of the story, that Nick *does* want to fish the swamp, and that Hemingway wants it for him. The river must be two-hearted, both healing and tragic.[3] The story closes with Nick cleaning the two big trout he has caught and walking back to his camp. "He looked back. The river just showed through the trees. There were plenty of days coming when he could fish the swamp" (232). The shift from restoration to conflict, from fishing as Walton's calm and innocent recreation to a threatening test of the individual spirit, from pastoral to tragedy—this is the indispensable Hemingway note. It continues, in our own time, to yield up new meanings for our consideration.

It was in the writing of "Big Two-Hearted River" that Hemingway first felt he had it in him to become a great writer. Before the waters of the big two-hearted river deepened to the Gulf Stream and Hemingway's greatest fish story of all—perhaps his greatest book of all—*The Old Man and the Sea*, nearly thirty years passed. In order to treat that late Hemingway masterwork adequately, it is necessary to consider the direction of his life and work in those intervening years. During this time the Hemingway legend formed itself around his rejoinder, both personal and literary, to what he perceived as a chaotic and murderous world. He had good evidence for such a view. George Steiner, in his book *In Bluebird's Castle*, cites the annihilation of 70 million people in Europe and Russia between the start of the First World War and the end of the Second, roughly the years of Hemingway's development as a writer. Reminding us of myriad smaller wars, as well as the two World Wars and the new possibility of global nuclear annihilation, Philip Young writes that "we may argue against Hemingway's world, but we should not find it easy to prove that it is not the world we have been living in" (*Ernest Hemingway* 45).

The famous Hemingway response was a world-model, narrow but compelling, that was to enclose and direct his writing for the remainder of his career. Two essential elements of that unique Hemingway consciousness were, first, a primitivistic conception of the natural world and one's proper behavior within it, and, second, a theory of literary tragedy. What follows here is a questioning of whether these two concepts were reconcilable, codifiable, in Hemingway's work. My contention is that they proceed from fundamentally warring assumptions and that their mutual antipathy finds its most memorable—but deeply troubling—expression in the story of the battle between fisherman and fish in *The Old Man and the Sea*.

Reconsidering Hemingway's Primitivism

In his introduction to *The Viking Portable Hemingway* in 1944, Malcolm Cowley reminded his readers that Hemingway was often described as a primitive. But, wrote Cowley, the term needed to be shifted from its artistic to its anthropological sense. Hemingway created, Cowley maintained, Indian-like heroes who survive in a world of hostile forces by acts of propitiation and ritual, and—in the face of the failure of these acts—by stoic acceptance of what must come. Memories of Indians whom Hemingway had encountered during his boyhood summers up in Michigan are reworked, as Cowley claimed, in *The Torrents of Spring*, in several of the Nick Adams stories, and in Robert Jordan's behavior in *For Whom the Bell Tolls* (Cowley xviii–xx). Responding in kind, Hemingway referred to himself, in a letter to Cowley occasioned by the 1949 reprinting of *The Portable Hemingway*, as an old Cheyenne. He wrote Charles Scribner that he had "a Cheyenne great-great grandmother" and called attention in another letter to his father's "Indian blood." Elsewhere, Hemingway proudly described his third son, Gregory, with his cool athletic prowess, as "a real Indian boy (Northern Cheyenne)" or as a "Northern Cheyenne Indian angel."[4] In essays published in the mid-1960s, Wallace Stegner reasserted Cowley's claim, concluding that Hemingway's were "essentially Indian virtues" (198, 184).

Recognizing that Cowley and Stegner were referring to the primitivism of Hemingway's fictional heroes and that the distinction between Hemingway the man and his literary creations must be acknowledged, it can nevertheless be maintained that the two are closely interconnected—Hemingway, for example, assuring Cowley and other recipients of his letters that he came by the Indianness of his fictional heroes honestly. More importantly, Hemingway's life and art share a paradoxical symbiosis with the natural world in which the author's primitivism is rooted. In this respect Hemingway's perceived Indian virtues deserve to be reexamined in a contemporary context for both their anthropological and their artistic significance.

In its broadest terms Hemingway's primitivism can be seen as a return to earth, Thoreau-like, to confront the essential facts of life and reduce life to its most elemental terms. Hemingway's primitivism found personal expression in his lifelong search for unspoiled natural settings and the elemental experiences that fed his appetite for conflict and violence: big-game hunting in Africa, bullfights and guerrilla warfare in Spain, World War I and II battle experiences, deep-sea fishing on the Gulf Stream, "high on the wild" in the mountains of Idaho, rejecting, as Richard Lehan notes, "all patterns of continuity—historical or literary—which took precedence over the self" (197). Hemingway put this rejection into a famous passage in *Green Hills of Africa:*

> A continent ages quickly once we come. The natives live in harmony with it. But the foreigner destroys, cuts down the trees, drains the water, so that the water supply is altered and in a short time the soil, once the sod is turned under, is cropped out and, next, it starts to blow away as it has blown away in every old country and as I had seen it start to blow away in Canada. The earth gets tired of being exploited. A country wears out quickly unless man puts back in it all his residue and that of all his beasts. When he quits using beasts and uses machines, the earth defeats him quickly. The machine can't reproduce, nor does it fertilize the soil, and it eats what he cannot raise. A country was made to be as we found it. We are the intruders and after we are dead we may have ruined it but it will still be there and we don't know what the next changes are. I suppose they all end up like Mongolia.
>
> . . . Our people went to America because that was the place to go then. It had been a good country and we had made a bloody mess of it and I would go, now, somewhere else as we had always had the right to go somewhere else and as we had always gone. . . . We always went in the old days and there were still good places to go.
>
> I knew a good country when I saw one. Here there was game, plenty of birds, and I liked the natives. Here I could shoot and fish. That, and writing, and reading, and seeing pictures was all I cared about doing (284–85).

The characteristic objection of Lehan and other critics to Hemingway's primitivism is that it is a denial of contemporary society and an avoidance of the issues faced in modern lives. But a further concern needs exploring: not that Hemingway rejects intellect and society in favor of primitive values and "rhythms of life and death and the land" (Lehan 196), but rather that he often turns against the earth itself in his version of primitivism, adopting an aggressive and isolated individualism that wars against those natural manifestations he reveres. "In rebellion against death," as Hemingway described himself, loving the sensations and pleasures of the natural world yet also hating its implacable cycle that denied him immortality, Hemingway seemed compelled to exact a retribution from nature before it could claim him. "I spend a hell of a lot of time killing animals and fish so I won't kill myself," A. E. Hochner reports Hemingway saying. "When a man is in rebellion against death as I am in rebellion against death, he gets pleasure out of taking to himself one of the godlike attributes, that of giving it."[5]

The Hemingway body count against the earth, both in fiction and in life, is startlingly high. The letters are particularly revealing on this score. When one attempts to derive a total from the photographs and letters and writing of a lifetime, the real-life Hemingway kill record is astonishing: not only big-game animals (lions, leopards, buffalo, rhinocerous, kudu, sable, bears, elk, and so forth) in Africa and the American West, including some of the last grizzly bears outside protected ares in America, but also shoals of marlin, tuna, dolphin, tarpon, kingfish, and sea turtles—and even a sixty-foot whale that he claimed to have harpooned and lost.[6] To this can be added the shooting of sharks for sport with a Thompson submachine gun and the killing of such nongame species as a flying eagle, giant bustards, cranes, magpies, coyotes, porcupines, and snakes.[7]

Then there is the "dirty joke" of shooting hyenas for entertainment, watching their "highly humorous" antics, "racing the little nickelled death inside," one circling madly, pulling out his own intestines and eating them as he died (*Green Hills* 37–38). Even when Hemingway is obviously fabricating, as when he claims, like his fictional Colonel Cantwell, to have killed 122 men "besides the possibles," the need for such assertion is itself revealing.[8] Thus Hemingway exacts a considerable price from the natural world. He overcomes his own sense of guilt saying, "I did nothing that had not been done to me" and "they all had to die" (*Green Hills* 148, 272).

The paradox of Hemingway's primitivism, then, arises from its countertendency to war against the earth, to exploit the natural world for self-aggrandizement. His unique brand of primitivism characteristically rejects those perceptions—the interconnectedness of all life, the harmonious sense of oneness with the world, the ability to understand and use complex natural processes without destroying them, the acceptance of death as part of an inevitable and nonthreatening flow of existence—that enable the actual indigenous people to exist in the sort of nondestructive relationship with their surroundings that Hemingway paradoxically admired, and that left the country as he liked to find it. True, Hemingway does not exclude himself from the pioneering exploiters of nature in the *Green Hills of Africa* passage. He says, "we are the intruders," and he claims the privilege of ruining new lands just as his white forebears had ruined ours. He understood firsthand how places like the Michigan old-growth forests were destroyed, as he reveals in the story, "The Last Good Country." But Hemingway also clearly considered himself a defender of and a spokesman for the natural world. We recall his claim to Maxwell

Perkins that the point of *The Sun Also Rises* "was that the earth abideth forever—having a great deal of fondness for the earth and not a hell of a lot for my generation. . . . I didn't mean the book to be a hollow or a bitter satire but a damn tragedy with the earth abiding forever as the hero" (*Selected Letters* 229).

Can there can be fashioned a tragedy with the earth abiding forever as the hero? This becomes a crucial question in Hemingway, perhaps even more so for his readers today and in the future. Tragedy, Joseph Meeker has claimed, is in its essence a denial of the earth and its nobility or heroism in favor of a vaulting human protagonist who refuses to accept even the natural bounds placed upon all people (*Comedy*, 1974, 51–59). While this sense of defiant individualism warring against the natural order is not found in all tragedy, and Meeker's generalization must be qualified, it is evident that much of Hemingway's work reflects this aggressive assertion of human will over the abiding earth. Hemingway's stoicism, his deference to ritual and taboo—these may be primitivistic, but they are accompanied by little evidence of the autochthon's humility before the powers of the natural world and the inevitability of death. For Hemingway death was a cruel and hateful trick, malevolently claiming the best and bravest for its first victims. Hemingway's aim is always to control and manage what he conceives of as hostile forces.

The characteristic Hemingway ethic places heroic selfhood above the wider sense of obligation to the earth to which the author's avowed primitivism might be expected to bind him. In Hemingway's famous definition, "moral is what you feel good after." This contrasts pointedly with an earth-centered ethic such as that expressed by Aldo Leopold, who wrote that "a thing is right when it tends to preserve the integrity, stability, and beauty of the biotic community."[9] Nature exists in Hemingway's work and life primarily as a backdrop for aggressive and destructive individualism, the same individualism which, written large, has authored ecological devastation and poisoned the organic origins of the contemporary society that Hemingway turned to nature to escape.

For Hemingway and the late nineteenth century into which he was born, the powerful evolutionary discoveries of the midcentury had been popularly distilled into Herbert Spencer's catchphrase "survival of the fittest," a partially understood concept that seemed to characterize the natural world as only a vast killing ground. It was a perception that shared at least one misunderstanding with the earlier romanticism it replaced: that nature was simple. A fuller comprehension of evolutionary nature by Hemingway might have understood fitness to include those best equipped by evolution to survive not only through their killing ability but through other means of adaptation by way of other natural processes, such as cooperation, reciprocation, niche filling, or simply leaving more offspring. It might have demonstrated to him that patterns of interdependence within nature and between organisms and their natural environment are even more complex and more rigorously demanding than those on the human, societal level and are not subsumable into the one paradigm of dog eat dog.

Something of Hemingway's biological thinking is evident in his passage dealing with the great, indifferent power of the sea to cleanse itself, as he described the Gulf Stream, into which Havana dumps its daily bargeloads of garbage: "The stream, with no visible flow, takes five loads of this a day when things are going well in La Habana and in ten miles along the coast it is as clear and blue and unimpressed as it was ever before the tug hauled out the scow; and the palm fronds of our victories, the worn-out light bulbs of our discoveries, and the empty condoms of our great loves float with no significance against one single, lasting thing—the stream" (*Green Hills* 150).

Yet Hemingway might have come to realize by the end of his life that even the sea—a brilliantly stylized metaphor for time in this passage, but also, still, the sea—was not inexhaustible in its powers of renewal. Recalling his father's claim that there would not be a trace of the Havana garbage a few miles downstream, Hemingway's son, Gregory, child of a later age, wrote in his memoir that "even the sea can endure only so much," as he described the degradation of the Gulf Stream waters in more recent times (25).

Hemingway, not as primitivist but as literary modern, had in an important sense left the world itself—the heroic, enduring earth—far behind. As a modern and as an artist, he was a *maker* of his world, and he found and refined his unique selfhood in repeated acts of will and creativity that shaped, over and over, world and event and character into the paradigm he perceived. But his *making*, his proclaiming of his own uniqueness, also necessitated a destruction or diminishment of the natural world that he loved and revered. The harmonious sense of self and world is not sufficient for the artist Hemingway. Instead, he turns—as had Nick Adams in the prophetic early story, "Big Two-Hearted River"—from the healing open river to the swamp, the stage setting of tragic adventure.

To summarize, those who find Hemingway engaged in returning us to our primitive origins may have so misunderstood primitivism as to assume that Hemingway's compulsive, ritualized repetition of the life-death confrontation was its central experience. Rather, it is the central experience of tragedy, an art form which, in its tradition in the literature of the Western world, is unique. Hemingway's imposition of a theory of literary tragedy upon his primitive settings and apparently primitivistic characters and value systems was not without its price.

Tragedy and *The Old Man and the Sea*

Originated by the Greeks and shaped by Judeo-Christian beliefs, literary tragedy is exclusively a product of the Western and modern world, a distinctive creation arising from the same aggressive conquest of nature that Hemingway recounts in his *Green Hills of Africa* statement. For the essence of much tragedy is its focus upon hubris, the elevation of the individual will above all other considerations. The tragic hero, as Meeker writes,

> demonstrates that unique human individuals are capable of experiences that go beyond the capacity of humanity in general. . . . Neither the laws of nature nor the laws of men are absolute boundaries to the tragic hero, but are rather challenges which he must test by attempting to transcend them. . . . The suffering which accompanies his struggle or results from it is merely a price that must be paid for his momentary freedom from the restraints accepted by all other creatures. . . . Personal greatness is achieved at the cost of great destruction . . . but . . . any price is justified for the fulfillment of the unique personality. (*Comedy*, 1974, 50–51)

Meeker may slight the extent to which, in modern tragedy, world and protagonist must jointly be found guilty in the fall of the individual. In "Tragedy and the Common Man," Arthur Miller, for example, argues both as critic and playwright that tragedy is born out of our sense of something wrongfully denied to the individual by society. But although a greater ambiguity may be present in the portrayal of outside forces and the individual in modern tragedy, Meeker's claim for the genre's insistence upon human uniqueness and self-fulfillment remains valid. That this central consideration is the unique product of Western thinking—and is thus not a human universal—is affirmed by several critics of tragedy and is underscored by the response of Asian scholar Naozo Ueno to *The Old Man and the Sea*. Of Santiago's defiant response that "man can be destroyed but not defeated," Ueno writes that this same assertion "echoes over and over again in the literature of the West, from the pronouncement of Lucifer in *Paradise Lost* to the final passage of Tennyson's 'Ulysses.' Man becomes supreme and different from any other creature on earth through his assertion of will power. This is where the Orient cannot follow."[10]

Biologist David Sloan Wilson claims, in this regard, that "[m]odern western thought is derived from the Greek system and is mistaken by western social scientists as universal human nature" (248). Tellingly, modern existential tragedy has claimed Hemingway as one of its primary exponents, as John Killinger's *Hemingway and the Dead Gods* reveals. Existential tragedy, Killinger argues, stresses even more strongly than its classical forebears the elevation of the individual as "separated from all other beings, human or nonhuman," "the only vital entity of existence," with all that such a concern implies as to the worth and relevance of all entities ouside the self (2, 97).

Man's need to achieve on a grand scale, to realize himself without any limitation, to attack that which hedges and limits him, even if it means an assault upon nature itself—this defiance informs much of the tragic spirit. The tradition of tragedy appealed strongly to Hemingway on one level, because it fused his desire to assert the importance of the individual with his need to strike back at what he regarded as cruel and purposeless fate. But on another level, tragedy located the author of that fate in the same nature whose evidences of unquestionable nobility and beauty likewise compelled Hemingway's allegiance.[11] Hemingway's aim, as much expressed by his last major novel as it was intended for his first—to write a tragedy with the earth abiding forever as the hero—was caught upon this dilemma: that tragedy depicts an earth which, although it may be present only metaphorically in the drama, must yield up its nobility to a human hero whose usurping of that nobility is accompanied by profound misgivings. For this vexation of the heart, the greatest primitivist Hemingway hero, Santiago, the fisherman of *The Old Man and the Sea*, gives evidence that tragedy is not something that one feels good after.

In *The Old Man and the Sea* the elements of primitivism and tragedy are given their most searching treatment, resulting in what has often been seen as the capstone of Hemingway's fictional achievement. Included in the high praise for the novel is the claim that it is Hemingway's final testament of acceptance, his coming to peaceful terms with the natural world.[12] This assessment of the novel as an all-embracing affirmation of life is commonly found in criticism of the book, indicating a widely shared reader experience.

At the same time the central figure of the story, an old Cuban fisherman who catches an enormous marlin far out on the Gulf Stream and then loses it to sharks before he can return to land, represents the indisputable tragic hero, strongly affirming the spirit of man in conflict with natural laws. That Hemingway can successfully hold in tension these competing forces, the abiding sea and the tragic will of man, through so much of the novel is in no small measure attributable to his choice of hero. Santiago is a virtual Pleistocene archetype in his keen biophilial awareness and his store of skills, which seem to be the distilled accumulation of generations of tradition. With his crude skiff and his hand lines, he is as close as one could imagine to a virtual Stone Age fisherman living in the mid-twentieth century. Santiago is intended to be both the vessel of his author's conception of primitivist natural nobility and of tragic consciousness. But he becomes, by the end of the story, a tragic hero whose sense of the nobility of nature proves inadequate and unequal to his pride.

Among the most thorough of all the treatments of naturalistic and humanistic elements in the book is Bickford Sylvester's "Hemingway's Extended Vision: The Old Man and the Sea." Sylvester argues for Hemingway's portrayal of "a fundamental natural principle of harmonious opposition," "a natural law man is permitted to follow" (85, 94). Yet such a principle, though operative through much of the story, does not adequately explain Santiago's persistent sense of sin as he struggles to justify to himself his killing of the nobility of nature, the great marlin, much as he loves the bodies of the heavens and thinks of them as his friends and yet would be challenged to destroy them, given the opportunity: "'The fish is my friend too,' he said aloud. 'I have never seen or heard of such a fish. But I must kill him. I am glad we do not have to try to kill the stars.' Imagine if each day a man must try to kill the moon, he thought. The moon runs away. But imagine if a man each day should have to try to kill the sun? We were born lucky, he thought" (75).

It is man's nature to kill, and Santiago is a man—more properly still, for all of his natural associations, a Hemingway man—in whom there is such pride as to lead him to strike, Ahab-like, at the sun and the stars themselves, had he been given the opportunity. Indeed, Santiago's claim is more outrageous than that of Ahab, who at least posited a sun that had insulted him. It is as if, for the Hemingway man, the sun's existence itself is sufficient insult.

Man was born lucky, thinks Santiago, not to have to face this challenge, since—the implication seems clear—he would accept any challenge offered him even if, as in the killing of the sun, it meant his own destruction and that of all life. Reading this in our own time, it seems impossible not to find irony in Santiago's readiness to wreak cosmic annihilation by his own hand. "I do not understand these things, he thought. But it is good that we do not have to try to kill the sun or the moon or the stars. It is enough to live on the sea and kill our true brothers" (75). That is, it is good that we are spared the irresistible opportunity to make war on the universe. It is sufficient to be limited to killing the noble creatures of the earth, our own true brothers. The latent irony here becomes stronger in the hours following the marlin's death, when the arguments about the rightness of his act move back and forth in Santiago's mind between guilt and necessity, those two elements which, as Paul Tillich claims, are the essence of tragedy (see Sewell 178).

So the book takes us more deeply than any of Hemingway's other works into the conflict between tragic individualism and the magnificence of nature. Conscious of the defects of his own moral system, Santiago is both his own assertive hero and his own chastising chorus, alternately proclaiming and questioning his tragic pride.

"The truly great killer . . . must be a simple man," Hemingway had once contended (*Death in the Afternoon* 232). Santiago reveals a compassion and a complexity in his repeated questioning of his killing of the marlin that makes him less than a good killer. A very special primitive, he has too much of the modern's—that is to say, Hemingway's—self-awareness for the naive, all-engrossing sense of simplicity that Hemingway saw in the great killers of the bullring. Santiago's failings as a killer are, at the same time, the reason for our interest in him and the mark of his advance over the assertive individualism of his predecessors in the Hemingway canon. Yet he is a killer, after all, and he goes down chanting, however uneasily, the old Hemingway verities.

One might posit, in Santiago's final dream of the lions at play on the beach, the image that closes the book, a new vision of a peaceable kingdom, an expiation of the sense of sinful killing with which Santiago has charged himself. Arvin Wells argues that the lions "have put aside their majesty and have grown domestic and familiar. It is as if they gave themselves up to the old man, to his love, without the necessity of further trial or guilt or suffering, and that they suggest a final harmony between the old man and the 'fierce heart of nature'" (101). But this dream of the lions must be balanced against the rest of the book, against Santiago's climactic cry for destruction but never defeat and his reminder to the boy, Manolin, that they must fashion a new killing lance to replace the one he has lost in his epic battle.[13]

As great as it is, *The Old Man and the Sea* is no testament of acceptance. The self-exaltation of tragedy does not permit it to be. In Hemingway's fine but narrow world, there is no room to maneuver except at the edge of death, no arresting of the cycle in which one must go forth to kill one's brothers, turning to the natural world as the arena for human greatness but effecting thereby its further diminishment.

For Santiago nature is something other than a system in which "each thing has its place in a giant symbiosis" (Williams 178). Rather, it is a "great sea with our friends and our enemies," creatures judged in Santiago's mind according to how they serve or hinder him (*Old Man and Sea* 120). The friends are those who promote Santiago's freedom and happiness, the enemies those who restrict that freedom and happiness. The two sides are clearly marked out in the narrative. The porpoises are good: "They play and make jokes and love one another. They are our brothers like the flying fish" (48). The Portuguese man-of-war is an enemy, *agua mala*, a "whore," beautiful but with filaments poisonous to man (though not to the small fish who swim among these filaments). Santiago loves to see the turtles (friends) eat the men-of-war, and he likes to walk on them, popping them under his feet, when they are washed up on the beach (35–36). The sharks are bad because they prey upon the turtles and upon his catch, although he admires the Mako shark for its bravery and beauty. The rest of the sharks are despised as scavengers. We are told that Santiago eats the eggs of the benevolent turtle for strength and that he drinks a cup of shark-liver oil each day as a protection against colds and grippe and to help his eyes (37). Whether Santiago recognizes his obligations to both his sea friends and enemies for his good health is not revealed.

If *The Old Man and the Sea* approaches a humanistic ethic or a truce with nature that pleased many of Hemingway's critics, one finds no evidence that this testament of acceptance could transcend its anthropocentrism. It does not include a recognition that the villainous shark, for example, is no less necessary to the nobility of the sea than the marlin and the porpoise and the turtle; that the elimination of the shark would threaten the other species on whom it preys; that, by taking the wounded or the feeble or the slow or the old, the shark ensures the survival of the healthiest and strongest; that the shark, by trimming the numbers of fish, keeps their proportions appropriate to the food supply. Hence there is more at issue in Santiago's self-doubts than Greek hubris or Christian pride. Beyond these, there is the greater folly of his assumption that the only order to the biotic world is that which his limited understanding can provide.

Aldo Leopold once claimed that we need to learn to think like a mountain, which depends on its predators to keep its deer population from exploding and denuding its slopes of vegetation, eventually causing starvation and erosion and thus the death of deer and mountain alike (137–41). Thinking like a man may characterize the shark and the man-of-war as our enemies. But thinking like the sea—if Hemingway could at last have fully conceived that tragedy in which the earth endures as hero—requires a longer view, an awareness that these creatures, too, are members of an ecosystem that man is not privileged to exterminate for real or assumed self-benefits, nor to attempt to shape to his own often self-destructive purposes.

As Chaman Nahal observes, in Santiago's "'They beat me, Manolin. They truly beat me,'" (124), "they" is "the plurality of life that surrounds the old man—the plurality that includes the old man, but also includes the gulf weed, the shrimp, the man-of-war bird, the delicate tern, the schools of bonito and albacore, the tuna and the flying fish, the dolphin, the turtle, the plankton, the warbler, the big marlin and all the sharks" (179). But this realization, the fullest implication of Santiago's "'I went out too far,'" seems to elude Santiago, who still attributes his beating to the sharks. To Manolin's "'He didn't beat you. Not the fish,'" Santiago replies, "'No. Truly. It was afterwards'" (124).

If *The Old Man and the Sea* is, as Clinton Burhans, Jr., claims, the "culminating expression" of Hemingway's concern for "the relationship between individualism and interdependence," it still falls short of considering that interdependence in its fullest sense (73). That conception could be realized only by integrating all parts of the world that the novel yearns to encompass into a perception larger than the transcendence or salvation of the individual human agent within it.

"The Earth Abiding Forever"

When Hollywood was filming *The Old Man and the Sea* off Cuba during the summer of 1955, Hemingway joined the film crew and led the hunt for a marlin of one thousand pounds or more to be used in the fish-fighting scenes. But although they caught four-hundred-pounders, the giant fish were not there that season and the filming had to be stopped. The following spring Hemingway and the film crew moved to Capo Blanco, Peru, reputed to have big marlin. After thirty-two days and only one suitable big fish—films of which were unusable because of bad light conditions—this expedition, too, was scrapped. The story was eventually filmed almost entirely in a tank on a Hollywood sound stage and featured a marlin made of foam rubber and plastic.[14]

Whether or not Hemingway might have seen some relationship between the scarcity of big fish in these later years and the general and unrestrained practice of hauling them in for photograph and market and freezer, we do not know. But Gregory Hemingway's account at this time of his father's returning a marlin to the sea ("something I'd never seen him do before" saying, "'I'd rather release him and give him his life back and have him enjoy it, than immortalize him in a photograph'" [73]) is perhaps significant in view of continuing references in Hemingway's later letters and writings to the unresolved dilemma expressed by Santiago.

In a hunting article published in 1951, Hemingway announced that "the author of this article, after taking a long time to make up his mind, and admitting his guilt on all counts, believes that it is a sin to kill any non-dangerous game animal except for meat" ("The Shot" 369). A year later he wrote to Harvey Breit, in a reference to Faulkner's "The Bear," that "I think it is a sin to kill a black bear, because he is a fine animal that likes to drink, that likes to dance, and that does no harm and that understands better than any other animal when you speak to him. . . . I have killed enough of them since I was a boy to know it is a sin. It isn't just a sin I invented."[15] During his 1953 African safari, Hemingway was more interested in watching animals than in killing them.[16]

These intimations of a change in sensibility, occurring at about the time of the writing of *The Old Man and the Sea*, suggest that Santiago's inner struggle between feelings of wrongdoing and necessity may be related to his creator's own questioning of long-held beliefs as he approached the end of his career. Hemingway's love for nature was a central and immutable tenet in his system of beliefs. Like some latter-day Antaeus, seemingly invincible so long as he remained in touch with his sustaining earth, Hemingway orchestrated his life and work to accommodate his need for that contact. Did he question at last whether the imposition of a tragic and aggressive individualism upon his loved earth had claimed too high a cost?

Certainly, up to the final stages of his career, Hemingway's was essentially not an Indian's but a mountain man's mentality in its relationship to the wild, an attitude that could assert that "a country was made to be as we found it" and yet could, in the name of defiant individualism, lead the assault by which it would be ruined. The next generation would find itself trying to make the best of a diminished thing. Hemingway's sons, whom he had carefully instructed in hunting and fishing, found, at last, that they could not follow these pursuits on their father's terms. Jack, the eldest, became a Fish and Game commissioner in his home state of Idaho, charged with enforcing the game laws for which his father, as a younger man, had had slight regard.[17] Patrick, the second son, became a professional hunter and then a teacher at the College of African Wildlife Management in Tanzania, where African students learn principles of wildlife preservation and management (4). Gregory, the youngest, also attempted, then gave up, a career as a hunting guide in Africa: "I shot eighteen elephants one month, God save my soul" (10).[18]

Yet it is the father's aggressive and tragic individualism that has memorably defined an age. Art, Hemingway said in *Green Hills of Africa*, was what lasted. "A country, finally, erodes and the dust blows away, the people all die and none of them were of any importance except those who practiced the arts. . . . a work of art endures forever" (109). Art endures, but the earth endures also, and whether it endures as poisoned wasteland or nuclear cinder—an ironic tribute to the assertive will and its goads to fame or power—or as the last good country is now a question of more than speculative importance. The earth has become—even in the evolutionary eye blink since *The Old Man and the Sea*—more than a protean form for the artist. It exists now as a locus of profound human concern, threatened as never before. The private anxieties of Nick Adams, back on the Big Two-Hearted River, have expanded to encompass a universal dread. To the great power of Hemingway's best work to make us see and feel, to teach us how it was, we can also add that it has dramatized for us how we have reached our precarious present.

It is, of course, unfair to hold Hemingway accountable to the ecological standards of a later time. The issues raised here go beyond those of contemporary environmentalism, looking back with twenty-twenty hindsight, because they have always been Hemingway's concerns as well. Despite his fixation upon the dealing of death, any summing up of the ecological Hemingway must acknowledge that among the animals his insights are as unmatched as his conquests. What ties us to animals, in literature or in life, is our evolutionary heritage and the deep sense of interconnection between us and them. W. D. Hamilton voiced a common sociobiological view in his claim that "[p]ractically none of our basic behaviour, perhaps only our linguistic behaviour and even that uncertainly, is wholly unique to humans" (259). Darwin postulated in his works a psychological as well as a biological line of continuity between humans and nonhuman animals. Hemingway's artistic portrayals of such encounters seem a dramatization of the validity of Darwin's hypothesis. One thinks of Santiago's memory of the female marlin he had once hooked, whose mate stayed with her all through the fight, and when she was hauled into the boat, "the male fish jumped high into the air beside the boat to see where the female was and then went down deep" and stayed down. "That was the saddest thing I ever saw with them" (49–50).[19] Similarly, the Hemingway reader may remember how, in "The Short, Happy Life of Francis Macomber," Hemingway takes us into the consciousness of the wounded lion and the animal's sense of what he must do, thus expanding our circle of moral awareness and responsibility beyond that of only the human participants.[20]

The more we study ethology, the less "anthropomorphism" seems readily dismissable, the less a "fallacy." As Reg Morrison points out in *The Spirit in the Gene*, anthropomorphism "used to be considered sloppy science," as if such thinking might undermine the respect due us as the only species possessing consciousness. We hear less of that today, Morrison notes, as increasing evidence of our close linkage to other animals becomes known. Yet, in an ironic sense, the taboo against anthropomorphism is correct: "Indeed, no animal displays human behavior. Quite the reverse. Humans display only animal behavior. Watch the action without the sound track and this truth becomes obvious" (xiv). Further, such movingly authentic depictions as Hemingway gives us of contact between human and nonhuman animal minds seem to support Frederick Turner's hypothesis of a sensory language that preceded the development of spoken language. Within such a perspective our relationship with animals reacquaints us with "a larger kind of sensing," an "ur-language we share with other parts of nature than ourselves" ("An Ecopoetics" 135–36).

So the author's level of understanding of these connections—Hemingway among the animals—is deep and insightful, even if its implications could not overcome his drive toward tragic individualism. Still, I hope not to seem to claim that Hemingway would have been a greater author if he had reflected sound environmental values. The opposite is nearer the truth. The great power of much of his work arises from the tensions between the competing pulls of defiant individualism and the abiding earth. But part of the cost of that greatness is a diminished earth and a version of primitivism whose price was still being reckoned by Hemingway at the end of his career, as it is by his audience even today.

The right relationships between self and earth were of such crucial importance to Hemingway—and to those readers who, like me, have been deeply influenced by his depictions of the individual in nature—that it seems likely that they would have continued to engross him, had his life and career carried forward into the environmental awareness of the late 1960s and beyond. Intimations of a threatened nature, the necessity for self-restraint, for a sense of stewardship toward the earth, do emerge in his later writing. And his posthumous novel, *The Garden of Eden*, which Hemingway worked on from 1946 until his death in 1961, is notable for the narrator's expression of his deep disgust, as a boy, at the excesses of elephant killing in Africa by his father. Indeed, the boy's loyalty shifts from his father to the elephants. It is an echo, or perhaps a premonition, of Gregory Hemingway's own appalled confession.

As Hemingway, at the end of his career, may have been essaying new relationships—less destructive forms of human dignification—with an enduring earth, so also, to the credit of his genius, he had already anticipated that his followers would move beyond him in a continuing development of consciousness. "Every novel which is truly written," he said in *Death in the Afternoon*, "contributes to the total of knowledge which is there at the disposal of the next writer who comes, but the next writer must pay, always, a certain nominal percentage in experience to be able to understand and assimilate what is available as his birthright and what he must, in turn, take his departure from" (192). In this account of the course of literary evolution, Hemingway has written his own best defense while also anticipating the necessary and inevitable departure from him of the next generation of writers, whose understanding of their own place in the natural world would be formed, in part, from Hemingway's tragic conflicts with the earth.

"I think I could turn and live with the animals, they are so placid and self-contained, / I stand looking at them long and long," says Whitman's speaker in "Song of Myself" (60). We turn, too, to look at the animals, and the appeal of their purposeful self-containment seems a check to the little wheel of striving and guile that turns endlessly within us. But though we look long and long, we turn away at last to our own strivings, demented, as Whitman says, with the mania of owning things. In our random-chance world, can we hope for a Utopia that would satisfy the yearnings of our nature? No American novelist was more struck by the chaotic uncertainties of everyday life and the appeal of the Utopian social reconstruction of human nature than William Dean Howells.

6

The Realist in Altruria: Evolution, Utopianism, and Ecology in William Dean Howells

. . . .

> Should a traveller give an account of men who were entirely divested of avarice, ambition, or revenge; who knew no pleasure but friendship, generosity, and public spirit, we should immediately detect the falsehood and prove him a liar with the same certitude as if he had stuffed his narration with centaurs and dragons.—David Hume, *Essays and Treatises*, 1771

> This was too many for me, but she told me what she meant—I must help other people, and do everything I could for other people, and look out for them all the time, and never think about myself. This was including Miss Watson, as I took it. I went out in the woods and turned it over in my mind a long time, but I couldn't see no advantage about it—except for the other people—so at last I reckoned I wouldn't worry about it any more, but just let it go.—Mark Twain, *Adventures of Huckleberry Finn*

For Alfred Kazin, in his classic study of modern American literature, *On Native Grounds*, William Dean Howells—with all his limitations—is identified as the central figure of literary interpretation in the country's radical social transformation during the 1880s and 1890s, out of which our modern literature emerged. Howells was this country's first major theorist and practitioner of realist fiction during the same period that Darwinian thought was challenging all previous conceptions of human nature. But in his often deeply conflicted efforts to make sense of this moral earthquake and the rapidly changing social and economic America he saw around him, Howells also struggled, in the realism that was his intellectual credo and in his brief attraction to Utopian fiction, with virtually the same individual and collective agonies that afflict us today.

While the social-constructionist perspective of recent critical studies has yielded some profitable readings of the works of American literary realists, the corresponding theoretical devaluing of realism may, as Lawrence Buell notes, have gone too far.[1] In reconsidering several novels of Howells, aspects of the genre can perhaps be reaffirmed from a new ecocriticial perspective, one that widens the context of social fiction.

In what follows I aim once again to stretch the social parameters of contemporary criticism in order to encompass matters biological and ecological as well as historical and social. I hope to expand the historicizing of several of Howells's novels by considering them from an evolutionary perspective, one outlined by Joseph Carroll, who argues for the conjoining of science and realism:

> The Darwinian theory of natural selection is inextricably enmeshed with the whole body of our scientific knowledge, and the evolutionary argument for linguistic verisimilitude presupposes the validity of what [Karl] Popper calls "scientific realism"—the idea that scientific knowledge corresponds to a reality that exists independently of our conceptions. As Popper declares, if the main body of our scientific knowledge is true, then "realism must also be true." . . . Philosophical arguments in support of scientific realism correspond to our powerful instinctive disposition to believe in a reality external to us. Even the most ingenious solipsist gets out of the way of an oncoming vehicle. . . . Evolutionary theory predicts this behavior as an adaptive response to conditions that exist independently of our perception of them, and our subjective belief, evidenced in our actual behavior, dovetails with this prediction. (100–101)

Those who have studied the impact of post-Darwinian biology upon late nineteenth-century American writers, artists, and thinkers generally conclude that Darwinism was rendered tolerable for its age by being subsumed under an optimistic new faith in progress. The so-called law of progress—it was seemingly given the authority of law, while Darwinism was only a theory—softened the harsh realities of evolutionary theory by martialing them to its own support. In the camp of John Fiske, American leader of these "soft" Darwinists, Howells occupied a somewhat uneasy place.[2] Acknowledging the new Darwinian paradigm intellectually, he was also deeply troubled by the blow it dealt to the human longing for immortality (Vanderbilt 16–21). But while he accepted—as did nearly all the artists and intellectuals of the time—the prevailing spirit of progress and the belief in an inclined moral plane leading the human race perpetually upward and out of what they perceived as the Darwinian jungle, his realist's credo sometimes led him to probe evolutionary issues more critically. This is especially the case in *The Landlord at Lion's Head* (1897), his last great work of literary realism and his best fictional treatment of evolutionary ideas—as well as one of his least-known and least-appreciated works.[3]

Evolution in *The Landlord at Lion's Head*

Looking back some years later upon the composition of *The Landlord at Lion's Head*, Howells recalled "a very becoming despair when at a certain moment in it, I began to wonder what I was driving at" (quoted in Lynn 306). Howells's despair and puzzlement with his novel in progress may be sensed by today's reader. This story of an artist-observer, Jere Westover, who witnesses the growth of young Jeff Durgin from a country boy in New Hampshire's White Mountains to landlord of the hotel built upon his family's farm, is a disturbing and complex mélange of late nineteenth-century social concerns, as well as a record of Howells's private doubts about the relevance of moral art in an increasingly amoral age.

If the writing of *Landlord* brought Howells to the edge of confusion and hopelessness, he may have only recorded his own age's sense of dislocation as it attempted to deal with two of its most profound cultural shocks. The first of these was Darwinian evolution. Howells repeatedly and conflictingly images Jeff Durgin as both a prehistoric savage, an animalistic throwback in the long evolutionary march, and as a contemporary survivor, one of the "fittest" for an increasingly materialistic present and future. Fears that evolution would deny individual free will, that moral choice would cease to function as a controlling force in social relationships, are vividly presented in the novel. Millennial progress upward, the hopeful side of Darwinism, is threatened in Howells's depiction of Jeff. Did Darwinian evolution posit the social and moral growth of the race, or did it, in its disquieting correspondences to the competitive, dog-eat-dog economic sphere, put forward the rapacious entrepreneur as the inevitable end product?

For Howells, the moral progress of the race found its microcosm in the development of man from the "savagery" of boyhood to the ethical consciousness of civilized adulthood. Howells's boys, as Tom H. Towers has shown, are depicted as "savages," prisoners of their mindless immersion in sensation and pleasure. In his portrait of Jeff, Howells seems to present the possibility of an arrestment of that metamorphosis from savagery to civilization. If Jeff is a representative new man, then the future of civilization itself may be threatened. Whether Jeff's virtues—

self-awareness, industriousness, a successful marriage—are sufficient to redeem what some would see as his problematic moral nature is a question that vexes Howells's novel.

The other dislocation in *Landlord* is related to the first but presents an even more radical threat, since it undercuts the entire process by which reality is perceived and rendered into artistic form. As Donald Pizer has explained, Howells had adopted an evolutionary analogy to defend and justify the growth and development of literary realism out of the "puerile, primitive, savage" tastes of the "unthinking multitude," as these barbaric tastes were to be found in romantic and meretricious fiction (100–101). But such evolutionary analogies, as Howells was to find in the writing of *Landlord*, were a two-edged sword that could cut away realism's scientific supports as readily as it might put to rout the romantic rabble. Evolution, for example, demonstrated geologically that the very earth itself was not static but in a condition of ceaseless flux. In selecting as his novel's central metaphor the mountain Lion's Head, Howells had chosen not an emblem of immutability, but a representation of ceaseless change. The implications for any assurance of perdurable moral order were not far out of sight. Through the influence of evolutionary discovery and theory, Howells's mountain had been transformed from coherent message to cryptogram.

What Charles Darwin had established was that our record of the natural world was fragmentary and confusing. He wrote in his *The Origin of Species* in 1859, "I look at the geological record as a history of the world imperfectly kept, and written in a changing dialect; of this history we possess the last volume alone, relating only to two or three countries. Of this volume, only here and there a short chapter has been preserved; and of each page, only here and there a few lines" (312).

It is curious that Darwin's analogy for the geological record is a deficient and virtually unreadable hieroglyph, for both Darwin's evolutionary theory and the decipherment of the ancient Egyptian hieroglyphics have been cited by John T. Irwin as probably the two strongest blows delivered by nineteenth-century learning to the faith of the age. More curious still—though perhaps less so when one considers Howells's seismic sense of widely felt and disturbing social concerns—is that both challenges lie at the heart of *The Landlord at Lion's Head.* Cryptic messages and Egypt figure increasingly in the story. And the mountain that gives the Durgin farm its name is in the form of a lion at rest, an implicit Sphinx, bearing the face of a man. But neither the geologic form nor the human counterpart seems to yield up its riddled meaning.

Thus a profound threat to the grounding of our epistemology, to the ability of the artist to assimilate and interpret the material world before him, pervades the novel. "The riddle of the painful earth," a favorite phrase of Howells from Tennyson's "Palace of Art," becomes, on both the natural and human levels, the writer's central concern. The novel's opening paragraph quickly establishes this enigmatic quality:

> If you looked at the mountain from the west, the line of the summit was wandering and uncertain, like that of most mountaintops; but seen from the east, the mass of granite showing above the dense forests of the lower slopes had the form of a sleeping lion. The flanks and haunches were vaguely distinguished from the mass; but the mighty head, resting with its tossed mane upon the vast paws stretched before it, was boldly sculptured against the sky. The likeness could not have been more perfect, when you had its profile, if it had been a definite intention of art; and you could travel far north and far south before the illusion vanished. In winter the head was blotted by the snows; and sometimes the vagrant clouds caught upon it and deformed it, or hid it, at other seasons; but commonly, after the last snow went in spring until the first snow came in the fall, the Lion's Head was part of the landscape, as imperative and importunate as the Great Stone Face itself. (1)

Howells immediately intimates the interpretive pitfalls. One's impression of the mountain depends upon one's point of view: from the west the line of the summit is vague and unclear; from the east it forms the figure of a lion. As William A. McMurray has noted, the opening thus invites a relativistic interpretation of the novel's central figure, Jeff Durgin. But the inquiry may also turn back upon the authorial maker here. Certainly the stylistic and rhetorical composition of the paragraph is weighted on the side of "composing" reality, the mountain, into a definite and coherent form. The illative "If . . . ; but . . ." structure of the opening sentence throws rhetorical emphasis upon the material following the semicolon, which gathers the force of its privileged ending position to assert—for the moment—the ascendancy of the formed over the formless. The second sentence follows a similar rhetorical strategy, seeming to claim primacy for the "boldly" formed head over the merely "vaguely" formed flanks and haunches. By the end of the paragraph, Lion's Head has been granted a typological significance like the imposing mountainside visage of Hawthorne's classic tale, "The Great Stone Face."

But Howells has also interspersed, in this beginning, ironic checks to such ready composing and symbolizing. The likeness, we are told, could not have been clearer "if it had been a definite intention of art," as if it is dryly recognized that art—and artists—are predisposed toward such bald intentionalizing. "Boldly sculptured" in the preceding sentence reinforces the suggestion of the artist's tendencies toward somewhat florid distortion. Further, he reminds us that the lion is but an "illusion" after all. Howells seems to be playing here with the relentless meaning-making proclivities of writers and readers, "lionizing" a natural feature that nevertheless remains both "imperative" and "importunate"—stubbornly demanding—at the end.

That Howells chooses an obsessive romantic image, the mountaintop, for deployment ought to alert us to the presence of a realist's ironies in this beginning. It does not so much offer a promise of Emersonian correspondences between nature and humankind as a cryptic Darwinian volume, tattered and virtually unreadable, a warning of the "blotted" and "deformed" text, "wandering and uncertain," which—when one puts aside the comfortable, ready-to-hand conventions of meaning-making—remains perversely resistant to interpretation. Lion's Head mountain is "silent" and imposes a silence upon chattering visitors as it rises above the forests that surround it like a "baffled sea" (4). As is often the case in Howells's most interesting fiction, the bottom is ready to drop out; a threatening void lies just beneath the controlled surface; in Auden's words, "the crack in the teapot opens / A lane to the land of the dead" (*Collected Poems* 115). The composed mountain from another perspective calls up conflicting translations, or worse, leaves us with the possibility of a bewildering confusion, a loss of any meaning whatsoever.

If the novel foregrounds several indecipherables, the attempted unraveling of their meanings becomes the primary interest of the novel. Most of the unraveling is left to Westover, the interpretive presence of the novel, who proves less than wholly reliable. Penetrating the secret meanings of nature and humankind is also the fascination of Whitwell, the cracker-barrel philospher, and Jackson Durgin, Jeff's tubercular older brother. Gripped by the disease that has claimed his father and all of the Durgin children except Jeff, Jackson has little time left. His mind runs to spiritual and biblical questions, and, upon Westover's suggestion, he undertakes a dying visit to Egypt.

For Westover, as for Howells and his audience at the time, Egypt was the source of belief in a future life. As Westover discourses learnedly to his rustic auditors, Whitwell and Jackson, on the pre-Christian Egyptian views of immortality, Whitwell cries irritatedly, "It don't stand to reason that folks without any alphabet, as you may say, and only a lot of pictures for words, like Injuns, could figure out the immortality of the soul. They got the idee by inspiration somehow" (191). But Egypt is another possible means of communication with the veiled infinite, and Jackson journeys there to spend his last few months of life studying its monuments and ethnology, writing letters home that stir the speculative spirits of the New Englanders.

The ancient Egypt that fills Jackson's dying days also raises the troubling shadow of a discontinuous, even regressive, history. Egypt forces upon the consciousness of Howells and his audience not only intimations of mortality, but the realization of the wholesale disappearance of a culture perhaps more advanced than that of the book's own time. Thus it projects paralyzing possibilities into the novel—a denial of the age's ascendant sense of inevitable human progress and a cancellation of historical and personal significance. Above all, ancient Egypt threatened the common Spencerian belief, largely shared by Howells and his audience, that moral and physical evolution were intertwined. The ancient civilization's achievements in art and science and architecture were shockingly offset by its barbarous mistreatment of its people. Howells himself had set forth this same troubling conflict in his *Atlantic Monthly* review, some years earlier, of Charles Dudley Warner's travel book, *Mummies and Moslems.* When Jackson returns from Egypt, he seems older than the rocks among which he has sat. He fades away quickly, as if stunned by his new awareness, communicating no more of his experiences than a numbing world-weariness.

It is left primarily to Westover, the central consciousness, to decipher the significance of Jeff, Jackson and Egypt, the doctrine of material and evolutionary progress, and a raft of other troubling matters. Though Howells reveals his realist's courage in confronting these matters, he has—as was often the case in his biggest and most engrossing novels—bitten off more than he could chew (in contrast to his friend and fellow novelist Henry James, who—it has been said—chewed more than he bit off). Not surprisingly, if there is the need for a Jamesian grasping imagination, Westover is not up to the task. For him, Jeff seems some kind of evil inversion of Emerson's Representative Man, a portent not of the advancement eventually to be reached and surpassed by humankind, as Emerson would have it, but of a rough beast slouching toward Bethlehem. In Emerson's words, however, and freed from Westover's narrow judgments, Jeff seems to represent a manifestation of the heroic and optimistic life force, "that famous aboriginal push [which] propagates itself through all the balls of the system, and through every atom of every ball"

(*Works* III, 184). And though it is, according to Emerson, "a long scale from the gorilla to the gentleman—from the gorilla to Plato, Newton, and Shakespeare," the upward line of progress may be seen in the "successive meliorations," in which Jeff might be accorded a place as a representative of the new commercial age (*Works* X, 186–87).

For Westover, Howells's not-wholly-reliable central consciousness, the hopeful meliorations have run aground in Jeff, whose actions have reversed the evolutionary climb and whose behavior, Westover claims bitterly at one point, "would have disgraced a Goth, or a gorilla. . . . You *are* a brute" (278–79). One can sense that in *Landlord* Howells repeats the compulsions of his Swedenborgian antecedents in seeking to interpret a now post-Darwinian, cryptic universe, to attempt once more to wrest significance from an otherwise chaotic randomness of matter, even while at the same time seeming to sense the folly of such efforts.

But after weighing his young protagonist as, alternately, an animalistic throwback and a fit survivor for the future, Howells circumvents his increasingly inadequate surrogate Westover, coming down, tentatively, on the side of Jeff as a survivor. Rather than a tragic evolutionary throwback, a New Hampshire McTeague, Jeff exits the novel as something of an evolutionary hero, a representative of the life force that turns out to be both adaptive and comic, a linking I shall return to later.

Westover, then—who at first seems to be the Howellsian moral arbiter and who can never quite relinquish his perception of Jeff as Goth or gorilla—is increasingly revealed to the reader as rigid and anachronistic, a finger-wagging prude, paralyzed by his idealism and ethical rigidity. Like Atherton of Howells's important early novel, *A Modern Instance*, Westover becomes a somewhat irrelevant figure whose insulation from the hard realities of life has left him trapped in his creed outworn. Westover is incapable of responding meaningfully to evolutionary change, as represented by the free-floating Jeff, who must be evaluated against the standards of a newer time that has passed Westover by and left him, in evolutionary terms, as something like the moral equivalent of a caudal appendage. In such a context adaptive rather than ancestral standards apply, and by such standards Howells's novel was a valid example of realism—a relatively objective, penetrating depiction of contemporary social life. As Howells wrote to his fellow-evolutionist Hamlin Garland during the composing of *Landlord*, "I have just begun a story . . . in which I study the growth of a brute boy into a pretty good man" (*Selected Letters*, Vol. 4, 104).

From a biological perspective, one can dispute Howells's perception that the moral progress of the race was mirrored in the development of the man from the "savagery" and demonic energy of boyhood to the ethical consciousness of civilized adulthood. But in allowing his main figure to trace a pattern of evolutionary complexity, as opposed to the closed moral rigidities of Westover and to some extent the author himself, Howells gives us a memorable example of how realism might address the Darwinian issues.

Howells's Altruistic Utopia

If *The Landlord at Lion's Head*, published in 1897, can be seen as perhaps Howells's fullest and most penetrating study of evolutionary principles at work in a contemporary social setting, it is revealing that this exemplary piece of realism is bracketed by the Utopian fiction of his Altrurian romances, *The Traveler from Altruria* (1894), *Letters from an Altrurian Traveler* (published individually in *Cosmopolitan* magazine in 1893 and 1894), and *Through the Eye of the Needle* (1907).[4] Edward Bellamy, the author of the immensely popular Utopian fantasy *Looking Backward, 2000–1887*, published in 1888, expressed his surprise and delight in reviewing the first installment of Howells's *The Traveler from Altruria*, that Howells, whom he rather uncharitably characterized as the creator of "the conventional types of polite fiction," had joined the Utopianists with "this glowing exposition of a nobler, higher, better life which beckons us on" (*The Altrurian Romances* xxii). While acknowledging the widespread popularity of Utopian fiction at the time, as well as Howells's growing commitment to socialism and his deeply felt need to speak out on issues of economic and social injustice in American life, readers today may find Utopian visions incongruous coming from the foremost theorist and practitioner of critical realism of his day. Having been given the realist principles of *Criticism and Fiction*, how are we to take this Howellsian flight into fantasy, a "glowing exposition" about a place that never was, on land or sea?

One response might be that there is a great deal of Howellsian realism in the Altrurian fictions, particularly in *The Traveler from Altruria*, where the Traveler, Mr. Aristedes Homos, visits America, confronts representative American types, and lectures local audiences upon the condition of Altruria before the bloodless revolution, or "Evolution" as he calls it, which led to the social millenium there. The barbaric conditions of early, pre-Evolution Altruria parallel precisely those of America in the 1890s, allowing Howells ample opportunity for realistic and satiric thrusts at contemporary social injustices. Howells's own scathing *North American Review* survey of America during the depression of 1894, the same year *The Traveler from Altruria* was published, closely resembles the Altrurian's assessments of his own country's benighted early state. Howells wrote of America,

> If we have built many railroads, we have wrecked many; and those vast continental lines which, with such tremendous expenditure of competitive force, we placed in control of the monopolies, have passed into the hands of receivers, the agents of an unconscious state socialism. The tramps walk the land like the squalid spectres of the laborers who once tilled it. The miners have swarmed up out of their pits to starve in the open air. In our paradise of toil, myriads of workmen want work. . . . The public domain, where in some sort the poor might have provided for themselves, has been lavished upon corporations, and its millions of acres have melted away as if they had been a like area of summer clouds. ("Are We a Plutocracy?" 194)

This is a close match with the Altrurian's description of his own country before "the Evolution":

> The land was filled with cities where the rich flaunted their splendor in palaces, and the poor swarmed in squalid tenements. The country was drained of its life and force, to feed the centers of commerce and industry. The whole land was bound together with a network of iron roads that linked the factories and foundries to the fields and mines, and blasted the landscape with the enterprise that spoiled the lives of men. (*The Altrurian Romances* 148)

To make sure his audience gets the point, Howells has the Altrurian interrupted by an old farmer in the audience who complains, "Look here! . . . When are you goin' to git to Altrury? We know all about Ameriky" (150). Sharply realistic depictions of American types are provided in Howells's satiric portraits of Mr. Twelvemough, the popular sentimental novelist who narrates *The Traveler from Altruria*, Mrs. Makely, the culture-vulture club woman who takes up the Altrurian as another oddity for her collection, and a banker, a lawyer, a professor, a manufacturer, and others, who play skeptical or amused foils to Mr. Homos's Utopian earnestness. These minor characters emerge as accurately realized characters in the realist tradition.

It is Altruria itself, and its traveling brochure, Mr. Homos, who are the cardboard grasshoppers here, creations that *ought* to be nobler and nicer than the real thing but often come across as lifeless and contrived. With his relentless one-upmanship and his instructive speeches, the Altrurian traveler represents the sort of moral uplift that can reduce any social gathering to stifling boredom. Few things are as hard to bear as a Good Example, as Mark Twain observed.[5]

Howells seems to sense the problem when he causes his shallow narrator, Mr. Twelvemough, the author of the sort of slight romances that Howells despised, to begin to wonder whether this outlandish visitor might not fit into one of his own graceful compositions: "Was he really a man, a human entity, a personality like ourselves, or was he merely a sort of spiritual solvent, sent for the moment to precipitate whatever sincerity there was in us, and show us what the truth was concerning our relations to each other? It was a fantastic conception, but I thought it was one that I might employ in some sort of purely romantic design, and I was professionally grateful for it" (99). Altruria, broadly described in *The Traveler from Altruria*, is examined more closely in *Through the Eye of the Needle*, which is to say that the latter is even more diffuse, a series of descriptions unleavened by the sharp, satiric characterizations of the earlier work.

Insofar as the Altrurian fictions remain anchored in American settings and characters, they are effective Howellsian realism. When Altruria and its mythical emissary take center stage, the works tend to become staged editorials. Of course Howells's Utopia must be taken as he doubtless intended it, as an emblem of possibility, a goad toward reformist thinking, a catalyst for social change. In this respect Altruria is consonant with Howells's long involvement in social reform, as Robert L. Hough, Daniel Aaron, James Woodress, and others have shown. Many of the causes Howells advocated have become part of public life in America. Still, the Altrurian romances were also clearly meant to be taken as a "blueprint for America" (*The Altrurian Romances* xxxiv). Accepting Mr. Homos's claim that "America prophesies another Altruria" (164), we are also invited, it seems, to consider the Altrurian model of the American future in the spirit of political reality.

In this spirit, it is tempting to imagine Howells as some clear-eyed Altrurian traveler from our own past, touching upon these shores today, a century later, to see how his prophecies have turned out. Would he confront in the United States today the realized White City of the future, a vision inspired by the World's Columbian Exposition in Chicago, which Howells and his Altrurian traveler visited in 1893? Or would he regard contemporary America as a Jeffersian perishing republic, shining garishly in the rich glow of its own decay?

The latter-day traveler would likely welcome evidence of progress, such as the emergence of women to play major roles in public life. The exclusion of women from American political affairs—even though they are better educated than men, whose entire energies and knowledge are business oriented—is met with shocked disbelief by the Alrurian Mr. Homos of a century ago.[6] But today's Howellsian visitor would recognize the same plutocracy still firmly entrenched that was depicted in the Altrurian romances as corrupting American democracy and undermining social progress. He would note a political system responsive primarily to large infusions of cash and the buying and selling of votes, poisoning democracy at its source. He would face an immense and gaudy materialism announcing that selfishness, the hateful target of the Altrurians, was yet rampant. Looking beyond America, he would see his visionary socialist systems in retreat on a universal scale, with theoretical socialists turning into practicing capitalists across the entire globe.

Turning back to regard the twentieth century, the Howellsian visitor would also be faced with the bloodiest century in human history, with the record of two World Wars and the unspeakable reality of between 100 and 200 million people murdered in these and other wars, in continuing genocides, and in other testaments to unchecked human cruelty and destructiveness, all in the name of making things better from the aggressors' perspective. The most unspeakable atrocities, he would be forced to note, were carried out by a nation nominally as Christian as Altruria. He would find hate-filled religious fundamentalists who believe that the bombing of airplanes and public places and the wholesale killing of men, women, and children accords the murderers a place in their own paradisical afterlife. Adding to this interhuman carnage—and related to it—the time traveler would see a superheated system of global production and consumption across the world, together with unprecedented population growth, using up the planet's resources and wiping out its diversity of species at a breakneck clip while loading its air, land, and waters with poisonous and corrosive wastes that increasingly threaten whole life systems.

As for the American public's cultural improvement, the Howellsian shape that haunts the dusk would find the contemporary romancers ascendant, still pushing the realists off the bookshelves, just as they were in his own time. If Howells found *McTeague* and *Sister Carrie* disquieting, sensationalized sex and violence in television, the movies, the paperbacks, magazines, and tabloids, would doubtless leave him staggered. There is evidence enough in all of this that the latter-day Howellsian traveler would find reason to recall the profound misgivings expressed in Howells's letter to Henry James in 1888 that "I'm not in a very good humor with 'America' myself. It seems to me the most grotesquely illogical thing under the sun . . . ; after fifty years of optimistic content with 'civilization' and its ability to come out all right in the end, I now abhor it, and feel that it is coming out all wrong in the end, unless it bases itself anew on real equality" (*Selected Letters*, Vol. 3, 231).

If the Altrurian romances pay an aesthetic penalty for their deviation from Howellsian realism, and if they suffer a serious credibility gap in their whistling-in-the-dark predictions for the American future, they are also marked by the biological, ecological, and evolutionary interpretations of their day, upon which a century of further study may offer interesting perspectives.

Altruism Revisited

In the context of today's scientific knowledge, the Altrurian fictions will not be praised for their farsightedness. Enlisting Darwinian biological precepts in the van of progress, as Howells does unquestioningly in his Altruria books, makes for bad science. As Stephen Jay Gould reminds us, Darwin himself avoided any Spencerian equating of evolution and progress by carefully insisting that "organic change led only to increasing adaptation between organisms and their environment and not to an abstract ideal of progress defined by structural complexity or increasing heterogeneity—never say higher or lower" (*Ever Since Darwin* 37). Howells handled these matters better—that is, questioningly—in his best novels like *The Landlord at Lion's Head*, where he presents the disquieting possibility that history has not been the celestial staircase leading humankind ever upward. But the received opinion of his day, to which Howells gave lip service, insisted upon the spiritual rather than the animal nature of humankind. What was accepted, as Frederick William Conner points out in his *Cosmic Optimism*, "was not so much the evolutionary theories of science as the old drama of providence revised according to these theories" (viii). From the standpoint of modern evolutionary thinking, human beings cannot hitch their fate to an inevitable celestial railroad. "We have no particular place to go," writes Harvard biologist Edward O. Wilson. "The species lacks any goal external to its own biological nature" (*On Human Nature* 3).

Wilson's sociobiological nemesis, Stephen Jay Gould, nevertheless agrees, in his *Ever Since Darwin*, putting Darwin's hard truth in terms even more blunt: "Natural selection dictates that organisms act in their own self-interest. They know nothing of such abstract concepts as 'the good of the species.' They 'struggle' continuously to increase the representation of their genes at the expense of their fellows. And that, for all its baldness, is all there is to it; we have discovered no higher principle in nature" (261).[7]

Even the optimism that underlay the doctrine of progress may itself be a genetic construct. Lionel Tiger, a social anthropologist, has argued as much in his study of human optimism. At the core of this study is the proposition that an evolved characteristic of human intelligence is the preference for the hopeful over the hopeless, the positive over the negative, the potentiality for success over that for failure. For Tiger, "making optimistic symbols and anticipating optimistic outcomes of undecided situations is . . . a part of human nature, of the human biology." He relates human optimism "to our general confidence in social arrangements to which a mammal with a lengthy phase of dependence will develop" and to our past as hunting and gathering primates. As our brain enlarged, Tiger posits, it began producing an increasing array of optimistic schemes and a belief in the possibilities for a desirable future that neither the awareness of mortality nor a realistic appraisal of human limitations could depress (15–16).

Reg Morrison, in his *The Spirit in the Gene*, argues from the same evolutionary perspective that the human gravitation toward spirituality—another manifestation of our yearnings for "progress"—underlies our need to see ourselves as separate from the rest of the animal world. Like Wilson, Jared Diamond, Carl Sagan, Alison Jolly, Richard Dawkins, and the other biologists cited in the earlier chapters of this book, Morrison argues that we are not unique from the rest of the mammals. But we are caught in a spiritual bind. Because many of us see ourselves as distinctive and exempt from our evolutionary heritage, "we will continue to be at least suspicious, if not thoroughly antagonistic, to Charles Darwin's heretical propositions" while still paying lip service to them in our assumption that only religious fundamentalists and the uneducated would deny them (xii–xiii). We tend, as Wilson claims, to be

> preoccupied with the last five thousand years of history, largely cultural in nature. But the human species was put together by two million years of history, from the first *Homo* [down to and including Howells' repre-

> sentative man, Mr. Homos]. Most of that history is genetic. It had to do with the way that the human brain evolved—a 3.2-fold increase in the cerebral cortex alone, an astonishing growth. That's biological. And the way we think, what we can smell, what we can sense, the bonding that we make—the things that are the commonalities of human nature—are the result of that genetic history, which tends to be totally ignored by scholars in the humanities. ("Ecology and the Human Imagination" 24)

To think of it in another way, consider not just the 2 million years of our development as a species, but only the last tiny fraction of that time. If we regard the last 50,000 years of human existence as composed of a series of contiguous human lifetimes, each about 62 years in length, then there have been about 800 such lifetimes. Of these 800 lifetimes, 650 were spent living in caves and temporary shelters (Toffler 15) and evolving the traits of the hunter and gatherer, which are, for better or worse, our genetic heritage. Looking back at Howells and his work today, we represent the 800th lifetime looking back at the 798th. It is not surprising that we still await the Altrurian millennium that Howells prophesied, in the teeth of evidence to the contrary.

In commenting upon the human preference for optimism from another perspective, economist and social critic Garrett Hardin pointedly observes that we have the word *melioristic* but no word *pejoristic.* "The Latin root *meliorare* means to become or to make better; *pejorare* means to become or make worse. . . . In the light of what we know of the power of Freudian denial, it is perhaps significant that meliorist is to be found in English dictionaries but pejorist is not" (Hardin 130). Hardin, noting that there are few melioristic processes and many pejoristic ones, argues for the efficacy of pejorism, which is not the same thing as pessimism and which provides an effective alternative to both sterile pessimism and fatuous optimism. Hardin's analysis is particularly relevant to our reading of Howells's Altrurian books:

> The distinction between pessimist and pejorist can be seen as rooted in motivation. A pessimist settles for describing the evils of the world without doing anything about it. It is no wonder that the generality of mankind represses the pessimist's descriptions. A pejorist, by contrast, looking for the providential workings of things, is likely to look also for ways of improving the system. In the realm of money, a pessimist may be satisfied to observe that everybody is so damned selfish, and to settle for the minimum policy of "Let every man look out for himself, and the devil take the hindmost."

> A good pejorist would refuse to regard this as acceptable policy; he would look for some way whereby men might collectively band together to create a more acceptable system. Laws that specify penalties for counterfeiting are the pejorist's reponse to the wishful thinking of the optimists and the cynicism of the pessimists. The pessimist is unhappy because he is cynical, the optimist because he is soon disillusioned; only a pejorist can be truly happy. He is busy trying to remake the world nearer to the heart's desire—and with occasional success. (131)

Basil March, Howells's familiar authorial presence, might be seen as something of a pejorist at the conclusion of *A Hazard of New Fortunes* when he and his wife Isabel discuss the interrelationships of social conditions and individual character and the capacity for society to reform itself through the democratic process (the same process by which Altruria threw off its hateful past and became the Utopian state). March's view is a rueful realist's assessment, promising no Altruria, but only the possiblity of some constructive change, assuming we are honest and do not sell our votes. Pejorism is the realist's position, a system that works, seeking out the pragmatic line between disdainful pessimism and hopelessly gullible optimism. But when he turned to his Altrurian fiction, Howells set aside his realist-pejorist concerns for what is in order to construct a vision of what ought to be.

He found in the word *altruism*—literally other-ism—the concept that would ideally direct the nation in its path of evolutionary progress. Auguste Comte, the putative founder of sociology, had first used the term in its current meaning in the 1850s, making it synonymous with his "religion of humanity" (Budd 40). Howells invented the name *Altruria* to designate the mythical island in the Aegean Sea where altruism was the guiding principle of government and social morality. Howells also had the example of Herbert Spencer, whose reading of Darwinism posited an evolutionary progression from egoism to altruism. In Spencer's view, "from a beginning point in pure egoism, individuals (and societies too) developed 'ego-altruistic' sentiments, that is, genuine ethical feelings based on the pleasure-pain nexus of social rewards and punishments. A fuller and finer level of development was reached when the individual was motivated by altruism, a product of intelligence and sympathy, and the opposite of egoism" (Martin 49–50). Howells parallels Spencer's terminology (as well as his evolutionary scenario) in his Altrurian romances, using phrases such as "the old egoistic conditions" and "the egoistic world" (159, 163). In Howells's final mention of Altruria in 1918, he tells of its war with a neighboring country, "the autocracy of Egoria" ("Editor's Easy Chair," *Harper's* 137, 589).

In establishing his Utopian state upon the principle of selflessness, Howells, as an ostensible student of evolution, could not have chosen a more problematic scientific basis for his mythical republic. Charles Darwin wrote before the discovery of genetics, but he seems aware that what we recognize today as genetic self-interest was in operation. He had risked his entire theory on the assertion, in chapter VI of his *Origin of Species*, that he could find no evidence of altruism between species in nature. Darwin writes,

> Natural selection cannot possibly produce any modification in a species exclusively for the good of another species; though throughout nature one species incessantly takes advantage of, and profits by, the structures of others. But natural selection can and does often produce structures for the direct injury of other animals. . . . If it could be proved that any part of the structure of any one species had been formed for the exclusive good of another species, it would annihilate my theory, for such could not have been produced through natural selection. (186–87)

While Darwin notes here the absence of altruism *between* species rather than *within* a species, as is the subject in the Altrurian fictions, Howells might have been warned that he was skating on thin ice, biologically speaking, given Darwin's srikingly bold willingness to stake his life's work on this statement.[8] And as many of today's biologists point out, unqualified, disinterested altruism within species is similarly unprecedented in biological theory. Richard D. Alexander argues that it is also the case that "all forms of genetic or reproductive altruism . . . within species are also contrary to evolutionary theory (*Darwinism and Human Affairs* 21). Geneticist Richard Dawkins describes pure, disinterested, and unselfish altruism as "something that has no place in nature, something that has never existed before in the whole history of the world" (*The Selfish Gene* 201). Edward O. Wilson calls altruism "the rarest and most cherished of all human behavior" (*On Human Nature* 149). In his then-controversial 1975 book, *Sociobiology*, Wilson singled out altruism as "the central problem of sociobiology" insofar as it represents behavior that must lessen the genetic fitness of the individual whose behavior benefits only another (3). Wilson asks, "How can altruism, which by definition reduces personal fitness, possibly evolve by natural selection?" (3).

Recognizing that his *Sociobiology* volume had been wrongly interpreted as a categorical argument that genes determine behavior, Wilson and a colleague from theoretical physics, Charles J. Lumsden, published two volumes, *Genes, Mind and Culture: The Coevolutionary Process* in 1981, directed at scientific specialists, and *Promethean Fire, Reflections on the Origin of Mind* in 1983, written for a wider public audience. In the latter work's second chapter, "The Sociobiology Controversy," in addition to summarizing the attack upon human applications of sociobiology by Wilson's colleagues at Harvard, including Marxists Stephen Jay Gould and Richard Lewontin and others, Lumsden and Wilson attempted to take the subject out of the old nature-nurture debate and to counter the belief that the denial of hereditary influence on human behavior was a necessary assumption for social justice. Their work involved challenging both the extreme anthropocentrism of the social sciences and the rigidity of biological determinism with a connection that links genes to culture in an interactive process of gene-culture coevolution. They conclude, "The theory of human nature that prevails in the end will be the one that aligns social behavior and history with all that is known about human biology" (*Promethean Fire* 85).[9] Gene-culture coevolutionary thinking, in various forms, is now common in biology.[10]

Although the subject of human altruism remains a vexing one, as Paul R. Ehrlich's recent book, *Human Natures: Genes, Cultures, and the Human Prospect*, details, most biologists agree that the deep structure of human altruism is based upon self-interest, marked by strong kinship allegiances and reciprocity and closely tied to social rewards and punishments.[11] One of these contemporary biologists, Bobbi Low, writes that all creatures, including humans,

> act as if they could "calculate" some kinds of costs and benefits arising from their actions; these costs and benefits are current ones, not far in the future, and local, not global; and the costs and benefits were not, and need not be, monetary. Our costs and benefits as a social primate are older than the invention of barter and money, though not older than family structure and reciprocity. We evolved as a highly social species, and reciprocity is a powerful force, one we have probably underestimated in our attempts to encourage sustainability. (257)

That is to say, these evolutionary scientists and Howells, were he alive today, might find some common ground in the widespread agreement that cultures can be designed to encourage altruism and other desirable social characteristics and that our predispositions toward reciprocity (and empathy) can be a force for greater social cooperation. (An eighteen-wheeler version of altruism's Golden Rule, overheard at a truck stop: "I always stop for somebody havin' trouble, because if I was havin' trouble, I'd want somebody to stop for me. And that's the whole ball a wax.")

Howells's depiction of Altruria is not so visionary as to deny that humans may be inherently selfish and competitive. But Altruria depicts Howells's assertion that institutions could be created that could leapfrog over even those Spencerian intermediate stages of social rewards and punishments, to completely and virtually immediately control selfish tendencies and allow altruism and genuine selflessness to prosper. What is the likelihood of this occurring? The response, pragmatically and politically, might be that Utopian designs have inevitably failed because their imposition of a single vision is certain to be unacceptable to many conflicting ambitions. This response is also subsumable into a sociobiological explanation and accords with the similarly negative considerations from this perspective. A small group of relatives and friends might constitute the basis for an altruistic community, but not for a large society. Even a few "cheaters" who elect to accept the benefits while ignoring their reponsibilities would be sufficient to scuttle the grand design. If the evolutionary process resulted in favoring the good of society rather than genes, as Low points out, "true genetic altruism would become as common as nepotism and reciprocity. . . . [T]here is, in fact, no evidence that any organism has evolved to assist unrelated individuals without reciprocation" (149).

But it is worth repeating, as do Low and many others, that the possibilities of expanding the circle of reciprocity are many and may offer our best hope for the future.[12] Matt Ridley, in *The Origins of Virtue*, argues, for example, that humans are hyper-social, extremely dependent upon other members of our species, and thus instinctively cooperative, but to understand this and to turn it to social advantage we need to move beyond the conventional social science model. This involves our recognizing that human nature involves instincts that are not immutably deterministic but should be understood and factored into our social thinking as important predispositions (5–7).

What *is*, in terms of our concept of what it means to be human, was forever altered by Darwin and by subsequent scientific discoveries. "We are the first generation," as Peter Singer reminds us in *A Darwinian Left*, "to understand not only that we have evolved, but also the mechanisms by which we have evolved and how this evolutionary heritage influences our behaviour" (63). Only a fraction of this information was current in Howells's lifetime. Genetics, for example, was unavailable to Howells (as it was unavailable to Darwin, Marx, and Freud); thus it could not have influenced his meliorist mission in the Altrurian fictions. Most of us, had we been alive at that time, would probably have thought as Howells did. He took the humanist's view of his age, that Darwinian thought applied only to the natural world and did not encompass the essential human spirit. He wrote, "We shall not have fraternity, human brotherhood, without trying for it. From nature, it did not come; it came from the heart of man, who in the midst of nature is above it" (Who Are Our Brethren?" 935).

But a century later the humanities are still conducted, for the most part, as if the monumental discoveries of Darwin and his followers had never taken place, as if we are "above nature." Yet the essence and basis of modern biology is that humans are a part of the animal world, sharing its evolutionary history and differing from it in degree, not in kind. Enlightened thinking today emphasizes the role of both biological and cultural processes in shaping human behavior. And allowing for these interrelated influences need not place the worthwhile goals of altruism beyond reach. Rather, such knowledge may help bring them closer, because the campaign can proceed from a position of understanding rather than one of ignorance or denial. As Richard D. Alexander states, "To say that we are *evolved* to serve the interests of our genes in no way suggests that we are *obliged* to serve them. . . . Evolution is surely most deterministic for those still unaware of it."[13]

Historian Bernard DeVoto once observed, as a writer, that the best thing about writing something down was that then you could change it. An evolutionary analogue with relevant moral implications might be that the greatest advantage of foregrounding our awareness that our behavior has genetic as well as cultural components is that then we can address the means to change it.

Socially conscious evolutionary biologists—and I have cited none who are not—seem to be as concerned as Howells and the humanists to move society in the direction of cooperation and unselfish behavior. Howells's Altrurian is quite right to condemn, as he does repeatedly, the phrase "That's human nature" when it is used to justify continuing ruthless or selfish social behavior. But to alter the culture that fosters such behavior requires something more than exhortations to be altruistic. "[P]ersuasive calls to be good are themselves a powerful human instinct; obeying them is not" (Ridley 225). Howells himself recognized the selfishness within. In an 1890 letter to his father he wrote with characteristic and rueful self-honesty that he and Mark Twain and their wives "are all of accord in our way of thinking: that is, we are theoretical socialists and practical aristocrats. But it is a comfort to be right theoretically, and to be ashamed of one's self practically" (*Selected Letters*, Vol. 3, 271).

To make an actual change in things calls upon us to acknowledge our obligation to keep learning the meaning of our humanity, to ask why Utopia has never evolved in actual human practice and why it has failed when imposed politically. We are challenged again to adopt something of Bertrand Russell's scientific spirit in refusing to regard our own wishes and hopes as the means of understanding the world. Edward O. Wilson argues convincingly that furthering the frontiers of biological knowledge in human behavior increases individual human freedom and reduces the likelihood of scientific tyranny. He seconds T. H. Huxley's guiding rule that "we must learn what is true in order to do what is right" (*Promethean Fire* vi).

What is true with regard to human altruism remains a topic of concern across the disciplines of evolutionary biology, psychology, anthropology, philosophy, and, to some extent, literary criticism. Literary scholar Joseph Carroll disputes with the sociobiologists on the issue of altruism. He posits sympathy as a distinct human motive outside of any reproductive advantage (as required by sociobiological explanations) but qualifies his argument for sympathy by finding it constrained by factors of group identification and socioeconomic class. From the perspective of evolutionary psychology, Elliott Sober and David Sloan Wilson, in their book *Unto Others: The Evolution and Psychology of Unselfish Behavior*, also pose group selection as a setting for the possible evolution of altruism. (Sociobiologists might respond that group-selected altruism is subsumable under the categories of cooperation or reciprocity, in which self-benefits are present along with benefits to others.)

Writer and English professor William Kittredge, in his *The Nature of Generosity*, discusses human selfishness and altruism from a biologically informed perspective but is moved to call for "long-loop altruism," which reaches beyond kin and group to include strangers as a means of preservation of "biological and cultural mutiplicity and possibility" and for reasons of personal fulfillment (34). Again, it would be pointed out by evolutionary theorists that there are elements of self-benefit as well as altruism in both (worthwhile) goals. Significantly, both Kittredge and the scientist authors of *Unto Others* bring literary texts to bear upon their arguments. Sober and D. S. Wilson use a key passage from Stephen Crane's classic story, "The Open Boat," as a sophisticated rendering of human experience in support of their central ideal of group-selected altruism (334–35). Their explication of Crane's story underscores the interdisciplinary opportunities that await literary scholars prepared to reverse the direction of productive border crossing shown by these two scientists.

The humanitarian spirit of the Altrurian romances and Howells's commitment to social reform, as well as his realist's pragmatic concern for how human nature influences human behavior, suggest that, were he alive today, he would be incorporating into his work such challenging thinking as is now being done in modern evolutionary biology and psychology and related fields.

Howells's treatment of Utopian and communal societies in his realistic fiction, such as the Shakers of *The Undiscovered Country* and *The Vacation of the Kelwyns*, reflects his long-standing interest in such social planning. At the same time his critical judgment did not blind him to the potentiality for disappointment and failure in such societies. The evolutionary cost of the Shaker doctrine of celibacy, for example, was not lost on Howells. (Most religions astutely promote high reproduction among their followers.) But in turning from his measured judgments of these experiments in his novels to the blue-sky meliorism of Altruria, Howells set aside his own realist's precepts and left himself open to the disillusionment that may accompany such optimism, a disillusionment that Howells revealed in a waspish introduction to *Through the Eye of the Needle*, the last of the Altrurian romances, which appeared in 1907. In that introduction Howells gives a sardonic account of the "progress" in social justice in America since the previous visit of the Altrurian traveler, Mr. Homos:

> The Altrurian Emissary visited this country when it was on the verge of the period of great economic depression extending from 1894 to 1898, but, after the Spanish war, Providence marked the divine approval of our victory in that contest by renewing in unexampled measure the prosperity of the Republic. With the downfall of the trusts, and the release of our industrial and commercial forces to unrestricted activity, the condition of every form of labor has been immeasurably improved, and it is now united with capital in bonds of the closest affection. (*The Altrurian Romances* 270–71)

Howells the optimist is driven to bitter irony here, as he often was when social conditions seemed most hopeless. Howells the pejorist, the author of "Editha," *The Rise of Silas Lapham*, *A Hazard of New Fortunes*, and *The Landlord at Lion's Head*, might have expected less and thus found some small victories in the genuine advancements in public life achieved in the dozen years of the Progressive era, advancements that are here lost sight of in the wave of disappointment that accompanied the ever-receding millennium.

The soft-Darwinian belief that mankind must distinguish itself ever more clearly from the animal world in order to achieve moral perfection does not seem to have been seriously questioned by Howells. Mark Twain had questioned it in the most caustic terms in his later works such as *The Mysterious Stranger* and *Letters from the Earth*. Twain's scornful attack upon humanity's pride in its "moral sense," which presumably lifted it above the animals, shows some affinity for biological thinking today, which would find human behavior—the admirable as well as the hateful—animal in origin.[14] But for Howells, the path seemed clear: from the gorilla to the Goth to Jeff Durgin, and then beyond to a Conrad Dryfoos, the saintly youth in *A Hazard of New Fortunes*, or to a Tolstoi, and finally to a nation of virtually instant Altrurians. It was an ill-conceived fast-forward, certain to disappoint.

Environmental Issues in the Altrurian Romances

If Howells had imbibed from his own times a faith in the doctrine of progress that would not survive the first decades of this century, he had also revealed an ecological and environmental awareness in the Altrurian romances that seems, in some respects, remarkably farsighted. As I have argued in chapter three, the enduring appeal of pastoral, one of the oldest of literary forms, seems closely related to our evolutionary history as creatures of the natural world. From the encounters between human society and nature presented in the Altrurian works, it seems clear that Howells looked beyond what Leo Marx has called the sentimental pastoral of illusion and escape and into the longtime implications of human destructiveness toward the natural world. Early in the first novel, the Altrurian stares in horror at a ravaged clear-cut forest near the country hotel (in Jeff Durgin's White Mountains) at which he is a guest. The damage—the narrator ruefully acknowledges—will take the forces of nature a century to repair, though he is not disposed, as is the Altrurian, to question the spirit of free enterprise and private property rights that has caused this affront to the general welfare.

The incident takes on added force for the modern reader, aware that the intervening century, while it may have healed the scars the novel's characters beheld in the New England woods, has seen the march of far greater destruction across the great timber stands of the Upper Midwest and the Pacific Northwest, not to mention the catastrophic destruction of the tropical rain forests. Though the cities of America are Howells's principal targets for satiric attack in the Altrurian fictions, he reveals in this early episode that the bang-and-grab ethics of business America are as evident in the rural retreats as in its great population centers.

The Altrurian's shock at this rape of the fair country is counterpointed in letter three of *Letters of an Altrurian Traveler*, which praises the sense of public life that could create Central Park. This famous urban park, which represented Frederick Law Olmstead's idea of what people thought of as "natural," impresses the Altrurian as "a bit of Altruria in New York," a vision of what America once was and a prophecy of the "truer state" it might become: "It [Central Park] stretches and widens away, mile after mile, in the heart of the city, a memory of the land as it was before the havoc of the city began, and giving to the city-prisoned poor an image of what the free country still is, everywhere" (226). Later, in looking at the park's menagerie, the Altrurian finds himself most interested not in the exotic foreign animals but in "the ragged bison pair . . . , unconscious of their importance as survivors of the untold millions of their kind, which a quarter of a century ago blackened the western plains for miles and miles. There are now only some forty or fifty left; for of all the forces of the plutocratic conditions, so few are conservative [conservationist] that the American buffalo is as rare as the old-fashioned American mechanic" (227). As Central Park suggests the potentiality for the generosity and communal spirit of public life in America, so the pathetic pair of surviving bison are reminders of how much of the common heritage has been wasted and lost.

These scenes relate to the fuller description of Altruria as a kind of pastoral paradise. The state of the country before its time of revolution—which, as has been noted, the Altrurians call "the Evolution" and which was brought about by plebiscite—is described by Mr. Homos as a kind of iron-dealt cleavage, an assault by the industrial juggernaut upon the peaceful garden of human and natural coexistence. The physical description of Altruria after its Evolution resembles a combination of Jeffersonian pastoralism with contemporary scientific technology, a harmonious pairing of the machine and the garden. The nation's old cities, with their ostentatious mansions for the rich and squalid tenements for the poor, are marked for extinction. They are succeeded by a series of smaller regional capitals and one capital for the country.

But it is in the land itself that Altruria finds its essence. All Altrurians share in the cultivation of the earth, which is the most honored occupation. The bioregional organization of the country and its marrying of respect for the earth with human-scale, manageable technology anticipate much of present-day organic and ecological thinking, but with one ominous exception: the massive physical alteration of the country. After a glowing description of the benefits of rearranging Altrurian land forms to benefit the climate (156–57), the Altrurian advises that the United States could have the same results "by cutting off the western shore of Alaska and letting in the Japanese current; and it could be done at the cost of any average war" (390).

We are also reassured that Altruria has "long been cleared of all sorts of wild beasts," emphasizing that the country's altruism extends only to its human inhabitants (390). From our perspective a century later, these paeans to a technology that blithely presumes to remake the world are met with a colder eye. The unparalleled loss of genetic and species diversity since the beginning of the twentieth century is now seen by biologists as a major environmental catastrophe. As Max Oelschlaeger notes, the twentieth century has painfully taught us that "nature is not simply a causal mechanism the technological society can control as an engineer does a train. There are environmental complexities and ecological interrelations that are incapable of being known through external relations and the mechanistic model" (*The Idea of Wilderness* 131).

We can recognize in Howells's visionary terra-forming another version of that technological sublime that has seen bright promises of abundance and ease turn into profound threats to our continued existence on the planet. The entire conception of a Shangri-la, a haven where one can "get away from it all," the very notion of an Altruria so blessed with isolation that it has withdrawn from the problems of the outside world, has today simply disappeared from enlightened thought. Howells may have sensed the implausibility, even in his own day, of such remoteness, especially in the well-traveled Aegean Sea, where he first locates Altruria. In the later Altrurian works, the country seems to have shifted location to somewhere in the vicinity of New Zealand. (Was Howells's evolutionary experiment edging its way toward the Galapagos?) But the point remains: There is no escape from the results of our environmental actions. There is no "away." The defining metaphor for the contemporary world is Kenneth Boulding's spaceship earth, a planetary vessel in which all human actions must be reckoned as part of a self-contained, closed system and in which actions that are apparently beneficial in one respect may have unanticipated and potentially disastrous consequences in another.

Once more, Howells's fictional realism was nearer the mark than his Utopian social planning. Silas Lapham's ham-fisted insistence that "the landscape was made for man, and not man for the landscape," resembles the Altrurians' policy of remaking their island home to suit human needs. But whereas in the Altrurian fictions the results of such thinking are an unexamined success story, in *The Rise of Silas Lapham* they are subjected to searching examination and irony, ranging from journalist Bartley Hubbard's sarcastic digs at Silas's decorating the rocks of the New England countryside with advertisements for his mineral paint; to Silas's losing his competitive advantage in the paint business to a rival paint baron whose appreciation of nature is doubtless no greater than Silas's but whose discovery of a vein of natural gas has given him, for the moment, control of the market; to Silas's final financial collapse and his humbling return to the land from which he arose, where he must finally eat his prideful words.

The Rise of Silas Lapham may thus be read as a kind of ecological parable with Silas as the rampant industrial hero, tearing his fortune from the earth, toward which he exhibits arrogance and disdain, defiling with broad swipes of his paintbrush the land that has sustained his forebears and yielded him, in a wild storm, the iron-ore treasure that becomes his paint mine. After leaving his New England farm for Boston, he indulges himself in a crass display of wealth and power that nevertheless fails to bring him and his family contentment or social acceptance. Finally, he is brought to ruin through equally mysterious economic and natural forces and retreats to the earth—in perhaps too pat an ending for realism—to put down new roots of spiritual regeneration.

The characteristic social note of Howells's best fiction is not the instructive editorials and canned lectures of the Altrurian romances. It is rather the sense that people are bumbling along somehow, accepting the limits of life, doing the best they can, as may be seen in Jeff Durgin's adaptive survival, married and with a child, at the end of *The Landlord at Lion's Head,* while Cynthia Whitwell, Jeff's old sweetheart, suffers a compensatory alliance with the biologically frozen Westover. So, too, can be seen the pluses and minuses with which *The Vacation of the Kelwyns* winds down, and the marriage of the irrepressible Fulkerson to the sensible Madison Woodburn, and the bewildered emergence of the Marches from the catastrophic fates of the Dryfooses and Lindau at the close of *A Hazard of New Fortunes,* or the newly married Penelope Lapham and Tom Corey, making their way despite the hovering family incompatibilities at the conclusion of *Silas Lapham.* As a "biological" reading might remind us, the evolutionary focus falls no longer upon the postreproductive elder Laphams, but upon the young couple who will carry the life force forward into the new century.

Realism, in many ways, shares the qualities of evolutionary comedy that Joseph Meeker celebrates in *The Comedy of Survival.* In considering the various literary genres from his evolutionary perspective, Meeker concludes that comedy best embodies the qualities of an ecologically and evolutionarily successful literature. "Comedy," says Meeker in a statement appropriate to Howells's mimetic successes, "is a celebration, a ritual renewal of biological welfare as it persists in spite of any reasons there may be for feeling metaphysical despair" (24). Howells had said it earlier, in 1901, reflecting that "the process of evolution is not always inspiring, but if we bring patience as well as hope to the spectacle we shall not be without entertainment though we provisionally fail of edification" ("Editor's Easy Chair," *Harper's* 103, 492).[15]

From Meeker's perspective, the tragic mode places human figures like Hemingway's Santiago in conflict with forces that are greater than they, "nature, the gods, moral law, passionate love. . . . Tragic literature and philosophy, then, undertakes to demonstrate that man is equal or superior to his conflict. The tragic hero takes his conflict seriously, and feels compelled to affirm his mastery and his greatness in the face of his own destruction" (22). The tragic spirit, Meeker reminds us, is limited to only a few of the world's cultures, whereas comedy appears in all human civilizations, because, he argues, it grows not from a particular and specialized ideology, but from the biological and evolutionary nature of life:

> Tragedy demands that choices be made among alternatives; comedy assumes that all choice is likely to be in error and that survival depends upon finding accommodations that will permit all parties to endure. Evolution itself is a gigantic comic drama, not the bloody tragic spectacle imagined by the sentimental humanists of early Darwinism. . . . Rather, the evolutionary process is one of adaptation and accommodation, with the various species exploring opportunistically their environments in search of a means to maintain their existence. Like comedy, evolution is a matter of muddling through. (33)

For the nonsurvivors, the battle of life may be more red in tooth and claw, more tragic, than Meeker allows. But for the survivors—and all of us who read this or who are alive today are the product of a line of survivors, at least to the point of reproduction, reaching far back into our evolutionary past—Meeker's judgment is provocative.

Howells's version of his country's future, his bright dream that America prophesies another Altruria, depended upon a straight line of evolutionary progress leading to a fixed apex—the sort of moral celestial staircase that biological thought since Darwin has denied. Life is better than Utopia, as Lewis Mumford, the notable student of Utopias, concluded at the end of his life (D. Miller xiii–xiv). It is also more interesting than a decreed Altruria, as Howells's other works reveal. Howells's altruistic fiat was not based upon evolutionary thought or his observation of human character, but on a visionary rewriting of human nature in which cosmic optimism triumphed over the realist's sharp sense of the probable. Howells's evolutionism finds its major achievements not in the forced meliorism of the Altrurian romances, but in his courageous commitment, seen in his best realist fiction, to the comedy of survival and to the questionable compensations of muddling through.

"So conflicted and ingenious a creature as humans," writes social novelist of today John Updike, "makes an endlessly interesting focus for the meditations of fiction. It seems to me true that *Homo sapiens* will never settle into any Utopia so complacently as to relax all its conflicts and erase all its perversity-breeding neediness" (quoted in Pinker 420). For Howells and for his fictional survivors, their uneasy acceptance of an ambiguous present and an uncertain future becomes their badge of modernity and their claim to our attention.

Afterword

. . . .

> We are in the fullest sense a biological species and will find little ultimate meaning apart from the remainder of life. The fiery circle of disciplines will be closed if science looks at the inward journey of the artist's mind, making art and culture objects of study in the biological mode, and if the artist and critic are informed of the workings of the mind and the natural world as illuminated by the scientific method. In principle at least, nothing can be denied to the humanities, nothing to science.—Edward O. Wilson, *Biophilia*

> Interpretation is the logical channel of consilient explanation between science and the arts.—Wilson, *Consilience*

Art—literature in our case—and science converge in what they may reveal about human nature, says Edward O. Wilson. The aesthetic uniqueness of the individual artistic creation fuses with deeply grounded epigenetic influences to form the texture of memorable language and feeling that comprises the literary experience. As readers and interpreters of literature, those of us in English depend upon assumptions about human nature in all that we do. But as Ian Jobling points out, following Joseph Carroll, "*these assumptions have never been clarified or justified*" (31).

In the preceding chapters I have tried to further the case that the study and criticism of literature have come to a turning point, that the nature-skeptical approaches of the past and present have played themselves out, that the postmodernist credo—borrowed from the social sciences—of human thought and behavior as formed by culture independent of biology has lost credibility, and that a new understanding which recognizes the role of our evolutionary past in shaping both human nature and culture is emerging. This conception holds particular promise for the study of literature and the environment. Literary studies today may find new purpose in redirecting human consciousness, through our teaching and scholarship, to a full consideration of our place in an undismissible but increasingly threatened natural world. Paradoxically, taking nature seriously in this way—embracing the social within the natural—may provide us with our best hope of recovering the disappearing social role of literary criticism.

As I write this, still in the shadow of September 11, 2001, and the catastrophic destruction of the World Trade Center, which claimed thousands of lives, I hear again and again that the world changed forever on that day. The way we conduct our daily lives, our sense of our social environment, our systems of domestic security, our foreign policy, our attitude toward strangers, toward travel, toward our families, toward the future—all has changed. That curiously repeatable loss, "The End of American Innocence," revisited regularly by social critics after each of the major upheavals of the last century—World War I, the Great Depression of the 1930s, the Second World War, Hiroshima, Vietnam, the worsening environmental crisis—is raised up for yet another final farewell.

This time our ingenuousness is the victim of festering tribal enmity. A new version of the old history of world conflict, often a matter of one group of people killing another over religion, must now be assimilated by us somehow, this time involving the increasing possibility of fundamentalist zealots carrying biochemical bombs in ordinary suitcases to lay waste the cities of the hated Others. The end of American innocence may this time be accompanied by a more radical sense of realism regarding the potentialities within our human heritage for more totalizing "ends." If there were any doubt about its destructive potentialities, "human nature" shoulders its way to the head of the line of our most serious concerns.

The ascendancy of this or that literary theory may seem like small potatoes at such a time, in such a world. But ecology's central lesson—everything is connected to everything else—still applies. We have to continue to learn what it is to be human. Steven Pinker faces, more directly than most of us are willing to face, the consequences of our continuing denial of human nature. "Acknowledging human nature," he argues, "does not mean overturning our personal world views. . . . It means only taking intellectual life out of its parallel universe and reuniting it with science and, when it is borne out by science, with common sense. The alternative is to make intellectual life increasingly irrelevant to human affairs, to turn intellectuals into hypocrites, and to turn everyone else into anti-intellectuals" (422).

Darwinian evolutionary theory and the modern life sciences offer the truest basis for dealing with the perils and opportunities of being human, as that awareness affects not only our work as teachers and scholars, but also our relationship with the nature that binds us to life on this decreasingly commodious sphere. Of the triumvirate of great intellects of the modern West, Darwin, Marx, and Freud, only Darwin remains virtually unexplored by literary scholars, even though his discoveries are unparalleled in their importance and influence. Students in the humanities are continuingly shortchanged by an education in which Darwin and the modern biology that is his heritage is ignored.

In a challenging new book, Loyal Rue writes that the epic of evolution is "everybody's story," the story capable of showing us a way out of the social and environmental madness that seems to be closing in upon us. The Apollo 8 photograph from space of the beautiful blue planet upon which we all live our preoccupied lives is Rue's evidence that *there is only one story*, which belongs to everybody. But with Rue my heart is laden, as I wonder along with him whether this one great epic story of our common evolutionary heritage and our only home place can hope to be heard above the babel of conflicting stories told by each culture, its tellers convinced of the veracity of their story and its superiority to all others. As Rue says, those who can tell everybody's story "must stand out there, at some distant remove, where the earth can be seen whole" (127).

Since only a few of us can be astronauts, that remove is available to the rest of us in tangible form only through the famous photograph that we nature-endorsers pin upon walls and tape to car windows. Biologists must have the concept in mind, if not the actual photograph, since, as Dobzhansky noted, nothing in biology makes any sense except as it relates to evolution. Is there room in the discipline of English for this epic evolutionary concept? Should we be telling everybody's story? The recent decoding of DNA repudiates theories of racism and creationism. It strengthens our bonds with other humans and with all forms of life. Does looking from a biological perspective at what we all have in common promise more human understanding and more informed literary study than focusing only upon our differences? Can we close in on an approach that unites the sciences and the humanities rather than driving them apart? Can we ground our idealism in reality rather than illusions?

Innovative thinkers such as Edward O. Wilson, Joseph Meeker, Joseph Carroll, Maxine Sheets-Johnstone, and many others cited in these pages have shown us the possibilities. Biologist Bobbi Low writes, "I would like to reach scholars in the traditional human disciplines with concepts that may be new and tantalizing to them" (xvi). Alison Jolly notes, " Biologists think they have a great deal to tell people. I am a biologist; I think we are right. What emerges is not just a heap of sexy or scary details. Biology offers an increasingly coherent view of human nature and humanity's place in nature" (1–2). Steven Vogel adds, "I'm a biologist. My professional biases start with the belief that we just can't understand history, literature, economics, art, and so forth without taking biology into consideration. . . . [I]n my view undeniable, is the idea that our behavior and even our aesthetic preferences reflect our evolutionary antecedents. . . . I remain persuaded that biology underpins the human world" (321–22).

To paraphrase Henry James, the house of criticism has many rooms. And some of them have hardly been looked into, let alone lived in. There may be nothing more worthwhile for the literary scholar and teacher today than informed interdisciplinary work. Further, I believe that no interdisciplinary study has more to offer us humanists now than evolutionary theory as it relates to biology, ecology, the neurosciences, psychology, anthropology, biogeography, linguistics, and related fields. From all of these and other evolving and emerging disciplines, evidence for the underlying universality of human nature and its complex interrelationship with cultural influences is increasingly affirmed. This is the new frontier of knowledge for the coming century. Thus, the understanding of human nature and human behavior may be redirected along truly ecological lines, allowing our place in the natural and social environment to be reopened for fresh interpretation.

Notes

Introduction

1. See Buell, *The Environmental Imagination* 290–308, for an analysis of Carson's literary and scientific abilities. Precursors to *Silent Spring* can be seen as extending back to the work of Thoreau, George Perkins Marsh, and others. The Carson book's most important immediate predecessor, especially in academic circles, was Aldo Leopold's *A Sand County Almanac* (1949). In *Visions of the Land* Michael A. Bryson studies Carson and Loren Eiseley as his latest exemplars of historical representations of science and nature in America between the 1840s and 1960s.

2. This anthology, *Ecological Crisis: Readings for Survival*, was published in 1970.

3. Early ecocritical articles, besides Rueckert's "Literature and Ecology: An Experiment in Ecocriticism," include those by Fred Erisman ("Western Fiction as an Ecological Parable"), Glen A. Love ("Ecology in Arcadia"), and Thomas J. Lyon ("The Ecological Vision of Gary Snyder"). Although its conception of "ecocriticism" is not, like mine, grounded in the environmental threats arising in the 1960s and 1970s, David Mazel's anthology, *A Century of Early Ecocriticism*, deserves mention here.

4. Among the most active early leaders were Cheryll Glotfelty, Scott Slovic, Michael Branch, and Ann Ronald.

5. These articles can be found on the "Introduction to Ecocriticism" page of *@sle Online* http://www.asle.umn.edu.

6. For a further description of ecocriticism's recent history, see Lawrence Buell's *The Environmental Imagination* and Cheryll Glotfelty's introduction to *The Ecocriticism Reader.*

7. An exception to this general indifference is the Society for Literature and Science. It has, unfortunately, little overlap with the Association for the Study of Literature and Environment.

8. Another and more specific use of the term "practical criticism," unrelated to that of I. A. Richards, is found in Michael J. McDowell's important essay, "The Bakhtinian Road to Ecological Insight," in *The Ecocriticism Reader.*

9. My antithesis would be found in the attitude toward nature ascribed to Michel Foucault. See Éric Darier 6. See also Didier Eribon, Foucault's biographer, who notes that Jacqueline Verdeaux, Foucault's companion on an auto trip

through the Alps, remembers "that Foucault detested nature. Whenever she showed him some magnificent landscape—a lake sparkling in the sunlight—he made a great show of walking off toward the road, saying, 'My back is turned to it'" (Eribon 46). It is also noted by Foucault scholars that he had virtually nothing to say in his writing about the environment or environmental problems. See Darier's anthology, *Discourses of the Environment*, especially the essays by Darier and Neil Levy. For a sustained analysis of Foucault from a Darwinian naturalistic perspective, see Carroll, *Evolution and Literary Theory*.

10. Soper's stance resembles that of my ecocritical colleague SueEllen Campbell, who, in an early and influential ecocritical essay, "The Land and Language of Desire: Where Deep Ecology and Poststructuralism Meet," also walks the divide between contemporary poststructuralist theory and nature-endorsement. In Campbell's conclusion, however, she seems to grant the edge to nature.

11. That is, Hemingway's observation that our sense of the power and dignity of an iceberg is due to the fact that "seven-eighths of it is underwater for every part that shows" (Plimpton 34).

12. See, for example, the descriptions of such tests in Robert Storey's *Mimesis and the Human Animal* and in the essays by Joseph Carroll, Gary Westphal, and Joseph D. Miller in *Biopoetics*, edited by Brett Cooke and Frederick Turner.

1. Why Ecocriticism?

1. See David W. Orr, "What is Education For?" 1, and Daniel D. Chiras, *Lessons From Nature* Ch. 1. A comprehensive current overview of the ecological state of Earth is found in Peter H. Raven's 2002 Presidential Address to the American Association for the Advancement of Science, "Science, Sustainability, and the Human Prospect."

2. Shifting perceptions of overpopulation in recent scientific, popular, and literary works are explored in Ursula K. Heise's "The Virtual Crowds." An anthropologist's perception of the dangers of urban overcrowding is treated in Tom Wolfe's "O Rotten Gotham." The increasing presence of such environmental issues in contemporary writing is addressed later in this chapter.

3. Some will dismiss this as a "just-so story." This complaint will be taken up in chapter 3.

4. Reported in *The Register-Guard*, Eugene, Oregon, 22 April 2001, A-11.

5. See Donald Worster, "Seeing Beyond Culture"; George Sessions, "Reinventing Nature"; Gary Snyder, "The Rediscovery of Turtle Island"; Michael Soulé and Gary Lease, eds., "Introduction," *Reinventing Nature?;* and Kevin R. Marsh, "'This Is Just the First Round,'" 212. Marsh points out that the postmodern attack on the wilderness idea, exemplified by Cronon, fails to recognize that wilderness debates in the last fifty years have focused not on ideas of primitive wilderness values, but on protecting specific places such as those Marsh studies, from industrial logging and mining of resources on public lands. William Cronon argues forcefully in his introduction to the 1996 paperback edition of *Uncommon Ground* that his book should not be linked with current anti-environmentalism.

6. Terry Gifford comments similarly on this issue: "The problem with the deconstructionists of the 'cultural studies' school is that their purely intellectual awareness of 'nature' seems to prevent them from communicating a direct experience of nature from any perspective whatsoever" (*Green Voices* 14).

7. See Sessions, "Reinventing Nature" 36; Worster, "Seeing Beyond Culture" 1144, 1146; and Snyder, "The Rediscovery of Turtle Island" 455–56.

8. Sessions writes as follows on this issue:

> As the only truly radical movement of the 20th century (as environmental historian Stephen Fox points out) it is perhaps understandable that the eco-centric Thoreau/Muir/Leopold/Carson–inspired environmental/ecology movement would eventually come under siege from both the left and the right ends of the political spectrum: the right denying that there is an ecological crisis, promoting continued economic growth and development "business as usual," while trying to destroy the environmental movement; the left apparently also ideologically blinded to the seriousness of the ecological crisis and attempting to coopt the movement towards its social justice agenda. Meanwhile world scientists, professional organizations, conservation biologists, the Wildlands Project, supporters of the Deep Ecology Movement, and many global, national, and local environmental groups try to stay the course. Of course, it is ultimately self-defeating for the international environmental movement to focus on social justice, or even urban pollution, if attention is thereby diverted away from providing realistic solutions to the various aspects of the global ecological crisis. It comes down to a matter of ecological perspectives in which urban pollution problems are seen as a subset of the larger global crisis ("Reinventing Nature" 36).

9. The survival of tribalism, with its attendant religious bigotry and exclusion of those "Others" outside the in-group as less than human, poses a continuing environmental and social threat, particularly when it is combined with a suicidal belief that dying by killing the inhuman Others guarantees one's eternal reward in some heavenly paradise. As Edward O. Wilson notes, 100,000 belief systems are estimated to have existed in history, and many practiced warfare and aggression. Further, "every major religion today is a winner in the Darwinian struggle waged among cultures, and none ever flourished by tolerating its rivals. The swiftest road to success has always been sponsorship by a conquering state" (*Consilience* 244).

10. For those who ponder the perfect response to the dismissive editor, it can be noted that there is a story that once Maclean's book was published by his own University of Chicago Press and became a best-seller, the offending editor, having forgotten his earlier rejection, wrote Maclean a fawning letter of praise, ending with the hope that his firm might have first choice at Maclean's *next* book. Maclean replied that "If the day should ever come when you are the last publisher in the world, and I am the last author, then that will be the end of books, as we know them."

11. A new edition of *The Comedy of Survival* was published in 1997 by the University of Arizona Press.

12. Snyder's pun is triply apt, encompassing not only the pagan nature god Pan and the sense of "applying to all," but also the genus name for the chimpanzee, our nearest genetic neighbor.

13. The work of Lopez himself, one of our very best nature writers, is steeped in science while still respectfully attuned to the mysteries that remain. He offers an important bridge between the politically contested domain of nature-endorsers versus nature-skeptics. (See Coles.)

14. Patrick D. Murphy's *Farther Afield in the Study of Nature-Oriented Literature* (2000) and Lawrence Buell's *Writing for an Endangered World* (2001) provide important new examples of the worldwide presence of evironmentally oriented literature and the wider possibilities of ecocriticism as it moves beyond its nature-writing origins. With its breadth of range and critical acumen, Buell's new book promises to prove as influential as his earlier *The Environmental Imagination.*

Among the recent anthologies are Thomas J. Lyon, ed., *This Incomperable Lande;* Ann Ronald, ed., *Words for the Wild;* Daniel Halpern, ed., *On Nature;* Robert Finch and John Elder, eds., *The Norton Book of Nature Writing;* Lorraine Anderson, Scott Slovic, and John P. O'Grady, eds., *Literature and the Environment;* Scott Slovic and Terrell F. Dixon, eds., *Being in the World;* William H. Shore, ed., *The Nature of Nature;* Scott Slovic, ed., *Getting Over the Color Green;* Susan Fox Rogers, ed., *Another Wilderness;* Chris Anderson and Les Runciman, eds., *A Forest of Voices;* Michael P. Branch and Daniel J. Philippon, eds., *The Height of Our Mountains;* and Bridget Keegan and James C. McKusick, eds., *Literature and Nature.*

Anthologies of ecocriticism include Patrick D. Murphy, ed., *Literature of Nature;* Michael Branch et al., eds., *Reading the Earth;* Patrick Murphy and Greta Gaard, eds., *Ecofeminist Literary Criticism;* John Cooley, ed., *Earthly Words;* Richard Kerridge, ed., *Writing the Environment;* Michael Bennett and David W. Teague, eds., *The Nature of Cities;* John Tallmadge and Henry Harrington, eds., *Reading Under the Sign of Nature;* David Mazel, ed., *A Century of Early Ecocriticism;* Jill Ker Conway, Kenneth Keniston, and Leo Marx, eds., *Earth, Air, Fire, Water;* and Karla Armbruster and Kathleen R. Wallace, eds., *Beyond Nature Writing.*

Among the critical studies of nature writing are Peter A. Fritzell, *Nature Writing and America;* Sean O'Grady, *Pilgrims to the Wild;* Sherman Paul, *For Love of the World;* Scott Slovic, *Seeking Awareness in American Nature Writing;* Don Scheese, *Nature Writing;* Ian Marshall, *Story Line;* Randall Roorda, *Dramas of Solitude;* and Mark Allister, *Refiguring the Map of Sorrow.* Other individual studies are noted in the text.

15. Two recent books, Joni Adamson's *Indian Literature, Environmental Justice, and Ecocriticism,* and Karla Armbruster and Kathleen R. Wallace's *Beyond Nature Writing,* demonstrate how this challenge can be met successfully.

16. Two perceptive essays on natural and environmental aspects of the novel are Dana Phillips's "Don DeLillo's Postmodern Pastoral" and Richard Kerridge's "Small Rooms and the Ecosystem." The Auden line is from his "As I Walked Out One Evening," in his *Collected Poems* 115.

17. See, for example, James Tarter's "Locating the Uranium Mine."

18. On the treatment of nature in Updike's earlier fiction, see Larry E. Taylor, *Pastoral and Anti-Pastoral Patterns.*

19. For a fuller treatment of this and related film themes, see David Ingram, *Green Screen.*

20. Lawrence Buell's chapter, "Toxic Discourse," in his *Writing for an Endangered World*, provides an excellent ecocritical overview of this subject. See also Love, "The Ecological Short Story."

21. Some humanist scholars who have investigated these opportunities include Michael Kowalewski, "Bioregional Perspectives"; Lawrence Buell, "Place," in *The Environmental Imagination* 252–79; and Peter Blakemore, "Writing Home."

22. For a thorough account of Muir's story and its history, see Ronald H. Limbaugh, *John Muir's "Stickeen" and the Lessons of Nature.*

23. An extensive modern account of research on consciousness is found in D. R. Griffin, *The Question of Animal Awareness.* See also Matt Cartmill, "Do Horses Gallop in Their Sleep?," and Ray Hyman, "The Psychology of Deception" 140–43. Animal-human relationships are also examined in Charles Bergman's "Academic Animals" and Barney Nelson's *The Wild and the Domestic.*

24. Representative recent anthologies of nature poetry include Robert Bly, ed., *News of the Universe;* Christopher Merrill, ed., *The Forgotten Language;* and Robert Pack and Jay Parini, eds., *Poems for a Small Planet.* Note also recent critical works on nature and poetry such as John Elder, *Imagining the Earth;* Andrew Elkins, *The Great Poem of the Earth;* Leonard Scigaj, *Sustainable Poetry;* David W. Gilcrest, *Greening the Lyre;* and Bernard W. Quetchenbach, *Back from the Far Field.*

25. Ecologically related readings of the novel can be found, for example, in Robert Zoellner, *The Salt-Sea Mastodon;* Robert M. Greenberg, *Splintered Worlds;* Joseph Andriano, "Brother to Dragons: Race and Evolution in *Moby-Dick*"; Elizabeth Schultz, "Melville's Environmental Vision in *Moby-Dick*"; and Eric Wilson, *Romantic Turbulence.* Bert Bender, in *Sea Brothers*, illustrates the novel's complexity in his counterargument that Melville's biological position in the novel left him within the confines of early nineteenth-century natural theology and that a pre-Darwinian universe allowed Melville to grant Ahab "diabolic grandeur" (37). Darwin influenced Melville, Bender says, but mostly after *Moby-Dick.* Lawrence Buell emphasizes the book's equivocal environmental elements in his rereading in *Writing for an Endangered World* 205.

26. A 1997 volume, *Steinbeck and the Environment*, ed. Susan F. Beegel, Susan Shillinglaw, and Wesley N. Tiffney, Jr., offers an impressive example of the cross-disciplinary possibilities.

27. In an as-yet-unpublished manuscript, "Evolution and 'the Sex Problem,'" Bender extends his study further into the twentieth century.

2. Ecocriticism and Science

1. See Chisholm 3, and Mumford, *The Pentagon of Power* 388.

2. A thorough record of the Sokal affair, including the original essay and many

of the responses and colloquies that it provoked, can be found in the 2000 volume *The Sokal Hoax: The Sham That Shook the Academy*, edited by the editors of *Lingua Franca*. (See Editors in Works Cited.)

3. On the misunderstanding and overstating of Kuhn's *The Structure of Scientific Revolutions*, see, for example, Horgan; Crews, *Skeptical Engagements* 167–68; Carroll, *Evolution* 454–64; Gross and Levitt 139; and Kuhn himself, in *The Essential Tension* xix–xiii, 293–339, and in an interview in Segerstråle 336 and 424. The applicability of Kuhn's thesis to biology is denied by the eminent biologist Ernst Mayr (xiii, 86, 91–104), as in this statement: "Virtually all authors who have attempted to apply Kuhn's thesis to theory change in biology have found that it is not applicable" (96). Even Kuhn's protestations that enthusiasts from the social sciences have carried his meaning too far have had little effect on his followers.

4. See, for example, defense of the scientific method in James E. Alcock; Fox; Gould, "Review of Ruth Bleier"; Gross and Levitt; and Sokal, "A Physicist."

5. See Hrdy xviii; Jolly 3; Tuana viii, 17, 37, 45–47; Gould, "Review of Ruth Bleier" 7. See also Nemecek 100, and Zuk 2–4, 36, 42–46, 200.

6. On these aptitudes, it should be noted that the neurosciences are discovering biological differences in brain activity between the sexes, another challenge to the blank-slate proponents. Besides Barash and Lipton, see Kimura; Carter 71, 77–78; Pinker 341–42, ch. 18; and Carroll 271–72.

7. For further comment on postmodern biology as it relates to ecocriticism, see James Tarter, "Collective Subjectivity and Postmodern Ecology."

8. My thinking on holistic science has been stimulated by conversations on the subject with Rhoda M. Love, by Jonathan Levin's essay, "Between Science and Anti-Science: A Response to Glen A. Love," and by the participation of Maxine Sheets-Johnstone, Michael Cohen, Gerd Bayer, Jonathan Levin, Robert Kern, and others in the session "Science, Faith, and Critical Practice" at the ASLE 2001 meeting in Flagstaff, Arizona. See also Kitano; McKusick 226–27; Vogel 321–23; and Gare 128–32.

9. On realism as concerned with the system that works, see Sterne 108.

10. For a lively contrasting of today's scientists and radical humanists on these matters, see Harold Fromm's "My Science Wars."

11. The coinage "ecolution" is Rhoda M. Love's, in conversation.

12. On the pope's position and on Catholicism and science, see the articles in *Science* by Holden and Seife. See also Pinker 186–87.

13. Quoted in Mayr 178.

14. University of Oregon biologist John Postlethwait has pointed out to me that creationism is not scientific, because it cannot meet one of the criteria of the scientific method—falsifiability. One cannot do an experiment to prove it false.

15. A recent issue of mainline sociology journal, *The American Sociologist* (Summer 1996), contains three articles warning that sociology must move in the direction of biological science if it is to survive. See Imber; Pearson; and Ellis.

16. For an overview of the new biology-literature movement, see "Biopoetics: The New Synthesis," in Cooke and Turner 3–25. W. John Coletta's 1989 doctoral thesis in English at the University of Oregon, "The Great Web of Being:

Ecological and Evolutionary Aesthetics and the Ideology of Biology," is a notable precursor of works from the 1990s. A particularly valuable introduction for the classroom teacher to the new synthesis of biology and culture is Boyd, "Jane, Meet Charles: Literature, Evolution, and Human Nature." See also Evans, "Evolution and Literature," and Pinker on the convergence of art, culture, and biology in *The Blank Slate* 404–20.

17. Maxine Sheets-Johnstone makes a related point in noting the absence of a foundationalist sense of experience, or the resulting possible description of experience, in postmodern thought: "Hence," she concludes, "the distance of postmodern thought and methodology from Darwinian evolutionary biology and from an acknowledgment of Nature to begin with" ("Descriptive Foundations" 172). See Rapp, *Fleeing the Universal,* for another rejoinder to postmodern and poststructuralist theory from a more traditional literary-philosophical position.

18. In his anthology, *Biopoetics,* Cooke collects Edward O. Wilson's statements on art from his various works and provides an informed commentary on them.

19. On the relationship of biodiversity to literature, see Howarth, "Literary Perspectives on Biodiversity."

20. See, for example, Pinker 108–12, 124, 132, 134, 135, 284, 285.

21. In addition to the works mentioned in the text, further support for sociobiology can be found in many books listed in the Works Cited, including those by Hamilton, Lopreato, Goldsmith, Breuer, John Alcock, Maxwell, Wright, Cronk, Barrett, and Cziko.

22. Edward O. Wilson, for example, writes that "most scientists have long recognized that it is a futile exercise to try to define discrete human races. Such entities do not exist" (*On Human Nature* 48). See also Tooby and Cosmides 34–38, and various index entries related to race in Olson and Pinker.

23. As an admirer of most of Berry's earlier work, I find his attack on Wilson extremely disappointing, an attack based, in its spiritual assertions, upon emotion, and in its targeting of "science," more properly directed at technology or the trappings of science. See Harold Fromm's incisive review, "A Crucifix for Dracula: Wendell Berry Meets Edward O. Wilson." For an unequivocal defense of science and spirituality, and of Wilson, see Deming 175.

24. See the preface to Heyes and Huber, eds., *The Evolution of Cognition.*

25. See also Mark Cladis's insightful modern georgic, "On the Importance of Owning Chickens." Cladis writes, "Knowing in the scientific sense need not be confined to the work of the professional scientist. We can all be scientists, if science is the art of careful observation" (204).

3. *Et in Arcadia Ego*

1. Marx also comments on this in his afterword to the 2000 edition of The Machine in the Garden, see 283–85.

2. Two recent articles in *Science* magazine illustrate the wide usage of the term. See Patricia Adair Gowaty, "Behavioral Just-So Stories Recast," and Michael Shermer, "Is God All in the Mind?" Further examples of popular dismissal of just-so stories can be found in John Alcock, *The Triumph of Sociobiology* 64–68, 220.

3. Similar critiques of Gould and/or Lewontin in this context are found in Richard D. Alexander, *The Biology of Moral Systems* 17–19, 223–24; Tooby and Cosmides 77; Pinker 109–33; and John Alcock *The Triumph of Sociobiology*, 64–68, 220. See also John Alcock's "Unpunctuated Equilibrium" and the full accounting in Dennett, particularly chapters 9 and 10. A recent overview of the field of evolutionary psychology (a term that has succeeded sociobiology in many quarters) and the problems of just-so stories can be found in David Sloan Wilson's book review of *Evolutionary Psychology: The New Science of the Mind*, by David M. Buss; see also Pinker 496, entries under "evolutionary psychology."

4. A similar disconnect between anthology editors and some contributors to their volume can be seen in Michael Soulé and Gary Lease's anthology, *Reinventing Nature*, which was planned to question the cultural constructionist assumptions in William Cronon's *Uncommon Ground.*

5. The epigraph to Edward O. Wilson's *On Human Nature* (1978) cites these sentences from David Hume's *An Inquiry Concerning Human Understanding*, published in 1748: "What though these reasonings concerning human nature seem abstract and of difficult comprehension, this affords no presumption of their falsehood. On the contrary, it seems impossible that what has hitherto escaped so many wise and profound philosophers can be very obvious and easy. And whatever pains these researches may cost us, we may think ourselves sufficiently rewarded, not only in point of profit but of pleasure, if, by that means, we can make any addition to our stock of knowledge in subjects of such unspeakable importance."

6. See Simon Schama's final chapter, "Arcadia Redesigned," in his *Landscape and Memory*, for a fuller treatment of pastoral's historical development. See also David M. Halperin, *Before Pastoral: Theocritus and the Ancient Tradition of Bucolic Poetry* esp. 75–89. Halperin calls attention to Leo Marx's idea that pastoral dates from the technological change accompanying the development of agriculture and fixed human settlements and the displacement of herding by farming (Halperin 86–7). That would date the pastoral impulse several millennia earlier than its first discovered written forms. See also Marx, "Environmental Degradation" 331.

7. Erwin Panofsky's famous 1936 essay on pastoral, discussed later in this chapter, offers relevant comments on many of Borgeaud's points.

8. Rhoda Love asked this question in reading a rough draft of this book. Greece is part of the region where the first encounters between the two groups probably took place, and the time of the meeting is not so far removed in the past as to preclude the possibility of the survival of such memories in myth and folklore.

9. On Wilson's literary explorations, see Brett Cooke, "Edward O. Wilson on Art."

10. Eminent biologist John Maynard Smith is reported as saying in 1994, "No one's a genetic determinist anymore." See Gowaty 610. See also William R. Clarke and Michael Grunstein's *Are We Hardwired? The Role of Genes in Human Behavior* (2000). They conclude,

> We have tried to make the case here that, contrary to the wishes of some, genes do play a very important role in human behavior; we pretend otherwise at our peril. But the truth lying at the end of this debate may very well

be that we will never be able completely to untangle genetics from environment, or to untangle either of these from a certain randomness in our behavior that sets up the possibility of free will. The working genes we as a species carry with us today have been repeatedly pounded and shaped by the environment; our DNA is itself a palimpsest on which previous experience with the environment has been repeatedly written and erased (270).

11. A brief overview of Dissanayake's theory and its adaptive capabilities can be found in her article, "'Making Special:' An Undescribed Human Universal and the Core of a Behavior of Art."

12. See *Lingua Franca*, October 2001, for Crain's essay, which includes a critical evaluation from Pinker, Tooby and Cosmides, and others of Dissanayake's thesis that art is an evolutionary adaptation. Crain's article also offers a helpful overview of evolutionary psychology's recent appearance in the field of literary criticism.

13. In a follow-up book on the biophilia hypothesis, Peter H. Kahn's *The Human Relationship with Nature: Development and Culture*, Kahn urges a theoretical approach that extends considerably beyond evolutionary biology, paying more attention to culture and development. He introduces new research on attitudes of children and others in Houston, Brazil, and Portugal. Generally affirming his belief in biophilia, Kahn presents important new research, theory, and pedagogy for the continued refinement of Wilson's hypothesis. See also Andrew Balmford, "Why Conservationists Should Heed Pokémon."

14. The paintings are reproduced in Panofsky, figs. 91–94.

15. William Empson argues in *Some Versions of Pastoral* that pastoral does not even require country settings. Empson applied the term *pastoral*, for example, to so urbanized a work as John Gay's *Beggar's Opera*. For Empson, the key strategy of pastoral is human reconciliation, such as between rich and poor social classes.

16. *Wilderness* is a term difficult to define for ecologists, as well as for ecocritics. But I follow Roderick Nash and Gary Snyder in seeing it in relative terms as one end—or virtually one end—of the spectrum, on the other end of which is civilization. Wilderness is land showing minimal human influence. See Nash, *Wilderness* 6, and Snyder, "The Rediscovery of Turtle Island" 456.

17. For a brief survey of new works in nature writing, see chap. 1, n. 14.

4. Place, Style, and Human Nature in Willa Cather's *The Professor's House*

1. Quoted in Casey, *The Fate of Place* ix.

2. Other testimonials to the power of place can be found in Lutwack's *The Role of Place in Literature.*

3. Leonard Lutwack's *The Role of Place in Literature* (1984) is a notable exception. Other place-related studies related to Cather's works can be found later in this chapter.

4. In his ecocritical study *Sustainable Poetry*, literary critic Leonard Scigaj persuasively applies Merleau-Ponty's phenomenological ideas, and those of his

interpreters such as David Abram in *The Spell of the Sensuous*, to four contemporary nature poets.

5. *The Philosophy of Literary Form* 8, 9, 37. See Randall Roorda, "KB in Green," for insightful connections between ecocriticism and Burke.

6. Many of these articles have appeared in the pages of *Western American Literature*, which, during the long tenure of Tom Lyon as editor, kept alive the sense of place and region when it was all but dismissed in other literary venues.

7. For further connections between Cather and science, see, for example, Love "The Cowboy in the Laboratory"; Quirk; and Reynolds.

8. "Tom Outland's Story" may seem to be confined to book two of the novel's tripartite structure, but the story of Tom Outland permeates the entire novel.

9. Epigenesis refers to "the total content, and results, of the interaction between genome and environment during development" (Lumsden and Wilson, *Genes, Mind and Culture* 259).

10. For a more recent interview with Midgley and her qualified support of sociobiology, see Segerstråle 74–77.

11. The history of the twentieth-century conflict over human nature versus culture is described in the books by Donald Brown; Degler; Ehrlich *(Human Natures);* Segerstråle; and Pinker.

12. See, for example, Donald Brown 54–87, 130–141; Dissanayake 20–23, 109–126; Singer 31–43; Sheets-Johnstone, *The Roots of Power* 328–29; Edward O. Wilson, *On Human Nature* 21–22; Carroll, *Evolution and Literary Theory* 158–59; and Pinker 55, 101–2, 435–39.

13. The editors of *The Adapted Mind*, Barkow, Cosmides, and Tooby, say in their introduction, "The central premise of *The Adapted Mind* is that there is a universal human nature, but that this universality exists primarily at the level of evolved psychological mechanisms, not of expressed cultural behaviors. On this view, cultural variability is not a challenge to claims of universality, but rather data that can give one insight into the structure of the psychological mechanisms that helped generate it" (5).

14. Judith Fryer, in her important essay, "Desert, Rock, Shelter, Legend," adds *Death Comes for the Archbishop* to this grouping as part of Cather's emotional attraction to the desert Southwest.

15. On Cather and heights see Love, "The Cowboy in the Laboratory" 118, 165, n. 15. See also McGiveron, "From a 'Stretch of Grey Sea' to the 'Extent of Space.'"

16. On this point see the discussion in Randall 217–18 and in Reynolds 124–49. Today's anthropologists would point out that though the cliff dwellings were abandoned over five hundred years ago, the people who inhabited them did not vanish but remained in the region as the Hopis and other presently existing cultures that claim Pueblo ancestry.

17. For a countering analysis to mine, see Michaels, *Our America* 35–38, 50–52, 69–70 *et passim.* Michaels explores Tom's identification with the Indians and Cather's anti-Semitism in the novel (the latter having been previously detailed in James Schroeter's essay on the novel in his *Willa Cather and Her Critics*) as these

relate to examples of virulent nativism in the 1920s. Criticism of American exceptionalism has now swung from the former emphasis on American innocence to one on American hegemony. One might question whether the notion of exceptionalism itself is not in need of questioning, in light of an evolutionary perception of human nature and history and what these reveal as a tendency for powerful groups everywhere and throughout time to victimize their weaker neighbors or to attempt to acculturate them to their own purposes. The United States, like all previous and existing cultures with the power to exercise such domination, doubtless has plenty to be ashamed of.

18. See n. 17. See also, for example, the material on Cather's novel in Eric Gary Anderson, *American Indian Literature and the Southwest.* Outland's later career as physicist-inventor has perhaps a more ominous dark side than his excavating sins. See Love, "The Cowboy in the Laboratory" 162–63.

19. The archetypal fear of, and fascination with, snakes is documented in *The Serpent's Tale: Snakes in Folklore and Literature*, ed. Gregory McNamee, who writes,

> We travel the world, and wherever we go there are snake stories to entertain us. That much suggests a human universal. But why all the attention to snakes? First and foremost, because we are primates, and venomous snakes cause sickness and death in primates and other mammals thoughout the world. For this reason all primates combine a native fear of snakes with a strange fascination for them. As human beings, our genetic aversion to snakes is ancient, bred in the bone, and those ancestral memories continue to rattle around in our brains. We would do better these days to fear guns, knives, and electricity, but instead we react with immediate dread when confronted with a snake. Even many who have never seen one have sweat-dream phobias about ophidians. Fear is a great inspirer of songs to dispel it. And from songs spring folktales, the root of literature (xiii).

20. See, for example, Edward O. Wilson, *Consilience* 74–81; Carroll 174–75; Storey 84–86. Likewise, Freudian discounting of place moves us even further from the explanatory power of evolutionary biology.

21. Later in his book, Storey explores the archetypes of C. G. Jung and points out that while many of Freud's original ideas have been replaced, Jung's are only now receiving appropriate attention (77–79).

22. In the Notes to *Consilience* (1998), Edward O. Wilson offers a useful bibliography of the main works, up to that time, contributing to the biological theory of the interpretation and history of the arts. See 313–14.

23. See Cather, "On *The Professor's House*" 30.

24. The Merleau-Ponty quotation is from Langer 154. The Shakespeare reference is found in *As You Like It*, Act II, Scene 1. On the knowledge of place as grounded in the senses, see also Kent C. Ryden, *Mapping the Invisible Landscape* 38–39.

25. Cather's biographer, E. K. Brown, notes the slight differences between Cather's and Longfellow's versions of the poem (244).

26. *On Writing* 42–43. For a fuller account of Cather's drive toward stylistic simplification, see Love "*The Professor's House.*"

27. Cather's own struggle with the "otherness" of anti-Semitism is revealed in Marsellus's problematic role and character and in the ambivalence with which he is received by the other characters. For a detailed analysis, see Schroeter, Michaels.

28. On entering unfamiliar country, see also Orians, G. H., and J. H. Heerwagen, "Evolved Responses to Landscapes," in Barkow et al., *The Adapted Mind.* The neuroscientific significance of coming into the country is described in David Bradley's "Moving Through the Landscape."

29. Joseph Conrad's affirmation of the author's need, above all, to make the reader *see* invokes and predicts neuroscientist Semir Zeki's recent assertion that "[o]ur inquiry into the visual brain takes us into the very heart of humanity's inquiry into its own nature" ("The Visual Image" 39).

30. See Appleby 25–26.

31. See Paul Shepard, "Place in American Culture" 32.

32. Cather's conception of the destruction of the Anasazis' fixed-emplacement "higher" civilization by roving hunter-gatherers contrasts interestingly with Paul Shepard's argument in *The Tender Carnivore and the Sacred Game* that the birth of agriculture and a settled existence marked the end of ecological health and harmony, which characterized hunting-gathering culture. In her early work Cather often praised the primitive spirit but admired those like the Anasazis whose art and architecture raised human achievement to a new level. For further questioning of Utopian assumptions about the hunter-gatherer period, see, for example, Storey 20; Pinker 57–58; and Flores.

33. There is recently discovered evidence of cannibalism among the Anasazis. See Holden, "Molecule"; Plog 150; and Pinker 305–7.

34. See entries indexed under "narrative" in Carroll, Storey, and Entrikin for further discussion of narrative in this context.

5. Hemingway among the Animals

1. As Keith Carabine points out, the story is "euphoric" despite the "nightmare at noontide" emphasis in most of the criticism (39–44). Philip Young's Preface to *The Nick Adams Stories* explains how the proper chronological placing of the story, after the World War I stories, makes its submerged anxieties more understandable.

2. Hovey 33. See also Monk.

3. The connections for Hemingway between fishing and tragedy are further revealed in his description to F. Scott Fitzgerald of his idea of heaven: "a big bull ring with me holding two barrera seats and a trout stream outside" (*Selected Letters* 165).

4. Hemingway, *Selected Letters* 681, 659, 867, 679, 847.

5. Hochner 152. Hemingway voices similar sentiments in *Death in the Afternoon* 233 and in *Selected Letters* 449. See also Drinnon 29.

6. See *Selected Letters* 277, 370, 374, 416, 636, 644, 648, 729, 771–72. See also Plimpton 35.

7. *Selected Letters* 416, 582. See also Leicester Hemingway 107, 120, and pictures between 224 and 225; Jack Hemingway 101.

8. See *Selected Letters* 697 and *Across the River* 123.

9. *Death in the Afternoon* 4; *A Sand County Almanac* 262. In his perceptive essay, "The Happiness of the Garden: Hemingway's Edenic Quest," John Leland reaches a similar conclusion to that expressed here, saying that "no real land can sustain the demands of the Hemingway hero."

10. Ueno 74. Meeker also sees tragedy as a peculiarly Western cultural tradition (42).

11. While Joseph Wood Krutch claimed in *The Modern Temper* in 1929 that tragedy was no longer possible in modern life because we have lost confidence in the nobility of humanity, tragedies, or some equivalent to them, continue to be written and critics to deal with them. Wirt Williams's *The Tragic Art of Ernest Hemingway* (1981) examines Hemingway's works from the perspective of the tragic condition, though not from the ecological viewpoint taken here. Major earlier critical books on Hemingway by Philip Young, Carlos Baker, and Jackson J. Benson all found tragedy to be central to Hemingway's art. In considering the possible endings of *The Garden of Eden*, Robert E. Fleming cites the pattern of tragedy running through all of Hemingway's work and thought as evidence that the optimistic ending of the Jenks edition of the novel is counter to Hemingway's probable intentions ("The Endings").

12. See, for example, Faulkner's tribute in *Shenandoah* and the essays by Gurko, Jobes, Burhans, and Sylvester in Jobes. Although he does not see the story as tragic, Earl Rovit perceptively links the novel to "Big Two-Hearted River," a connection that I have followed here.

13. Wolfgang Wittkowski underscores the combative fighter-in-the-ring quality of Santiago, and how this opposes and subsumes his Christian aspects.

14. For details of the filming, see Laurence.

15. *Selected Letters* 771–72. On Hemingway's verbal rapport with bears, see Hochner 32.

16. See Burwell 77, 137, 208. See also Hemingway, *True at First Light* 98.

17. See Donaldson 83–84. For a remembrance of Hemingway's positive fishing ethics and of the changes in his attitude toward "killing your limit" over his later years, see Jack Hemingway 18, 80.

18. Gregory Hemingway's daughter, Lorian Hemingway, grew up rebellious and followed a chaotic existence as a drifter and alcoholic for many years. She broke free at last, through fishing and the help of fishing elders, and caught herself a life, as she records in her remarkable memoir, *Walk on Water.* Fishing in her life became the healing restorative, the redemption through water, that was never enough for her grandfather, whose legacy haunted her.

19. The male fish may have jumped for other reasons, Harvard animal behaviorist Marc D. Hauser might caution. In his book *Wild Minds*, Hauser questions many interpretations of animal behavior but also finds that animals have core emotions, communicate, use tools, solve problems using symbols, learn by

imitation, and so forth. See, for example, 4–10, xviii–xix. Generally, Hauser's judgments accord closely with Hemingway's observations.

20. See Love, "The Ecological Short Story" 50–55. Further connections between Hemingway and animals are explored in several articles in Robert Fleming, ed., *Hemingway and the Natural World.*

6. The Realist in Altruria

1. See Buell, *The Environmental Imagination* 87–88. See also J. P. Sterne, *On Realism;* Tom Wolfe, "Stalking the Billion-Footed Beast"; and Frederick Turner, "In Praise of the Real: Reforming the Humanities."

2. For general background, see Frederick William Conner, *Cosmic Optimism.* The principal scholarship on Howells and evolution is summarized by Donald Pizer in his essay, "The Evolutionary Foundation of William Dean Howells' *Criticism and Fiction.*" An important recent addition to the study of Howells and Darwin is Bert Bender's *The Descent of Love: Darwin and the Theory of Sexual Selection in American Fiction, 1871–1926.*

3. For explication of the novel in addition to that presented here, see Love, "*The Landlord at Lion's Head.*" For the critical reaction to the novel, see John W. Crowley, "Giving a Character."

4. All three works are included in the Indiana University Press edition of *The Altrurian Romances,* from which all citations are taken. For the full publishing history, see the introduction to this edition by Clara and Rudolph Kirk.

5. A character in Ursula LeGuin's *Always Coming Home* seems to have the Altrurian's number when she says, "I never did like smartass utopians. Always so much healthier and saner and sounder and fitter and kinder and tougher and wiser and righter than me and my friends. People who have the answers are boring, niece. Boring, boring, boring" (335). The passage was pointed out to me by Nick O'Connell, to whom I am grateful.

6. The Altrurian Romances reflect the majority attitudes of their time in focusing upon social differences in white America. They have almost nothing to say about issues of race and ethnicity. Howells's banker at one point enlightens the Altrurian on the inequalities of the time, saying, "You are no more likely to meet a workingman in American society than you are to meet a colored man" (39).

7. Robert Storey (37) cites this passage to undercut Gould's attack on Wilsonian sociobiology. For further analysis of Gould's equivocation on this issue, see Dennett.

8. I am indebted to Garrett Hardin's essay for bringing this important point to my attention.

9. Joseph Lopreato's *Human Nature and Biocultural Evolution* (1984) provides an early balanced perspective on the sociobiology controversy that acknowledges Wilson's occasional ambiguities on the extent of genetic conditioning, but also notes his sensitivity to cultural influence and its place in sociobiological thinking. See, especially, 17–36. See also the defense of Wilson against charges of genetic determinism by distinguished biologist Ernst Mayr in his *This Is Biology*

203–5. Note also the general acceptance of sociobiology as normal science and its alliance of genetic with social, historical, personal, and other influences on human behavior described in preceding chapters in this book.

10. For a listing of other models of gene-culture coevolution, see Edward O. Wilson, *Consilience* 306, and Blackmore 108.

11. We can and do alter genetic evolution with cultural evolution (insofar as the two can be spoken of as disentagled), as Ehrlich emphasizes. "Genetic instructions are of great importance to our natures, but they are not destiny" (9).

Kinship alliances have been studied historically most notably by biologists J. B. S. Haldane, George Price, and William Hamilton. Reciprocal altruism, detailed in the work of Robert Trivers, William Hamilton, Robert Axelrod, Richard D. Alexander, and others, finds that altruistic acts are performed in the expectation that the person benefited will return the favor in the future. Many of the biologists and other students of human nature cited earlier employ these basic sociobiological considerations in their work. Matt Ridley's *The Origins of Virtue* offers a useful overview of the self-interest basis of altruism.

12. Susan Blackmore, in *The Meme Machine*, explores Richard Dawkins's positing of the possible existence of the "meme," a sociocultural equivalent of the biological gene. From a "memetic" standpoint, Blackmore puts forth the possibility of an "altruism trick," in which a meme that enhances an individual's image as kind and generous, or his or her identification with altruistic beliefs, will increase the possibility of that meme's being spread (162–74). But evolutionary biologist Lee Cronk would give this a conventional biological explanation, which he attributes to Richard D. Alexander: "In 'direct' reciprocity, I do something nice for you because there is a good chance that you will some day return the favor. In 'indirect' reciprocity, I do something nice for you even if you are totally incapable of returning the favor, because someone else may be watching, and I may be able to get a reputation as an especially nice, 'moral' guy who helps his fellow man in need" (Cronk 97).

13. From Alexander's *The Biology of Moral Systems* 40. Quoted in Barlow 191.

14. See, for example, Edward O. Wilson "Human Decency Is Animal"; Ridley; and Pinker 166–67.

15. Howells's choice of the word *entertainment* underscores Kermit Vanderbilt's judgment that, after Howells's unsuccessful defense of the Haymarket anarchists in the late 1880s, he came to realize that his theory of aesthetic realism was incompatible with direct advocacy of social reforms (181). Howells's frustrations in this regard, as Vanderbilt notes, "reveal the continuing lack of resolution in the mind of a natural conservative with a humanitarian conscience who was trying, but ultimately was unable, to respond to the radical democracy of the new industrialism in the East" (142).

Works Cited

Abbey, Edward. *Desert Solitaire: A Season in the Wilderness.* New York: Ballantine, 1968.

Abram, David. *The Spell of the Sensuous.* New York: Random, 1996.

Acocella, Joan. *Willa Cather and the Politics of Criticism.* Lincoln: U of Nebraska P, 2000.

Adamson, Joni. *American Indian Literature, Environmental Justice, and Ecocriticism: The Middle Place.* Tucson: U of Arizona P, 2001.

Alcock, James E. "The Propensity to Believe." *The Flight From Science and Reason.* Eds. Paul R. Gross, Norman Levitt, and Martin W. Lewis. New York: NY Academy of Sciences, 1996. 64–78.

Alcock, John. *The Triumph of Sociobiology.* New York: Oxford UP, 2001.

———. "Unpunctuated Equilibrium in the *Natural History* Essays of Stephen Jay Gould." *Evolution and Human Behavior* 19 (1998): 321–36.

Alexander, Richard J. *The Biology of Moral Systems.* Hawthorne, NY: de Gruyter, 1987.

———. *Darwinism and Human Affairs.* Seattle: U of Washington P, 1979.

Allister, Mark. *Refiguring the Map of Sorrow: Nature Writing and Autobiography.* Charlottesville: UP of Virginia, 2001.

Anderson, Chris, and Lex Runciman, eds. *A Forest of Voices: Reading and Writing the Environment.* Mountain View, CA: Mayfield, 1995.

Anderson, Eric Gary. *American Indian Literature and the Southwest.* Austin: U of Texas P, 1999.

Anderson, Lorraine, Scott Slovic, and John P. O'Grady, eds. *Literature and the Environment: A Reader on Nature and Culture.* New York: Longman, 1999.

Andriano, Joseph. "Brother to Dragons: Race and Evolution in *Moby-Dick*," *American Transcendental Quarterly* 10 (1996): 141–53.

Appleton, Jay. *The Symbolism of Habitat.* Seattle: U of Washington P, 1990.

Applewhite, James. "Postmodernist Allegory and the Denial of Nature." *Kenyon Review, New Series* 11.1 (Winter 1989): 1–17.

Argyros, Alexander J. *A Blessed Rage for Order: Deconstruction, Evolution, and Chaos.* Ann Arbor: U of Michigan P, 1991.

Aristotle. *The Poetics of Aristotle.* Trans. Stephen Halliwell. Chapel Hill: U of North Carolina P, 1987.

Armbruster, Karla, and Kathleen R. Wallace, eds. *Beyond Nature Writing: Expanding the Boundaries of Ecocriticism.* Charlottesville: UP of Virginia, 2001.

Auden, W. H. *Collected Poems.* Ed. Edward Mendelson. New York: Random House, 1976.

———. "Introduction: Concerning the Unpredictable." *The Star Thrower.* By Loren Eiseley. New York: Harcourt, 1978. 15–24.

Balmford, Andrew. "Why Conservationists Should Heed Pokémon." *Science* 295 (29 March 2002): 2367.

Barash, David P., and Judith Eve Lipton. *Gender Gap: The Biology of Male-Female Differences.*" New Brunswick: Transactions, 2002.

Barkan, Elazar. *The Retreat of Scientific Racism.* Cambridge: Cambridge UP, 1992.

Barkow, Jerome H., Leda Cosmides, and John Tooby, eds. *The Adapted Mind: Evolutionary Psychology and the Generation of Culture.* New York: Oxford UP, 1992.

Barlow, Connie, ed. *From Gaia to Selfish Genes: Selected Writings in the Life Sciences.* Cambridge, MA: MIT P, 1991.

Barrett, Louise, Robin Dunbar, and John Lycett. *Human Evolutionary Psychology.* Princeton, NJ: Princeton UP, 2002.

Bate, Jonathan. *Romantic Ecology: Wordsworth and the Environmental Tradition.* London: Routledge, 1991.

———. *The Song of the Earth.* Cambridge, MA: Harvard UP, 2000.

Beardsley, Monroe. "Style and Good Style." *Contemporary Essays on Style.* Ed. Glen A. Love and Michael Payne. Glenview, IL: Scott, 1969. 3–15.

Beegel, Susan F., Susan Shillinglaw, and Wesley N. Tiffney, Jr., eds. *Steinbeck and the Environment: Interdisciplinary Approaches.* Tuscaloosa: U of Alabama P, 1997.

Bellamy, Edward. *Looking Backward, 2000–1887.* Boston: Houghton, 1917.

Bender, Bert. *The Descent of Love: Darwin and the Theory of Sexual Selection in American Fiction, 1871–1926.* Philadelphia: U of Pennsylvania P, 1996.

———. "Evolution and 'the Sex Problem': Soundings of Life and Love in American Fiction during the Eclipse of Darwinism." Unpublished book manuscript.

———. *Sea-Brothers: The Tradition of American Sea Fiction from Moby-Dick to the Present.* Philadelphia: U of Pennsylvania P, 1988.

Bennett, Michael, and David W. Teague, eds. *The Nature of Cities: Ecocriticism and Urban Environments.* Tucson: U of Arizona P, 1999.

Bergman, Charles. "Academic Animals: Making Nonhuman Creatures Matter in Universities." *ISLE* 9.1 (Winter 2002): 141–47.

Berry, Wendell. *Life Is a Miracle: An Essay Against Modern Superstition.* Washington, DC: Counterpoint, 2000.

Birch, Charles. "The Postmodern Challenge to Biology." *The Reenchantment of Science.* Ed. David Ray Griffin. Albany: State U of New York P, 1988. 69–78.

Blackmore, Susan. *The Meme Machine.* New York: Oxford UP, 1999.

Blakemore, Peter. "Writing Home: Inhabitation and Imagination in American Literature." Diss. U of Oregon, 1998.

Bly, Robert, ed. *News of the Universe: Poems of Twofold Consciousness.* San Francisco: Sierra Club Books, 1980.

Borgeaud, Phillipe. *The Cult of Pan in Ancient Greece.* Trans. Kathleen Atlass and James Redfield. Chicago: U of Chicago P, 1988.

Boulding, Kenneth. "The Economics of the Coming Spaceship Earth." *Ecological Crisis.* Ed. Glen A. Love and Rhoda M. Love. New York: Harcourt, 1970. 307–19.

Bowers, C. A. *The Culture of Denial: Why the Environmental Movement Needs a Strategy for Reforming Universities and Public Schools.* Albany: State U of New York P, 1997.

Boyd, Brian. "Jane, Meet Charles: Literature, Evolution, and Human Nature." *Philosphy and Literature* 22.1 (April 1998): 1–30.

Bradley, David. "Moving Through the Landscape." *Science* 295 (29 March 2002): 2385–86.

Branch, Michael P., et al. *Reading the Earth: New Directions in the Study of Literature and Environment.* Moscow: U of Idaho P, 1998.

Branch, Michael P., and Daniel J. Philippon, eds. *The Height of Our Mountains.* Baltimore: Johns Hopkins UP, 1998.

Breur, Georg. *Sociobiology and the Human Dimension.* Cambridge: Cambridge UP, 1982.

Brown, Donald. *Human Universals.* Philadelphia: Temple UP, 1991.

Brown, E. K. *Willa Cather: A Critical Biography.* New York: Knopf, 1953.

Bryson, Michael A. *Visions of the Land: Science, Literature, and the American Environment from the Era of Exploration to the Age of Ecology.* Charlottesville: UP of Virginia, 2002.

Budd, Louis J. "Altruism Arrives in America." *American Quarterly* 8 (1956): 40–52.

Buell, Lawrence. *The Environmental Imagination: Thoreau, Nature Writing, and the Formation of American Culture.* Cambridge, MA: Harvard UP, 1995.

———. *Writing for an Endangered World.* Cambridge, MA: Harvard UP, 2001.

Burhans, Jr., Clinton. "*The Old Man and the Sea:* Hemingway's Tragic Vision of Man." *Twentieth Century Interpretations of The Old Man and the Sea.* Ed. Katharine T. Jobes. Englewood Cliffs, NJ: Prentice, 1968. 72–80.

Burke, Kenneth. *The Philosophy of Literary Form: Studies in Symbolic Action.* Louisiana State UP, 1941.

———. "Psychology and Form." *Counter-Statement.* Los Altos, CA: Hermes, 1953. 29–44.

Burwell, Rose Marie. *Hemingway: The Postwar Years and the Posthumous Novels.* New York: Cambridge UP, 1996.

Butler, Octavia. *Parable of the Sower.* New York: Warner, 1993.

Campbell, SueEllen."The Land and Language of Desire: Where Deep Ecology and Poststructuralism Meet." *The Ecocriticism Reader.* Ed. Cheryll Glotfelty and Harold Fromm. Athens: U of Georgia P, 1996. 124–36.

Carabine, Keith. "'Big-Two-Hearted River': A Reinterpretation." *The Hemingway Review* 1.2 (Spring 1982): 39–44.

Carroll, Joseph. "The Deep Structure of Literary Representations." *Evolution and Human Behavior* 20 (1999): 159–73.
———. *Evolution and Literary Theory.* Columbia: U of Missouri P, 1995.
Carson, Rachel. *Silent Spring.* New York: Fawcett, 1962.
Carter, Rita. *Mapping the Mind.* Berkeley: U of California P, 1998.
Cartmill, Matt. "Do Horses Gallop in Their Sleep?" *The Key Reporter* 66:1 (Autumn 2000): 6–9.
Casey, Edward S. *The Fate of Place: A Philosophical History.* Berkeley: U of California P, 1997.
———. *Getting Back into Place: Toward a Renewed Understanding of the Place World.* Bloomington: Indiana UP, 1993.
Cather, Willa. *Alexander's Bridge.* 1912. New York: Meridian, 1988.
———. *Death Comes for the Archbishop.* 1927. New York: Knopf, 1967.
———. *My Ántonia.* 1918. Boston: Houghton, 1949.
———. "The Novel Démeublé." *On Writing.* New York: Knopf, 1949. 35–43.
———. "On the Art of Fiction." *On Writing.* New York: Knopf, 1949. 101–4.
———. "On *The Professor's House.*" *On Writing.* New York: Knopf, 1949. 30–32.
———. *On Writing.* New York: Knopf, 1949.
———. *The Professor's House.* 1925. New York: Random, 1973.
———. *The Song of the Lark.* 1915. Boston: Houghton, 1937.
———. *Willa Cather in Person.* Ed. L. Brent Bohlke. Lincoln: U of Nebraska P, 1986.
Chiras, Daniel D. *Lessons From Nature: Learning to Live Sustainably on the Earth.* Washington, DC: Island, 1992.
Chisholm, Anne. *Philosophers of the Earth: Conversations with Ecologists.* New York: Dutton, 1972.
Cladis, Mark. "On the Importance of Owning Chickens." *ISLE* 7.2 (Summer 2000): 199–211.
Clark, William R., and Michael Grunstein. *Are We Hardwired?: The Role of Genes in Human Behavior.* New York: Oxford UP, 2000.
Cohen, Michael P. *A Garden of Bristlecones: Tales of Change in the Great Basin.* Reno: U of Nevada P, 1998.
Cokinos, Christopher. "A Hawk in the Margin's Cage: Robinson Jeffers and the Norton Anthologies." *ISLE* 1.2 (Fall 1993): 25–44.
Coles, Romand. "Ecotones and Environmental Ethics: Adorno and Lopez." *The Nature of Things: Language, Politics, and the Environment.* Ed. Jane Bennett and William Chaloupka. Minneapolis: U of Minnesota P, 1993. 226–49.
Coletta, W. John. "The Great Web of Being: Ecological and Evolutionary Aesthetics and the Ideology of Biology." Diss. U of Oregon, 1989.
Conner, Frederick William. *Cosmic Optimism: A Study of the Interpretation of Evolution by American Poets from Emerson to Robinson.* Gainesville: U of Florida P, 1949.
Conway, Jill Ker, Kenneth Keniston, and Leo Marx, eds. *Earth, Air, Fire, Water: Humanistic Studies of the Environment.* Amherst: U of Massachusetts P, 1999.

Cooke, Brett. "Edward O. Wilson on Art." *Biopoetics: Evolutionary Explorations in the Arts*. Ed. Brett Cooke and Frederick Turner. Lexington, KY: ICUS, 1999. 97–118.

Cooke, Brett, and Frederick Turner, eds. *Biopoetics: Evolutionary Explorations in the Arts*. Lexington, KY: ICUS, 1999.

Cooley, John, ed. *Earthly Words: Essays on Contemporary American Nature and Environmental Writers*. Ann Arbor: U of Michigan P, 1994.

Crain, Caleb. "The Artistic Animal." *Lingua Franca* 11.7 (Oct. 2001): 28–37.

Crews, Frederick. Foreword. *After Poststructuralism: Interdisciplinarity and Literary Theory*. Ed. Nancy Easterlin and Barbara Riebling. Evanston, IL: Northwestern UP, 1993.

Cronk, Lee. *That Complex Whole: Culture and the Evolution of Human Behavior*. Boulder, CO: Westview Press, 1999.

Cronon, William, ed. *Uncommon Ground: Rethinking the Human Place in Nature*. 1995. New York: Norton Paperback Edition, 1996.

Crowley, John W. "Giving a Character: Howellsian Realism in *The Landlord at Lion's Head*." *Harvard Library Bulletin* 5.1 (Spring 1994): 53–66.

———. "Howells in the Eighties: A Review of Criticism, Part 1." *ESQ* 32 (1986): 253–77.

Cziko, Gary. *The Things We Do: Using the Lessons of Bernard and Darwin to Understand the What, How, and Why of Our Behavior*. Cambridge, MA: MIT P, 2000.

Darier, Éric, ed. *Discourses of the Environment*. Oxford: Blackwell, 1999.

Darwin, Charles. *The Descent of Man, and Selection in Relation to Sex*. 1871. Princeton, NJ: Princeton UP, 1981.

———. *The Expression of the Emotions in Man and Animals*. 1872. New York: Oxford UP, 1998.

———. *The Origin of Species*. 1859. New York: Mentor, 1958.

Dawkins, Richard. *River Out of Eden*. New York: Basic, 1995.

———. *The Selfish Gene*. Oxford: Oxford UP, 1989.

Degler, Carl N. *In Search of Human Nature: The Decline and Revival of Darwinism in American Social Thought*. New York: Oxford UP, 1991.

Deitering, Cynthia. "The Postnatural Novel: Toxic Consciousness in Fiction of the 1980s." *The Ecocriticism Reader*. Ed. Cheryll Glotfelty and Harold Fromm. Athens: U of Georgia P, 1996. 196–203.

DeLillo, Don. *White Noise*. New York: Viking, 1998.

Deming, Alison Hawthorne. *The Edges of the Civilized World: A Journey in Nature and Culture*. New York: Picador, 1998.

Dennett, Daniel C. *Darwin's Dangerous Idea: Evolution and the Meaning of Life*. New York: Simon, 1995.

deWaal, Franz. *Tree of Origin: What Primate Behavior Can Tell Us About Human Social Evolution*. Cambridge, MA: Harvard UP, 2001.

Diamond, Jared. *Guns, Germs, and Steel: The Fates of Human Societies*. New York: Norton, 1997.

———. *The Third Chimpanzee: The Evolution and Future of the Human Animal.* New York: Harper, 1992.

Dick, Philip K. *I Hope I Shall Arrive Soon.* London: Gollancz, 1986.

Dillard, Annie. *Pilgrim at Tinker Creek.* New York: Bantam, 1975.

Dissanayake, Ellen. *Homo Aestheticus: Where Art Comes From and Why.* Seattle: U of Washington P, 1995.

———. "'Making Special': An Undescribed Human Universal and the Core of a Behavior in Art." *Biopetics.* Ed. Brett Cooke and Frederick Turner. Lexington, KY: ICUS, 1999. 27–46.

———. *What Is Art For?* Seattle: U of Washington P, 1988.

Donaldson, Scott. *By Force of Will: The Life and Art of Ernest Hemingway.* New York: Viking, 1977.

Drinnon, Richard. "In the American Heartland: Hemingway and Death." *Psychoanalytic Review* 52 (Summer 1965): 5–31.

Easterlin, Nancy. "Do Cognitive Predispositions Predict or Determine Literary Value Judgments? Narrativity, Plot, and Aesthetics." *Biopoetics: Evolutionary Explorations in the Arts.* Ed. Brett Cooke and Frederick Turner. Lexington, KY: ICUS Books, 1999. 241–62.

Easterlin, Nancy, and Barbara Riebling, eds. *After Poststructuralism: Interdisciplinarity and Literary Theory.* Evanston, IL: Northwestern UP, 1993.

Editors of *Lingua Franca*, eds. *The Sokal Hoax: The Sham That Shook the Academy.* Lincoln: U of Nebraska P, 2000.

Ehrenfeld, David. *The Arrogance of Humanism.* New York: Oxford UP, 1978.

Ehrlich, Paul R. *Human Natures: Genes, Cultures, and the Human Prospect.* Washington, DC: Island, 2000.

Ehrlich, Paul R., and Anne H. Ehrlich. *Betrayal of Science and Reason.* Washington, DC: Island, 1996.

Eiseley, Loren. *The Star Thrower.* San Diego: Harcourt, 1978.

Elder, John. *Imagining the Earth: The Poetry and Vision of Nature.* Urbana: U of Illinois P, 1985.

Elkins, Andrew. *The Great Poem of the Earth: A Study of the Poetry of Thomas Hornsby Ferril.* Moscow: U of Idaho P, 1997.

Ellis, Lee. "A Discipline in Peril: Sociology's Future Hinges on Curing Its Biophobia." *The American Sociologist.* 27.2 (Summer 1996): 21–41.

Emerson, Ralph Waldo. *The Complete Works of Ralph Waldo Emerson.* Centenary Edition. Ed. Edward Waldo Emerson. Vol. 4. Boston: Houghton, 1903–1904.

Empson, William. *Some Versions of Pastoral.* London: Chatto, 1935.

Entrikin, J. Nicholas. *The Betweenness of Place.* Baltimore: Johns Hopkins UP, 1991.

Eribon, Didier. *Michel Foucault.* Trans. Betsy Wing. Cambridge, MA: Harvard UP, 1991.

Erisman, Fred. "Western Fiction as an Ecological Parable." *Environmental Review* 6 (1978): 15–23.

Evans, David Allen. "Evolution and Literature." *South Dakota Review* 36.4 (Winter 1998): 33–45.

Evernden, Neil. "Beyond Ecology: Self, Place, and the Pathetic Fallacy." *The Ecocriticism Reader.* Ed. Cheryll Glotfelty and Harold Fromm. Athens: U of Georgia P, 1996. 92–104.

Faulkner, William. "Review of *The Old Man and the Sea.*" *Shenandoah* 3 (Autumn 1952): 55.

Fiedler, Leslie. *Love and Death in the American Novel.* New York: Criterion, 1960.

Finch, Robert, and John Elder, eds. *The Norton Book of Nature Writing.* New York: Norton, 1990.

Fleming, Robert. "The Endings of Hemingway's *Garden of Eden.*" *American Literature* 61 (1989): 261–70.

———, ed. *Hemingway and the Natural World.* Moscow: U of Idaho P, 1999.

Flores, Dan. "Nature's Children: Environmental History as Human Natural History." *Human/Nature: Biology, Culture, and Environmental History.* Ed. John P. Herron and Andrew G. Kirk. Albuquerque: U of New Mexico P, 1999. 11–30.

"Forum on Literatures of the Environment." *PMLA* 114 (1999): 1089–1104.

Fox, Robin. "State of the Art/Science in Anthropology." *The Flight from Science and Reason.* Ed. Paul R. Gross, Norman Levitt, and Martin W. Lewis. New York: NY Academy of Sciences, 1996. 327–45.

Fritzell, Peter A. *Nature Writing and America: Essays upon a Cultural Type.* Ames: Iowa State UP, 1990.

Fromm, Harold. "A Crucifix for Dracula: Wendell Berry Meets Edward O. Wilson." *Hudson Review* 53 (2001): 657–64.

———. "My Science Wars." *Hudson Review* 49 (1997): 599–609.

Frye, Northrop. *Anatomy of Criticism.* Princeton, NJ: Princeton UP, 1957.

Fryer, Judith. "Desert, Rock, Shelter, Legend." *The Desert Is No Lady.* Ed. Vera Norwood and Janice Monk. New Haven: Yale UP, 1987.

———. *Felicitous Space: The Imaginative Structures of Edith Wharton and Willa Cather.* Chapel Hill: U of North Carolina P, 1986.

Gaard, Greta, and Patrick D. Murphy, eds. *Ecofeminist Literary Criticism: Theory, Interpretation, Pedagogy.* Urbana: U of Illinois P, 1998.

Gadgil, Madhav. "Of Literature and Artifacts." *The Biophilia Hypothesis.* Ed. Stephen R. Kellert and Edward O. Wilson. Washington, DC: Island Press, 1993. 365–80.

Gare, Arren E. *Postmodernism and the Environmental Crisis.* London: Routledge, 1995.

Giannone, Richard. "Willa Cather and the Human Voice." *Five Essays on Willa Cather: The Merrimac Symposium.* Ed. John J. Murphy. North Andover, MA: Merrimac College, 1974. 51–74.

Gifford, Terry. *Green Voices: Understanding Contemporary Nature Poetry.* Manchester: Manchester UP, 1995.

———. *Pastoral.* London: Routledge, 1999.

Gilcrest, David W. *Greening the Lyre: Environmental Poetics and Ethics.* Reno: U of Nevada P, 2002.

Ginsburg, Carlo. *Clues, Myths, and the Historical Method.* Trans. John and Anne Tedeschi. Baltimore: Johns Hopkins UP, 1989.

Glotfelty, Cheryll. "Introduction: Literary Studies in an Age of Environmental Crisis." *The Ecocriticism Reader.* Ed. Cheryll Glotfelty and Harold Fromm. Athens: U of Georgia P, 1996. xv–xxxvii.

Glotfelty [Burgess], Cheryll. "Literary Studies and Environmental Issues: An Introduction to Ecocriticism." Unpublished paper, MLA Convention, Dec. 1991.

———. "Toward an Ecological Literary Criticism." Unpublished paper, Western American Literature Association Annual Conference, Coeur d'Alene, ID, Oct. 1989.

Glotfelty, Cheryll, and Harold Fromm, eds. *The Ecocriticism Reader: Landmarks in Literary Ecology.* Athens: U of Georgia P, 1996.

Goldsmith, Timothy H. *The Biological Roots of Human Behavior.* New York: Oxford UP, 1991.

Gould, Stephen Jay. *Ever Since Darwin.* New York: Norton, 1977.

———. Rev. of *Science and Gender,* by Ruth Bleier. *New York Times Book Review* 2 Aug. 1984: 7.

———. "Sociobiology: The Art of Story-Telling." *New Scientist* 80 (1978): 530–33.

Gowaty, Patricia Adair. "Behavioral Just-So Stories Recast." *Science* 293 (27 July 2001): 610–11.

Greenberg, Robert M. *Splintered Worlds: Fragmentation and the Ideal of Diversity in the Work of Emerson, Melville, Whitman, and Dickinson.* Boston: Northeastern UP, 1993.

Griffin, D. R. *The Question of Animal Awareness.* New York: Rockefeller UP, 1976.

Gross, Paul R., and Norman Levitt. *Higher Superstition: The Academic Left and Science.* Baltimore: Johns Hopkins UP, 1994.

Gross, Paul R., Norman Levitt, and Martin W. Lewis, eds. *The Flight from Science and Reason.* New York: NY Academy of Sciences, 1996.

Gunn, Giles. *Beyond Solidarity: Pragmatism and Difference in a Globalized World.* Chicago: U of Chicago P, 2001.

Haggett, N. Peter. *The Geographer's Art.* Oxford: Blackwell, 1990.

Halperin, David M. *Before Pastoral: Theocritus and the Ancient Tradition of Bucolic Poetry.* New Haven: Yale UP, 1983.

Halpern, Daniel, ed. *On Nature: Nature, Landscape, and Natural History.* San Francisco: North Point, 1987.

Hamilton, W. D. *Narrow Roads of Gene Land.* Vol. I of *Evolution of Social Behavior.* New York: Freeman, 1996.

Hardin, Garrett. "Rewards of Pejoristic Thinking." *Managing the Commons.* Ed. Garrett Hardin and John Baden. San Francisco: Freeman, 1977. 126–34.

Harrell, David. *From Mesa Verde to The Professor's House.* Albuquerque: U of New Mexico P, 1992.

Harrison, Robert Pogue. *Forests: The Shadow of Civilization.* Chicago: U of Chicago P, 1992.

Hauser, Marc D. *Wild Minds: What Animals Really Think.* New York: Holt, 2000.

Hayles, N. Katherine. *Chaos Bound: Orderly Disorder in Contemporary Literature and Science.* Ithaca, NY: Cornell UP, 1990.

Heerwagen, Judith H., and Gordon H. Orians. "Humans, Habitats, and Aesthetics." *The Biophilia Hypothesis.* Ed. Stephen R. Kellert and Edward O. Wilson. Washington, DC: Island, 1993. 138–72.

Heise, Ursula K. "The Virtual Crowds: Overpopulation, Space, and Speciesism." *ISLE* 8.1 (Winter 2001): 1–29.

Hemingway, Ernest. *Across the River and into the Trees.* New York: Scribner's, 1950.

———. "Big Two-Hearted River." *The Short Stories of Ernest Hemingway.* New York: Scribner's, 1953. 209–32.

———. *Death in the Afternoon.* New York: Scribner's, 1932.

———. *Ernest Hemingway: Selected Letters, 1917–1961.* Ed. Carlos Baker. New York: Scribner's, 1981.

———. *A Farewell to Arms.* New York: Scribner's, 1929.

———. *The Garden Of Eden.* New York: Scribner's, 1986.

———. *Green Hills of Africa.* New York: Scribner's, 1935.

———. *The Nick Adams Stories.* New York: Scribner's 1972.

———. *The Old Man and the Sea.* New York: Scribner's, 1952.

———. "The Shot." Repr. *By Line: Ernest Hemingway.* Ed. William White. New York: Bantam, 1968.

———. *True at First Light.* Ed. Patrick Hemingway. New York: Scribner's, 1999.

———. *The Viking Portable Hemingway.* Ed. Malcolm Cowley. New York: Viking, 1944.

Hemingway, Gregory. *Papa: A Personal Memoir.* Boston: Houghton, 1976.

Hemingway, Jack. *Misadventures of a Fly Fisherman.* Dallas: Taylor, 1986.

Hemingway, Leicester. *My Brother, Ernest Hemingway.* Cleveland: New World, 1962.

Hemingway, Lorian. *Walk on Water: A Memoir.* New York: Simon, 1998.

Hemingway, Patrick. "My Papa, Papa." *Playboy* 15:2 (December 1968): 197–98, 200, 263–64. 268.

Herron, John P., and Andrew G. Kirk, eds. *Human/Nature: Biology, Culture, and Environmental History.* Albuquerque: U of New Mexico P, 1999.

Heyer, Paul. *Nature, Human Nature, and Society: Marx, Darwin, Biology, and the Human Sciences.* Westport, CT: Greenwood Press, 1982.

Heyes, Cecilia, and Ludwig Huber, eds. *The Evolution of Cognition.* Cambridge, MA: MIT P, 2000.

Hochner, A. E. *Papa Hemingway.* New York: Bantam, 1967.

Hogan, Linda. *Power.* New York: Norton, 1998.

———. *Solar Storms.* New York: Scribner's, 1995.

Hogan, Patrick Colm. "Literary Universals." *Poetics Today* 18 (Summer 1997): 223–49.

Holden, Constance. "Molecule Shows Anasazi Ate Their Enemies." *Science* 289 (8 Sept. 2000): 1663.

———. "The Vatican's Position Evolves." *Science* 274 (1 Nov. 1996): 717.

Horgan, John. "Profile: Reluctant Revolutionary." *Scientific American* (May 1991): 40, 49.

Hovey, Richard. *Hemingway: The Inward Terrain.* Seattle: U of Washington P, 1968.

Howarth, William. "Literary Perspectives on Biodiversity." *Encyclopedia of Biodiversity.* Ed. Simon Asher. Vol. 3. San Diego: Academic Press, 2001. 739–46.

———. "Some Principles of Ecocriticism." *The Ecocriticism Reader.* Ed. Cheryll Glotfelty and Harold Fromm. Athens: U of Georgia P, 1996. 69–91.

Howells, W. D. *The Altrurian Romances.* Ed. Clara and Rudolf Kirk. Bloomington: Indiana UP, 1968.

———. "Are We a Plutocracy?" *North American Review* 158 (Feb. 1894): 185–96.

———. "Editor's Easy Chair." *Harper's Monthly Magazine* 103 (Aug. 1901): 490–95.

———. "Editor's Easy Chair." *Harper's Monthly Magazine* 137 (Sept. 1918): 589–92.

———. *A Hazard of New Fortunes.* 1890. New York: Signet, 1965.

———. *The Landlord at Lion's Head.* 1896. New York: International, 1900.

———. *A Modern Instance.* 1882. Cambridge, MA: Riverside, 1957.

———. Rev. of *Mummies and Moslems,* by Charles Dudley Warner. *Atlantic Monthly* 38 (July 1876): 108–12.

———. *The Rise of Silas Lapham.* 1885. New York: Penguin, 1983.

———. *Selected Letters, Vol. 3: 1882–1891.* Ed. Robert C. Leitz III. Boston: Twayne, 1980.

———. *Selected Letters, Vol. 4: 1892–1901.* Ed. Thomas Wortham. Boston: Twayne, 1981.

Hrdy, Sarah Blaffer. *Mother Nature: Maternal Instincts and How They Shape the Human Species.* New York: Ballantine, 1999.

Huxley, Aldous. *Literature and Science.* New York: Harper and Row, 1963.

———. "The Politics of Population/Second Edition." *Ecological Crisis: Readings for Survival.* Eds. Glen A. Love and Rhoda M. Love. New York: Harcourt, 1970. 321–31.

Hyman, Ray. "The Psychology of Deception." *Annual Review of Psychology* (1989): 133–54.

Imber, Jonathan B. "Editor's Column: Predestinations." *The American Sociologist* 27.2 (Summer 1996): 3–7.

Ingram, David. *Green Screen: Environmentalism and Hollywood Cinema.* Exeter: U of Exeter P, 2000.

Irwin, John T. *American Hieroglyphics.* New Haven: Yale UP, 1980.

James, William. *Pragmatism and Other Writings.* Ed. Giles Gunn. New York: Penguin, 2000.

Jobes, Katharine T., ed. *Twentieth Century Interpretations of The Old Man and the Sea.* Englewood Cliffs, NJ: Prentice, 1968.

Jobling, Ian. "Personal Justice and Homicide in Scott's *Ivanhoe:* An Evolutionary Psychological Perspective." *Interdisciplinary Literary Studies* 2 (Spring 2001): 29–43.

Jolly, Alison. *Lucy's Legacy: Sex and Intelligence in Human Evolution.* Cambridge, MA: Harvard UP, 1999.

Jones, Mary McAllester. *Gaston Bachelard, Subversive Humanist: Texts and Readings.* Madison: U of Wisconsin P, 1991.

Kahn, Peter H., Jr. *The Human Relationship with Nature: Development and Culture.* Cambridge, MA: MIT P, 1999.

Katcher, Aaron, and Gregory Wilkins. "Dialogue with Animals: Its Nature and Culture." *The Biophilia Hypothesis.* Ed. Stephen R. Kellert and Edward O. Wilson. Washington, DC: Island, 1993. 173–200.

Kazin, Alfred. *On Native Grounds.* New York: Harcourt, 1942.

Keegan, Bridget, and James C. McKusick, eds. *Literature and Nature: Four Centuries of Nature Writing.* Upper Saddle River, NJ: Prentice, 2001.

Keller, Evelyn Fox. *A Feeling for the Organism: The Life and Times of Barbara McClintock.* San Francisco: Freeman, 1983.

Kellert, Stephen R. "Coda." *The Biophilia Hypothesis.* Ed Stephen R. Kellert and Edward O. Wilson. Washington, DC: Island, 1993. 456–58.

Kellert, Stephen R., and Edward O. Wilson, eds. *The Biophilia Hypothesis.* Washington, DC: Island, 1993.

Kern, Robert. "Ecocriticism—What Is It Good For?" *ISLE* 7.1 (Winter 2000): 9–32.

Kerridge, Richard. "Small Rooms and the Ecosystem: Environmentalism and DeLillo's *White Noise.*" *Writing the Environment: Ecocriticism and Literature.* New York: St. Martin's, 1998. 182–95.

———. *Writing the Environment: Ecocriticism and Literature.* New York: St. Martin's, 1998.

Killinger, John. *Hemingway and the Dead Gods.* Lexington: U of Kentucky P, 1960.

Kimura, Doreen. "Sex Differences in the Brain." *Mind and Brain: Readings from Scientific American Magazine.* New York: Freeman, 1993. 78–89.

Kirk, Andrew G., and John P. Herron. Introduction. *Human/Nature: Biology, Culture, and Environmental History.* Ed. John P. Herron and Andrew G. Kirk. Albuquerque: U of New Mexico P, 1999. 1–8.

Kitano, Hiroki. "Systems Biology: A Brief Overview." *Science* 295 (1 March 2002): 1662–64.

Kittredge, William. *The Nature of Generosity.* New York: Vintage, 2001.

Kollin, Susan. "Toxic Subjectivity: Gender and the Ecologies of Whiteness in Todd Haynes' *Safe.*" *ISLE* 9.1 Winter 2002): 121–39.

Kowalewski, Michael. "Bioregional Perspectives in American Literature." *Regionalism Reconsidered.* Ed. David Jordan. New York: Garland, 1994. 252–79.

———. "Writing in Place: The New American Regionalism." *American Literary History* 6 (1994): 171–83.

Kroeber, Karl. *Ecological Literary Criticism: Romantic Imagining and the Biology of Mind.* New York: Columbia UP, 1994.

Krutch, Joseph Wood. *The Measure of Man.* New York: Bobbs, 1954.

———. *The Modern Temper.* New York: Harcourt, 1929.

———. *More Lives Than One*. New York: Sloane, 1962.

Kuhn, Thomas S. *The Essential Tension: Selected Studies in Scientific Tradition and Change*. Chicago: U of Chicago P, 1977.

———. *The Structure of Scientific Revolutions*. 2nd ed. Chicago: U of Chicago P, 1970.

Lakoff, George, and Mark Johnson. *Philosophy in the Flesh: The Embodied Mind and Its Challenge to Western Thought*. New York: Basic, 1999.

Langer, Monica M. *Merleau-Ponty's Phenomenology of Perception: A Guide and Commentary*. Tallahassee: Florida State UP, 1989.

Lash, Jonathan. "Dealing with the Tinder as Well as the Flint." *Science* 294 (30 November 2001): 1789.

Laurence, Frank M. *Hemingway and the Movies*. Jackson: U of Mississippi P, 1981.

Lawrence, D. H. *Studies in Classic American Literature*. 1923. Garden City: Doubleday, 1951.

Lear, Linda. *Rachel Carson: Witness for Nature*. New York: Holt, 1997.

Le Guin, Ursula. *Always Coming Home*. New York: Bantam, 1987.

Lehan, Richard. "Hemingway Among the Moderns." *Hemingway In Our Time*. Ed. Richard Astro and Jackson J. Benson. Corvallis: Oregon State UP, 1974.

Leland, John. "The Happiness of the Garden: Hemingway's Edenic Quest." *The Hemingway Review* 3.1 (Fall 1983): 44–53.

Lentricchia, Frank. Introduction. *New Essays on White Noise*. Ed. Frank Lentricchia. New York: Cambridge UP, 1991.

Leopold, Aldo. *A Sand County Almanac*. 1949. San Francisco: Sierra Club/Ballantine, 1966.

Leshner, Alan. "Science and Sustainability." *Science* 297 (9 August 2002): 897.

Levin, Jonathan. "Between Science and Anti-Science: A Response to Glen A. Love." *ISLE* 7:1 (Winter 2000):1–8.

Levin, Richard. "The New Interdisciplinarity in Literary Criticism." *After Poststructuralism: Interdisciplinarity and Literary Theory*. Ed. Nancy Easterlin and Barbara Riebling. Evanston: Northwestern UP, 1993. 13–43.

Limbaugh, Ronald H. *John Muir's "Stickeen" and the Lessons of Nature*. Fairbanks: U of Alaska P, 1996.

Livingston, Paisley. *Literary Knowledge: Humanistic Inquiry and the Philosophy of Science*. Ithaca, NY: Cornell UP, 1988.

Lodge, David. *Thinks*. London: Secker, 2001.

Lopez, Barry. "Barry Lopez." *On Nature*. Ed. Daniel Halpern. San Francisco: North Point, 1987. 295–97.

Lopreato, Joseph. *Human Nature and Biocultural Evolution*. Boston: Allen, 1984.

Love, Glen A. "The Cowboy in the Laboratory." *New Americans: The Westerner and the Modern Experience in the American Novel*. Lewisburg, PA: Bucknell UP, 1982. 107–69.

———. "Ecocriticism and Science: Toward Consilience?" *New Literary History* 30 (1999): 561–76.

———. "The Ecological Short Story." *The Columbia Companion to the Twentieth-Century American Short Story*. Ed. Blanche H. Gelfant. New York: Columbia UP, 2000. 50–55.

———. "Ecology in Arcadia." *Colorado Quarterly* 21 (1972): 175–85.

———. "*Et in Arcadia Ego:* Pastoral Theory Meets Ecocriticism." *Western American Literature* 25.3 (Fall 1992): 195–207.

———. "Hemingway's Indian Virtues: An Ecological Reconsideration." *Western American Literature* 22.3 (November 1987): 201–13.

———. "*The Landlord at Lion's Head:* Howells and 'The Riddle of the Painful Earth.'" *The Old Northwest* 10 (Spring 1984): 107–25.

———. "Nature and Human Nature: Interdisciplinary Convergences on Cather's Blue Mesa." *Cather Studies Vol. 5: Willa Cather's Ecological Imagination.* Ed. Susan J. Rosowski. Lincoln: U of Nebraska P, 2003. 1–27

———. "*The Professor's House:* Cather, Hemingway, and the Chastening of American Prose Style." *Western American Literature* 24 (1990): 295–311.

———. "Revaluing Nature: Toward an Ecological Criticism." *Western American Literature* 25 (1990): 201–15. Rpt. in *The Ecocriticism Reader.* Ed. Cheryll Glotfelty and Harold Fromm. Athens: U of Georgia P, 1996. 225–40.

———. "Science, Anti-Science, and Ecocriticism." *ISLE* 6.1 (Winter 1999): 65–81.

———. "Slouching Toward Altruria: Evolution, Ecology, and William Dean Howells." *Harvard Library Bulletin* 5.1 (1994): 29–44.

Love, Glen A., and Rhoda M. Love, eds. *Ecological Crisis: Readings for Survival.* New York: Harcourt, 1970.

Low, Bobbi S. *Why Sex Matters: A Darwinian Look at Human Behavior.* Princeton, NJ: Princeton UP, 2000.

Lowenthal, David. "Geography, Experience, and Imagination: Toward a Geographical Epistemology." *Annals of the Association of American Geographers* 51 (1961): 241–60.

Lumsden, Charles J., and Edward O. Wilson. *Genes, Mind, and Culture: The Coevolutionary Process.* Cambridge, MA: Harvard UP, 1981.

———. *Promethean Fire: Reflection on the Origin of Mind.* Cambridge, MA: Harvard UP, 1983.

Lutwack, Leonard. *The Role of Place in Literature.* Syracuse: Syracuse UP, 1984.

Lynn, Kenneth S. *William Dean Howells.* New York: Harcourt, 1971.

Lyon, Thomas J. "The Ecological Vision of Gary Snyder." *Kansas Quarterly* 2 (Spring 1970): 117–24.

———, ed. *This Incomperable Lande.* Boston: Houghton, 1989.

Maclean, Norman. *A River Runs Through It and Other Stories.* Chicago: U of Chicago P, 1976.

Marsh, Kevin R. "'This Is Just the First Round': Designating Wilderness in the Central Oregon Cascades, 1950–1964." *Oregon Historical Quarterly* 103.2 (Summer 2002): 210–33.

Marshall, Ian. *Story Line: Exploring the Literature of the Appalachian Trail.* Charlottesville: UP of Virginia, 1998.

Martin, Ronald E. *American Literature and the Universe of Force.* Durham, NC: Duke UP, 1981.

Marx. Leo. Afterword. *The Machine in the Garden: Technology and the Pastoral Ideal in America.* New York: Oxford UP, 2000. 367–85.

———. "Environmental Degradation and the Ambiguous Social Role of Science and Technology." *Earth, Air, Fire, Water: Humanistic Studies of the Environment.* Ed. Jill Ker Conway, Kenneth Keniston, and Leo Marx. Amherst: U of Massachusetts P, 1999. 320–38.

———. *The Machine in the Garden: Technology and the Pastoral Ideal in America.* New York: Oxford UP, 1964.

———. Pastoralism in America." *Ideology and Classic American Literature.* Ed. Sacvan Berkovitch and Myra Jehlen. New York: Cambridge UP, 1986. 36–69.

Maxwell, Mary, ed. *The Sociobiological Imagination.* Albany: State U of New York P, 1991.

Mayr, Ernst. *This Is Biology.* Cambridge, MA: Harvard UP, 1997.

Mazel, David, ed. *A Century of Ecocriticism.* Athens: U of Georgia P, 2001.

McDowell, Michael J. "The Bakhtinian Road to Ecological Insight." *The Ecocriticism Reader.* Ed. Cheryll Glotfelty and Harold Fromm. Athens: U of Georgia P, 1996. 372–91.

McGiveron, Rafeeq. "From a 'Stretch of Grey Sea' to the 'Extent of Space': The Gaze Across Vistas in Cather's *The Professor's House.*" *Western American Literature* 34 (2000): 388–408.

McKibben, Bill. *The End of Nature.* New York: Random, 1989.

McKusick, James C. *Green Writing: Romanticism and Ecology.* New York: St. Martin's, 2000.

McMurray, William A. "Point of View in Howells' *The Landlord at Lion's Head.*" *American Literature* 34 (1962): 207–14.

McNamee, Gregory, ed. *The Serpent's Tale: Snakes in Folklore and Literature.* Athens: U of Georgia P, 2000.

McRae, Murdo William, ed. *The Literature of Science: Perspectives on Popular Scientific Writing.* Athens: U. of Georgia P, 1993.

Meeker, Joseph. *The Comedy of Survival: Literary Ecology and the Play Ethic.* 3rd ed. Tucson: U of Arizona P, 1997.

———. *The Comedy of Survival: Studies in Literary Ecology.* New York: Scribner's, 1974.

Melville, Herman. *Moby-Dick.* 1851. Indianapolis: Bobbs, 1964.

Merrill, Christopher, ed. *The Forgotten Language: Contemporary Poets and Nature.* Salt Lake City: Peregrine, 1991.

Michaels, Walter Benn. *Our America: Nativism, Modernism, Pluralism.* Durham, NC: Duke UP, 1995.

Midgley, Mary. *Beast and Man: The Roots of Human Nature.* Ithaca, NY: Cornell UP, 1978.

———. *Evolution as a Religion: Strange Hopes and Stranger Fears.* London: Metheun, 1985.

Miller, Arthur. "Tragedy and the Common Man." Rpt. *Tragedy: Plays, Theory, and Criticism.* Ed. Richard Levin. New York: Harcourt, 1960.

Miller, Donald, L. *Lewis Mumford: A Life.* New York: Weidenfeld, 1989.

Monk, Donald. "Hemingway's Territorial Imperatives." *Yearbook of English Studies* 8 (1978): 125–40.

Morris, David Copland. "Inhumanism, Environmental Crisis, and the Canon of American Literature." *ISLE* 4.2 (Fall 1997): 1–16.

Morrison, Reg. *The Spirit in the Gene: Humanity's Proud Illusion and the Laws of Nature*. Ithaca, NY: Cornell UP, 1999.

Morton, Peter. *The Vital Science: Biology and the Literary Imagination, 1860–1900*. London: Allen, 1984.

Muir, John. "Stickeen." In Ronald H. Limbaugh, *John Muir's "Stickeen" and the Lessons of Nature*. Fairbanks: U of Alaska P, 1996. 99–128.

Mumford, Lewis. *The Pentagon of Power*. New York: Harcourt, 1970.

Murphy, Patrick D. "Centering Connections." *ISLE* 2.2 (Summer 1996): v–ix.

———. *Farther Afield in the Study of Nature-Oriented Literature*. Charlottesville: UP of Virginia, 2000.

———, ed. *Literature of Nature: An International Sourcebook*. Chicago: Fitzroy, 1998.

Nabhan, Gary Paul, and Sara St. Antoine. "The Loss of Floral and Faunal Story." *The Biophilia Hypothesis*. Ed. Stephen R. Kellert and Edward O. Wilson. Washington, DC: Island, 1993. 229–50.

Nahal, Chaman. *The Narrative Pattern in Ernest Hemingway's Fiction*. Rutherford, NJ: Fairleigh Dickinson UP, 1971.

Nash, Roderick Frazier. *The Rights of Nature: A History of Environmental Ethics*. Madison: U of Wisconsin P, 1989.

———. *Wilderness and the American Mind*. New Haven: Yale UP, 1967.

Nelson, Barney. *The Wild and the Domestic: Animal Representations, Ecocriticism, and Western American Literature*. Reno: U of Nevada P, 2000.

Nelson, Richard. *The Island Within*. San Francisco: North Point, 1989.

———. "Searching for the Lost Arrow: Physical and Spiritual Ecology in the Hunter's World." *The Biophilia Hypothesis*. Ed. Stephen R. Kellert and Edward O. Wilson. Washington, DC: Island, 1993. 201–28.

Nemecek, Sasha. "The Furor over Feminist Science." *Scientific American* 276 (January 1997): 98–100.

Oates, David. *Earth Rising: Ecological Belief in an Age of Science*. Corvallis: Oregon State UP, 1989.

Odum, Eugene P. *Ecology: A Bridge Between Science and Society*. Sunderland, MA: Sinauer, 1997.

Oelschlaeger, Max. *The Idea of Wilderness: From Prehistory to the Age of Ecology*. New Haven: Yale UP, 1991.

———. Introduction. *Postmodern Environmental Ethics*. Ed. Max Oelschlaeger. Albany: State U of New York P, 1995. 1–20.

———, ed. *The Wilderness Condition: Essays on Environment and Civilization*. San Francisco: Sierra Club, 1992.

O'Grady, Sean. *Pilgrims to the Wild: Everett Ruess, Henry David Thoreau, John Muir, Clarence King, Mary Austin*. Salt Lake City: U of Utah P, 1993.

Olson, Steve. *Mapping Human History: Discovering the Past Through Our Genes*. Boston: Houghton, 2002.

Orians, Gordon H., and J. H. Heerwagen. "Evolved Responses to Landscapes."

The Adapted Mind: Evolutionary Psychology and the Generation of Culture. Ed. Jerome H. Barkow, Leda Cosmides, and John Tooby. New York: Oxford UP, 1992. 555–79.

Ornstein, Robert, and Paul Ehrlich. *New World New Mind: Moving Toward Conscious Evolution*. New York: Simon, 1990.

Orr, David W. "Love It or Lose It: The Coming Biophilia Revolution." *The Biophilia Hypothesis*. Ed. Stephen R. Kellert and Edward O. Wilson. Washington, DC: Island, 1993. 415–40.

———. "What Is Education For?" *Earth Ethics* 3.3 (Spring 1992): 1–5.

"OSU Biologist to Discuss Environment." *Register Guard* [Eugene, Oregon] 10 Feb. 1997: D1, 5.

Pack, Robert, and Jay Parini, eds. *Poems for a Small Planet: Contemporary American Nature Poetry*. Hanover, NH: Middlebury College P, 1993.

Panofsky, Erwin. *Meaning in the Visual Arts*. Chicago: U of Chicago P, 1982.

Paul, Sherman. *For Love of the World: Essays on Nature Writers*. Iowa City: U of Iowa P, 1992.

Pearson, David E. "Sociology and Biosociology." *The American Sociologist* 27:2 (Summer 1996): 8–20.

Phillips, Dana. "Don DeLillo's Postmodern Pastoral." *Reading the Earth: New Directions in the Study of Literature and Environment*. Ed. Michael P. Branch, et al. Moscow: U of Idaho P, 1998. 235–46.

Pinker, Steven. *The Blank Slate: The Modern Denial of Human Nature*. New York: Viking, 2002.

Pizer, Donald. "The Evolutionary Foundation of William Dean Howells' *Criticism and Fiction*." *Philological Quarterly* 40 (1961): 91–103.

———. "Evolutionary Literary Criticism and the Defense of Howellsian Realism." *Journal of English and Germanic Philology* 61 (1962): 296–304.

Plimpton, George. "An Interview with Ernest Hemingway." *Hemingway and His Critics: An International Anthology*. Ed. Carlos Baker. New York: Hill, 1961. 19–37.

Plog, Stephen. *Ancient Peoples of the American Southwest*. London: Thames, 1997.

Popper, Karl R. *Objective Knowledge: An Evolutionary Approach*. Oxford: Clarendon, 1972.

Porter, Theodore M. *Trust in Numbers: The Pursuit of Objectivity in Science and Public Life*. Princeton, NJ: Princeton UP, 1995.

Quantic, Diane Dufva. *The Nature of the Place: A Study of Great Plains Fiction*. Lincoln: U of Nebraska P, 1995.

Quetchenbach, Bernard W. *Back from the Far Field: American Nature Poetry in the Late Twentieth Century*. Charlottesville: UP of Virginia, 2000.

Quirk, Tom. *Bergson and American Culture: The Worlds of Willa Cather and Wallace Stevens*. Chapel Hill: U of North Carolina P, 1990.

Randall, John H. *The Landscape and the Looking Glass: Willa Cather's Search for Value*. Boston: Houghton, 1960.

Rapp, Carl. *Fleeing the Universal: The Critique of Post-Rational Criticism*. Albany: State U of New York P, 1998.

Raven, Peter H. "Science, Sustainability, and the Human Prospect." *Science* 297 (9 August 2002): 954–58.

Reynolds, Guy. *Willa Cather in Context: Progress, Race, Empire.* London: Macmillan, 1996.

Richards, I. A. *Practical Criticism: A Study of Literary Judgment.* New York: Harcourt, 1929.

Richards, Robert J. *Darwin and the Emergence of Evolutionary Theories of Mind and Behavior.* Chicago: U of Chicago P, 1987.

Ridley, Matt. *The Origins of Virtue.* New York: Viking, 1996.

Rogers, Susan Fox, ed. *Another Wilderness: New Outdoor Writing by Women.* Seattle: Seal, 1994.

Ronald, Ann, ed. *Words for the Wild: The Sierra Club Trailside Reader.* San Francisco: Sierra Club, 1987.

Roorda, Randall. *Dramas of Solitude: Narratives of Retreat in American Nature Writing.* Albany: State U of New York P, 1998.

———. "KB in Green: Ecology, Critical Theory, and Kenneth Burke." *ISLE* 4.2 (Fall 1997): 39–52.

Rosedale, Steven, ed. *The Greening of Literary Scholarship: Literature, Theory, and the Environment.* Iowa City: U of Iowa P, 2002.

Rosenberg, Alexander. *Instrumental Biology, or, The Disunity of Science.* Chicago: U of Chicago P, 1994.

Rosenblatt, Roger. "All the Days of the Earth." Special Edition: Earth Day 2000 of *Time* 155.17 (April–May 2000): 8–15.

Rosowski, Susan J. "Willa Cather's Ecology of Place." *Western American Literature* 30 (1995): 37–51.

Rosowski, Susan J., and Bernice Slote. "Willa Cather's 1916 Mesa Verde Essay: The Genesis of *The Professor's House.*" *Prairie Schooner* 58 (1984): 81–92.

Roszak, Theodore. *Person/Planet: The Creative Disintegration of Industrial Society.* Garden City: Doubleday, 1978.

Rourke, Constance. *American Humor.* 1931. Garden City: Doubleday, 1953.

Rovit, Earl. *Ernest Hemingway.* New York: Twayne, 1963.

Rue, Loyal. *Everybody's Story: Wising Up to the Epic of Evolution.* Albany: State U of New York P, 2000.

Rueckert, William. "Literature and Ecology: An Experiment in Ecocriticism." *Iowa Review* 9.1 (Winter 1978): 71–86.

Russell, Bertrand. "Science as an Element in Culture." *Cultures in Conflict.* Ed. David K. Cornelius and Edwin St. Vincent. Chicago: Simon, 1979. 104–10.

Ryden, Kent C. *Mapping the Invisible Landscape.* Iowa City: U of Iowa P, 1993.

Sack, Robert David. *Homo Geographicus: A Framework for Action, Awareness, and Moral Concern.* Baltimore: Johns Hopkins UP, 1997.

Sagan, Carl. *The Demon-Haunted World.* New York: Random, 1995.

Sale, Kirkpatrick. *Dwellers in the Land: The Bioregional Vision.* San Francisco: Sierra Club, 1985.

Sanders, Scott Russell. "Speaking a Word For Nature." *The Ecocriticism Reader.* Ed. Cheryll Glotfelty and Harold Fromm. Athens: U of Georgia P, 1996. 182–95.

Schama, Simon. *Landscape and Memory*. New York: Random, 1996.

Scheese, Don. *Nature Writing: The Pastoral Impulse in America*. New York: Twayne, 1996.

Scholtmeijer, Marian. *Animal Victims in Modern Fiction: From Sanctity to Sacrifice*. Toronto: U of Toronto P, 1993.

Schroeter, James. "Willa Cather and *The Professor's House*." *Willa Cather and Her Critics*. Ed. James Schroeter. Ithaca, NY: Cornell UP, 1967. 363–81,

Schultz, Elizabeth. "Melville's Environmental Vision in *Moby-Dick*." *ISLE* 7.1 (Winter 2000): 97–114.

Scigaj, Leonard M. *Sustainable Poetry: Four American Ecopoets*. Lexington: U of Kentucky P, 1999.

Searle, John R. *The Rediscovery of the Mind*. Cambridge, MA: MIT P, 1992.

Segerstråle, Ullica. *Defenders of the Truth: The Battle for Science in the Sociology Debate and Beyond*. New York: Oxford UP, 2000.

Seife, Charles. "Science and Religion Advance Together at Pontifical Academy." *Science* 291 (23 February 2001): 1472–74.

Sessions, George, ed. *Deep Ecology for the Twenty-First Century*. Boston: Shambhala, 1995.

———. "Reinventing Nature, The End of Wilderness? A Response to William Cronon's *Uncommon Ground*." *The Trumpeter: Journal of Ecosophy* 13:1 (1996): 33–38.

Sewell, Richard. "The Tragic Form." *Tragedy: Plays, Theory, and Criticism*. Ed. Richard Levin. New York: Harcourt, 1960.

Sheets-Johnstone, Maxine. "Descriptive Foundations." *ISLE* 9.1 (Winter 2002): 165–79.

———. *The Primacy of Movement*. Philadelphia: John Benjamin, 1999.

———. *The Roots of Power: Animate Form and Gendered Bodies*. Chicago: Open Court, 1994.

———. *The Roots of Thinking*. Philadelphia: Temple UP, 1990.

Sheffer, Victor B. "Environmentalism: Its Articles of Faith." *The Northwest Environmental Journal* 5:1 (Spring/Summer 1989): 99–109.

Shepard, Paul. *Coming Home to the Pleistocene*. Ed. Florence R. Shepard. Washington, DC: Island, 1998.

———. "Introduction: Ecology and Man—A Viewpoint." *The Subversive Science*. Ed. Paul Shepard and Daniel McKinley. Boston: Houghton, 1969. 1–10.

———. *Nature and Madness*. San Francisco: Sierra Club. 1982.

———. *The Others: How Animals Made Us Human*. Washington, DC: Island, 1996.

———. "Place in American Culture." *North American Review* 262 (Fall 1977): 22–32.

———. *The Tender Carnivore and the Sacred Game*. New York: Scribner's, 1973.

Shermer, Michael. "Is God All in the Mind?" *Science* 93 (6 July 2001): 54.

Shore, William H., ed. *The Nature of Nature: New Essays from America's Finest Writers on Nature*. New York: Harcourt, 1994.

Silko, Leslie Marmon. *Almanac of the Dead*. New York: Penguin, 1992.

———. *Ceremony.* New York: Viking, 1977.

Singer, Peter. *A Darwinian Left: Politics, Evolution and Cooperation.* New Haven: Yale UP, 1999.

Slovic, Scott. *Seeking Awareness in American Nature Writing: Henry Thoreau, Annie Dillard, Edward Abbey, Wendell Berry, Barry Lopez.* Salt Lake City: U of Utah P, 1992

———, ed. *Getting Over the Color Green: Contemporary Environmental Literature of the Southwest.* Tucson: U of Arizona P, 2001.

Slovic, Scott, and Terrell F. Dixon, eds. *Being in the World: An Environmental Reader for Writers.* New York: Macmillan, 1993.

Snow, C. P. *The Two Cultures and the Scientific Revolution.* Cambridge: Cambridge UP, 1959.

———. "The Two Cultures: A Second Look." *The Two Cultures* Canto Ed. Cambridge: Cambridge UP, 1993.

Snyder, Gary. "Four Changes." *Deep Ecology for the Twenty-First Century.* Ed. George Sessions. Boston: Shambhala, 1995. 141–50.

———. "The Place, the Region, and the Commons." *The Practice of the Wild.* San Francisco: North Point, 1990. 25–47.

———. "The Rediscovery of Turtle Island." *Deep Ecology for the Twenty-First Century.* Ed. George Sessions. Boston: Shambhala, 1995. 454–62.

———. *Turtle Island.* New York: New Directions, 1974.

Sober, Elliot, and David Sloan Wilson. *Unto Others: The Evolution and Psychology of Unselfish Behavior.* Cambridge, MA: Harvard UP, 1998.

Sokal, Alan. "A Physicist Experiments with Cultural Studies." *Lingua Franca* 6.4 (May/June 1996): 62–64.

———. "Transgressing the Boundaries: Toward a Transformational Hermeneutics of Quantum Gravity." *Social Text* No. 46 (Spring/Summer 1996): 217–52.

Soper, Kate. *What Is Nature?: Culture, Politics, and the Non-Human.* Cambridge: Blackwell, 1995.

Soulé, Michael, and Gary Lease, eds. *Reinventing Nature? Responses to Postmodern Deconstruction.* Washington, DC: Island, 1995.

Sperber, Dan. *Explaining Culture: A Naturalistic Approach.* Oxford: Blackwell, 1996.

Stegner, Wallace. *The Sound of Mountain Water.* New York: Dutton, 1980.

Steiner, George. *In Bluebeard's Castle: Some Notes Toward the Definition of Culture.* New Haven: Yale UP, 1971.

Sterne, J. P. *On Realism.* London: Routledge, 1973.

Stevens, Russell B. Rev. of *Lucy's Legacy,* by Alison Jolly. *The Key Reporter* 65 (Summer 2000): 12.

Storey, Robert. *Mimesis and the Human Animal: On the Biogenetic Foundations of Literary Representation.* Evanston, IL: Northwestern UP, 1996.

———. Rev. of *Evolution and Literary Theory,* by Joseph Carroll. *Modern Philology* 94 (1997): 350–54.

Swift, John N. "Memory, Myth and *The Professor's House.*" *Western American Literature* 20 (1986): 301–14.

Sylvester, Bickford. "Hemingway's Extended Vision: *The Old Man and the Sea.*" *Twentieth Century Interpretations of The Old Man and the Sea.* Ed. Katharine T. Jobes. Englewood Cliffs, NJ: Prentice, 1968. 81–96.

Tallmadge, John. Rev. of *The Norton Book of Nature Writing,* ed. Robert Finch and John Elder, and *This Incomperable Lande,* ed. Thomas J. Lyon. *Orion Nature Quarterly* 9 (Summer 1990): 63–64.

Tallmadge, John, and Henry Harrington, eds. *Reading Under the Sign of Nature.* Salt Lake City: U of Utah P, 2000.

Tanner, Stephen L. "Hemingway's Trout Fishing in Paris: A Metaphor for the Uses of Writing." *The Hemingway Review* 19.1 (Fall 1999): 79–91.

Tarter, James. "Collective Subjectivity and Postmodern Ecology." *ISLE* 2.2 (Winter 1996): 65–84.

———. "Locating the Uranium Mine: Place, Multiethnicity, and Environmental Justice in Leslie Marmon Silko's *Ceremony.*" *The Greening of Literary Scholarship.* Ed. Steven Rosedale. Iowa City: U of Iowa P, 2002. 97–110.

Taylor, Larry E. *Pastoral and Anti-Pastoral Patterns in John Updike's Fiction.* Carbondale: Southern Illinois UP, 1971.

Thomas, Lewis. "Are We Fit to Fit In?" *Sierra* 67.2 (March/April 1982): 49–52.

Thoreau, Henry David. *Walden and Resistance to Civil Government.* 2nd ed. Ed. William Rossi. New York: Norton, 1992.

Tiffney, Wes. "Re: more nature or the lack . . . ." E-mail to asle@unr.edu.network. 27 Jan. 1995.

Tiger, Lionel. *Optimism: The Biology of Hope.* New York: Simon, 1979.

Toffler, Alvin. *Future Shock.* New York: Random, 1970.

Tooby, John, and Leda Cosmides. "The Psychological Foundations of Culture." *The Adapted Mind: Evolutionary Psychology and the Generation of Culture.* Ed. Jerome H. Barkow, Leda Cosmides, and John Tooby. New York: Oxford UP, 1992. 19–136.

Towers, Tom H. "Savagery and Civilization: The Moral Dimensions of Howells' *A Boy's Town.*" *American Literature* 40 (1969): 499–509.

Toynbee, Arnold. *Mankind and Mother Earth.* New York: Oxford UP, 1976.

Tuana, Nancy, ed. *Feminism and Science.* Bloomington: Indiana UP, 1989.

Tucker, Herbert F. "From the Editors." *New Literary History* 3 (1999): 505.

Turner, Frederick. *The Culture of Hope.* New York: Free P, 1995.

———. "An Ecopoetics of Beauty and Meaning." *Biopoetics: Evolutionary Interpretations in the Arts.* Lexington, KY: ICUS, 1999. 119–38.

———. "In Praise of the Real: Reforming the Humanities." *Interdisciplinary Literary Studies* 2.2 (Spring 2001): 93–103.

Turner, Mark. *Reading Minds: The Study of English in the Age of Cognitive Science.* Princeton, NJ: Princeton UP, 1991.

Twain, Mark. *The Adventures of Huckleberry Finn.* 1883. Berkeley: U of California P, 1985.

———. "The Man That Corrupted Hadleyburg." *Great Short Works of Mark Twain.* Ed Justin Kaplan. New York: Harper, 1967. 231–77.

———. *The Mysterious Stranger. Great Short Works of Mark Twain.* Ed. Justin Kaplan. New York: Harper, 1967. 278–366.

Ueno, Naozo. "An Oriental View of *The Old Man and the Sea.*" *East-West Review* 2 (Spring 1965): 67–76.

Ulrich, Roger S. "Biophilia, Biophobia, and Natural Landscapes." *The Biophilia Hypothesis.* Ed. Stephen R. Kellert and Edward O. Wilson. Washington, DC: Island, 1993. 73–137.

Updike, John. *Rabbit at Rest.* New York: Knopf, 1990.

Vanderbilt, Kermit. *The Achievement of William Dean Howells: A Reinterpretation.* Princeton, NJ: Princeton UP, 1968.

Van Ghent, Dorothy. *Willa Cather.* Minneapolis: U of Minnesota P, 1961.

Vogel, Steven. *Prime Mover: A Natural History of Muscle.* New York: Norton, 2001.

Walton, Isaac. *The Compleat Angler: 1653–1736.* Ed Jonquil Bevan. Oxford: Clarendon, 1983.

Watson, James D. Foreword. *Discovering the Brain.* By Sandra Ackerman. Washington, DC: National Academy, 1992.

Weaver, Richard M. *The Ethics of Rhetoric.* Chicago: Regnery, 1953.

Wells, Arvin. "A Ritual of Transfiguration: *The Old Man and the Sea.*" *Twentieth-Century Interpretations of* The Old Man and the Sea. Ed. Katharine T. Jobes. Englewood Cliffs, NJ: Prentice, 1968. 56–63.

Westling, Louise. *The Green Breast of the New World: Landscape, Gender, and American Fiction.* Athens: U of Georgia P, 1996.

Whitman, Walt. *Leaves of Grass.* 1855. Ed. Sculley Bradley and Harold W. Blodgett. New York: Norton, 1973.

Williams, Raymond. *The Country and the City.* London: Hogarth, 1973.

Williams, Terry Tempest. *Refuge: An Unnatural History of Family and Place.* New York: Pantheon, 1991.

Williams, Wirt. *The Tragic Art of Ernest Hemingway.* Baton Rouge: Louisiana State UP, 1981.

Wilson, David Sloan. Rev. of *Evolutionary Psychology: The New Science of the Mind,* by David M. Buss. *Evolution and Human Behavior* 20 (1999): 279–87.

Wilson, Edward O. *Biophilia.* Cambridge, MA: Harvard UP, 1984.

———. *Consilience: The Unity of Knowledge.* New York: Knopf, 1998.

———. *The Diversity of Life.* New York: Norton, 1992.

———. "Ecology and the Human Imagination." *Writing Natural History: Dialogues with Authors.* Ed. Edward Lueders. Salt Lake City: U of Utah P, 1989. 9–35.

———. *The Future of Life.* New York: Knopf, 2002.

———. "Human Decency Is Animal." *New York Times Magazine* (12 Oct. 1975): 38–50.

———. *Naturalist.* Washington, DC: Island, 1994.

———. "On Art." *Biopoetics: Evolutionary Explorations in the Arts.* Ed. Brett Cooke and Frederick Turner. Lexington, KY: ICUS, 1999. 71–96.

———. *On Human Nature.* Cambridge, MA: Harvard UP, 1978.

———. *Sociobiology: The New Synthesis.* Cambridge, MA: Harvard UP, 1975.

Wilson, Edward O., with Bert Hölldobler. *The Ants.* Cambridge, MA: Belknap Press of Harvard UP, 1984.

Wilson, Eric. *Romantic Turbulence: Chaos, Ecology, and American Space.* New York: St. Martin's, 2000.

Winters, Laura. *Willa Cather: Landscape and Exile.* Selingsgrove, PA: Susquehanna UP, 1993.

Withgott, Jay. "Amphibian Decline: Ubiquitous Herbicide Emasculates Frogs." *Science* 296 (19 April 2002): 447–48.

Wittkowski, Wolfgang. "Crucified in the Ring: Hemingway's *The Old Man and the Sea.*" *The Hemingway Review* 3.1 (Fall 1983): 2–17.

Wolfe, Tom. "O Rotten Gotham." *Literature and the Environment.* Ed. Lorraine Anderson, et al. New York: Longman, 1999. 53–61.

———. "Stalking the Billion-Footed Beast." *Harper's* 279 (Nov. 1989): 45–56.

Worster, Donald. "Seeing Beyond Culture." *Journal of American History* 76 (1990): 1142–47.

Wright, Robert. *Three Scientists and Their Gods.* New York: Times Books, 1988.

Yam, Philip. "The Media's Eerie Fascination." *Scientific American 276* (Jan. 1997): 100–101.

Young, Philip. *Ernest Hemingway.* Minneapolis: U. of Minnesota P, 1965.

———. *Ernest Hemingway: A Reconsideration.* University Park: Pennsylvania State UP, 1966.

Zeki, Semir. "Artistic Creativity and the Brain." *Science* 293 (6 July 2001): 51–52.

———. "The Visual Image in Mind and Brain." *Mind and Brain: Readings from Scientific American Magazine.* New York: Freeman, 1993. 27–39.

Zoellner, Robert. *The Salt-Sea Mastodon: A Reading of Moby-Dick.* Berkeley: U of California P, 1973.

Zuk, Marlene. *Sexual Selections: What We Can and Can't Learn from Animals.* Berkeley: U of California P, 2002.

Index

Under the Sign of Nature: Explorations in Ecocriticism

RACHEL STEIN *Shifting the Ground: American Women Writers' Revisions of Nature, Gender, and Race*

IAN MARSHALL *Story Line: Exploring the Literature of the Appalachian Trail*

PATRICK D. MURPHY *Farther Afield in the Study of Nature-Oriented Literature*

BERNARD W. QUETCHENBACH *Back from the Far Field: American Nature Poetry in the Late Twentieth Century*

KARLA ARMBRUSTER AND KATHLEEN R. WALLACE, EDITORS *Beyond Nature Writing: Expanding the Boundaries of Ecocriticism*

STEPHEN ADAMS *The Best and Worst Country in the World: Perspectives on the Early Virginia Landscape*

MARK ALLISTER *Refiguring the Map of Sorrow: Nature Writing and Autobiography*

RALPH H. LUTTS *The Nature Fakers: Wildlife, Science, and Sentiment* (reprint)

MICHAEL A. BRYSON *Visions of the Land: Science, Literature, and the American Environment from the Era of Exploration to the Age of Ecology*

ROBERT BERNARD HASS *Going by Contraries: Robert Frost's Conflict with Science*

IAN MARSHALL *Peak Experiences: Walking Meditations on Literature, Nature, and Need*

GLEN A. LOVE *Practical Ecocriticism: Literature, Biology, and the Environment*